VIETNAM'S WAR OF HATE

DEDICATION

— To Chris, Victor, and Delta —
Selfless "WE *not* ME"[1, i] lives best lived

Christopher C. Webster: October 23, 1947 to August 12, 1969

A life on earth cut short, like so many others in Vietnam, during or prior to that youthfully targeted twenty-first year . . . legal recognition as an adult. May you have carried your contagious exhilaration for this life into the next. And may your name be synonymous with honor and pride, the manner in which you and your fallen comrades served. If those of us touched by your memory and theirs can draw upon the strength and courage—the dedication and self-esteem—residing therein, we will be more worthy for it, each and every one of us.

Dr. Victor W. Westphall: October 13, 1913 to July 22, 2003

A life on earth that will live forever. A truly remarkable, inspirational healer who dedicated his life to military veterans after his eldest son, David, was killed in Vietnam. Your name *is* synonymous with honor and pride, as is the swept-wing chapel, the Vietnam Veterans Memorial, you and your family shaped and nurtured in the Land of Enchantment. Countless Vietnam veterans and loved ones of those lost in Vietnam drew upon your strength and courage—the dedication and self-esteem—residing therein and they are more worthy for it. You saved untold numbers of lost souls. May you rejoice in the memory of the thousands upon thousands who love and miss you. You can finally rest. They can now carry your eternal flame.

Delta Brothers: 1969

And to my selfless "WE *not* ME" Brothers in Delta Company, 2nd Battalion, 3rd Infantry, 199th Light Infantry Brigade: Your service to America was "Number 1;"[ii] the welcome home was "Number 10."[iii] Nonetheless, we know honor and pride; they never will.

VIETNAM'S WAR OF HATE

PROUD MILITARY VETERANS VILIFIED AT HOME

R. W. TREWYN

Pen & Sword
MILITARY
AN IMPRINT OF PEN & SWORD BOOKS LTD.
YORKSHIRE - PHILADELPHIA

First published in Great Britain in 2025 by
PEN AND SWORD MILITARY
An imprint of
Pen & Sword Books Limited
Yorkshire – Philadelphia

ISBN 978 1 03611 004 8

Typeset in Times New Roman 10/12 by
SJmagic DESIGN SERVICES, India.
Printed and bound in the UK by CPI Group (UK) Ltd.

The Publisher's authorised representative in the EU for product safety is
Authorised Rep Compliance Ltd., Ground Floor, 71 Lower Baggot Street,
Dublin D02 P593, Ireland.
www.arccompliance.com

For a complete list of Pen & Sword titles please contact
PEN & SWORD BOOKS LIMITED
George House, Units 12 & 13, Beevor Street, Off Pontefract Road,
Barnsley, South Yorkshire, S71 1HN, England
E-mail: enquiries@pen-and-sword.co.uk
Website: www.pen-and-sword.co.uk

or

PEN AND SWORD BOOKS
1950 Lawrence Rd, Havertown, PA 19083, USA
E-mail: uspen-and-sword@casematepublishers.com
Website: www.penandswordbooks.com

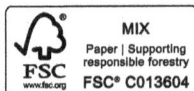

MIX
Paper | Supporting
responsible forestry
FSC
www.fsc.org   FSC® C013604

CONTENTS

CONTENTS

Introduction

YOU'RE NOT WELCOME HERE . . . IN AMERICA

Pride in service TO America was stolen BY America.

VIETNAM'S WAR OF HATE recounts what returning from Vietnam was like for me in 1969, proud of my combat service and proud of my Delta Company brothers. As a draftee who was discharged from the Army five months early with shrapnel a couple inches from my heart, I knew I was lucky to be alive. Inconceivably, five months later I was ready to go back to Vietnam. Dying with brothers in war looked better to me than living with haters in America while going to college in the anticipated refuge of my childhood hometown.

VIETNAM'S WAR OF HATE is about my struggles trying to comprehend the animosity toward Vietnam veterans in the United States back then. The magnitude was overwhelming. It's also about the evolution of my understanding of the war overall and my battles against the common misrepresentations of the largely patriotic, valorous soldiers who deployed to Southeast Asia.

It took me over thirty years to feel welcome in America, to experience a homecoming commensurate with the sacrifices made. Unfortunately, the erroneous portrayal of U.S. forces in Vietnam persists in popular culture and in the conventional wisdom of far too many Americans. The image of those who served remains tainted to this day including, most tragically, perception of the fifty-eight thousand men and eight women who died in Vietnam. Pride in their service *to* America was stolen from them *by* America. It was ripped from the hearts of their loved ones. VIETNAM'S WAR OF HATE describes my arduous journey entangled in this awful saga. Importantly, its causes are exposed along the way, which is of significance today.

Alarmingly, America has experienced the same type of strife and convulsions in recent years that I came home to in 1969. The bitterness and polarization of that period have resurfaced. As a result, the long trek charted in VIETNAM'S WAR OF HATE offers both timely and enduring lessons for America's current era.

Prologue

GULLY OF THE SHADOWS OF DEATH LESSONS FOR LIFE

"WE" gave strength to those not killed by Groundhog Day shadows.

....

THE SPIRIT OF WE[1, i]
... "WE *not* ME" ...

A life best lived should always be about YOU,
It should never be about ME;
But, the times to really cherish and hold on to
Are those all too fleeting moments in life
That are truly about WE!

....

DAILY STAFF JOURNAL OR DUTY OFFICER'S LOG (AR 220-346 & FM 101-5)				PAGE NO. 1		NO. OF PAGES 9	
ORGANIZATION OR INSTALLATION Combined Staff Journal 2d Bn, 3d Inf 199th Inf Bde (Sep)(Lt)		LOCATION XT7120 CONFIDENTIAL		PERIOD COVERED			
				FROM		TO	
				HOUR 0001	DATE 2 Feb 69	HOUR 2400	DATE 2 Feb 69
ITEM NO	TIME		INCIDENTS, MESSAGES, ORDERS, ETC.		ACTION TAKEN		INL
	IN	OUT					
1	0001		(U) Journal Opened by Sgt E-5 Horcha DNCO		JSF		JH
2	0100		(U) Sitrep negative		2/25		JH

Medic! . . . Man Down!! . . . *MEDIC!!!* . . . MEN DOWN!!!! . . . *MEDIC!!!!!*

Morning shadows slinking from concealed burrows made for a dire Groundhog Day forecast. Punxsutawney Phil's was not among them.

February 2, 1969 was my first encounter with "the Spirit of WE"[1] fleeting moments in life. The verse describing it emerged 50 years later.

Delta Company hadn't had a casualty of any kind for months and I had been in Vietnam with them less than 3 weeks. However, our WIA/KIA counts—wounded-in-action and killed-in-action[ii]—came quickly from hidden tunnels that day. So did my exposure to "WE *not* ME"[2, iii] in combat; selfless service where your brothers' lives take precedence over your own.

The initial notations in the battalion log regarding enemy contact were items 12–15 below. There were *many* more to come.

The 0831 report of Delta Company's 1st Platoon (#2 Eagle) being ambushed by a Vietcong (VC) *squad* was a disastrous misjudgment. An after-action analysis concluded it was a *battalion* of North Vietnamese regular Army troops, not a rag-tag guerrilla squad.

So, the size of the enemy force was *massively* larger than first reported and *immeasurably* better trained. We paid a heavy price for that bloodletting bad guess.

Combined Staff Journal: 2d Bn, 3d Inf, 199th Bde (Sep) (Lt); 2 Feb 69

Item No.	Time In	Incidents, Messages, Orders, etc.
12	0831	(C) Co D #2 Eagle has contact with VC Sqd; Reported grid XT685218 for contact.
13	0835	(C) Requested LFT from 2/25
14	0840	(C) Co D (-) ordered to move out into contact
15	0900	(C) Requested urgent dustoff of 5 WIA, 2 KIA

The 0835 entry was a helicopter light fire team (LFT) being called in to provide gunship support against the "few" enemy fighters. A squad it might have handled; numbers orders of magnitude larger, *not!*

At 0840, Delta Company's 2nd and 3rd Platoons were ordered to move out to support 1st Platoon. As a staff sergeant graduate of the Army's shake 'n' bake NCO school,[iv] my position at the time was 3rd Squad Leader in 2nd Platoon, and we had yet to encounter the enemy in our few times in the field together. By the end of the day, we had a lifetime of combat experience, and I would be 2nd Platoon Leader, replacing our lieutenant, who took over as Delta's commanding officer (C.O.) when our captain was killed.

The 0900 entry—dustoff of 5 WIA, 2 KIA—tells the story. And, tragically, there were many more such entries before our day was done.

Combined Staff Journal: 2d Bn, 3d Inf, 199th Bde (Sep) (Lt); 2 Feb 69

Item No.	Time In	Incidents, Messages, Orders, etc.
31	0925	(C) Co D arrived at point of contact.
135	1813	(C) Starting sweep from West to East with two units
138	1837	(C) Request dustoff Co C two litter, two ambu (1 was for Cpt ▮▮▮▮▮)

The 0925 entry denotes when we linked up with 1st Platoon, and it was the first of innumerable thereafter where crucial details were lacking.

We could see 1st Platoon to our front with troops just milling around while some were tending to wounded. Our assumption was the VC had hit and run, but when we were about 40 meters away, the tree line to our right exploded with automatic small arms fire. Somehow, everyone dove for cover fast enough so no one got hit, but I don't know how.

Lucky!

We were within hand grenade range when they opened fire.

Artillery and 4.2 mortars bombarded the enemy position on and off all day and pairs of F-4 fighters screamed in three different times, dropping napalm canisters and 500-pound bombs. Nonetheless, whenever we would advance on the tree line during ceasefires, our casualties kept mounting . . . *substantially!*

Plus, the enemy's firepower seemed to intensify with each assault. Only AK-47s at first . . . with belt-fed machine guns next . . . then RPGs (rocket-propelled grenades).

Well, it intensified until 1813.

Delta was one of the two units—Bravo and Charlie Companies had joined us during the day—and we finally made it well inside the tree line to a massive gully . . . obscured until we were nearly upon it.

"BOOM!

Then, [SH]IT hit the fan—*BIGTIME!"*[3, v]

When the 1813 sweep turned apocalyptic at the gully, "WE *not* ME" saved numerous lives; regrettably, not all lives. "With the first machinegun burst from a shadowy hole in the side of the gully, our KIA/WIA numbers jumped again."[3]

And, the 138th entry 24 minutes later, at 1837, was wrong.

The casualties were Delta's, not Charlie's, and our captain was KIA, not litter or ambulatory WIA. Another machinegun burst from the gully killed him as he tried to catch a glimpse of our guy below. Two of us dragged his body away from the edge and there was *no* question . . . he died instantly.

Thankfully, though, 1 KIA and 3 WIA were *finally* our last for the day. Total Gully of the Shadows of Death U.S. casualties: 7 KIA; 27 WIA.

Truly horrible numbers, but it was also my first exposure to combat selfless service that "the Spirit of WE"[1] is meant to describe. Everyone performed remarkably, covering each other's backs time and time again.

The fact that there were MANY concealed tunnel openings *behind us* when we reached the ravine, meant we could have lost lots, lots more. But, "the Spirit of WE"[1]— "WE *not* ME"[2]—got some of us through it, preparing us for the battles ahead.

Combined Staff Journal: 2d Bn, 3d Inf, 199th Bde (Sep) (Lt); 3 Feb 69

Item No.	Time In	Incidents, Messages, Orders, etc.
3	0040	(C) Co's C, B, D and tanks returning at this time from contact area vic 695210
8	0255	(C) All els ref item 3 closed NDP's
25	1145	(C) Little Bear 847 on station Pick up KIA

After midnight, twenty-eight of thirty members of Delta Company still there, along the Bravo and Charlie Companies, departed for our night defensive positions (NDP's; i.e., camps) two-plus hours away. It was a *LONG* day!

Delta's 2nd Platoon RTO (radio telephone operator) stayed behind with Alpha Company, the late arrival night shift, to retrieve our 3rd Squad brother at the bottom of the gully. Recon Platoon joined for ambush duty. In the morning, there was no sign of the enemy; just deserted tunnels and a cavernous underground hospital.

A Huey medevac, Little Bear 857, finally arrived at the gully at 1145 to evacuate 2nd Platoon's fallen comrade.

Russell, Delta's RTO, walked out with Alpha Company. He finally made it back to us three or four days later.

VIETNAM'S WAR OF HATE provides Groundhog Day specifics, but the recurring examples of "WE *not* ME"[2] valor are ingrained *forever.*

INCREDIBLE!!!

A couple decades after my time in Vietnam, I visited the National Archives and perused the 2nd Battalion logs (DA Form 1594) for the months I was there. Each day had one report that started at 1 minute after midnight (0001) and ended at midnight (2400) with one exception, Groundhog Day.

It had two quite different versions. *Very strange.*

Many of the entries were identical on both and others were similar, but with a few words or times changed. However, one of them had sixty-three fewer entries than the other (95 vs. 158).

Since the 2nd Battalion C.O. was relieved of command a couple weeks later, I presume he was responsible. And based on multiple names being absent on the 95-entry version compared to the 158, I'm guessing he didn't want those individuals questioned about his actions that day.

There were good reasons for that too.

Those of us on the ground while he was flying overhead—*SAFE*—knew he had his head up his ass when he ordered on-line assaults again and again against a tunnel complex. He was intent on chalking up a BIG enemy body count and he got a large number . . . *but for us!*

Regardless, soldiers follow orders, even stupid-ass ones.

As to the two versions, I'd bet a battalion NCO figured out what the jerk was up to and squirreled away a copy of the original so it wasn't destroyed. Senior NCOs *always* know how to bury assholes that need burying!

Chapters 3 and 4 provide additional details about the Gully of the Shadows of Death and thereafter until I joined Delta's WIA club on April 18. Recuperating for 4 months in Okinawa, I had no clue the war back home would be worse than combat . . . worse than Groundhog Day.

Astonishingly, the shrapnel 2 inches from my heart soon became "no sweat" by comparison. I damned near reenlisted to go back to Vietnam five months after coming home. At five and a half months, Molotov cocktails and a massive inferno pissed me off enough to stay and fight.

And that's what I did; suck it up and battle . . . day by day.

Of course, it took me three decades to find the elusive welcome home that was lost in the smoke and haze of 1969–1970, but I got there . . . *eventually!* Then, a mere 106 days later, America was attacked—September 11, 2001. But even with as horrible as that day was, on day 107, the country united in a manner unseen since Pearl Harbor in 1941.

For me, a country finally united sealed it . . . welcome home!

* * *

Two-plus decades after that—2019-2020—America was back where it was in 1969–1970 . . . at war domestically. NOT GOOD!

Shockingly and repulsively, I was seeing the same groups of anti-America anarchists at work that I encountered during my thirty-year quest to feel welcome at home. The one upside, perhaps, is that the five categories of these Benedict Arnolds are delineated in VIETNAM'S WAR OF HATE.

Twelve of twenty-three chapters highlight "anti-America Americans . . . Lady Liberty's Achilles' heel."[vi] They include: "(1) socialist-loving 'intellectuals;' (2) screw-the-public profiteers (politicians and bureaucrats); (3) mass media manipulators; (4) antimilitary/antiauthority zealots; and (5) sanctimonious amoral moralists."[4, vii] These traitors were an existential threat to freedom during the Vietnam era, as they still are today.

All must be confronted and exposed for what they are: anti-America "ME/FU" self-servants bent on destroying liberty and freedom as we know it. They failed fifty years ago; they could succeed this time. Stopping them will require American patriots—believers in the U.S. Constitution and in "We the People"—to be "WE *not* ME" selfless servants and fight back.

Being a patriot—on the back side of over-the-hill, but a patriot nonetheless—I felt compelled to raise the alarm.

Learn from history for Christ's sake!
"WE" can't keep going through this crap.
WAKE UP, AMERICA!!!

R.W. Trewyn, Army SSG
Delta Company, 2nd Battalion
3rd Infantry (The Old Guard)
199th Light Infantry Brigade
Republic of Vietnam, 1969

Chapter 1

PRIDE . . . NOW YOU SEE IT; NOW YOU DON'T

Adios, mother! Hello, mom and apple pie.

"Welcome Home!"

For being nothing more than eleven letters stuck on some spare, unused poster paper, the two words those few characters created sure looked great up there on the garage door at my mother and dad's farm. Xuan Loc, Cu Chi, Binh Chan. Those "mothers" were finally—*forever*—names in the past. For me, the ordeal in Southeast Asia was over.

The would-be corpse made it home . . . corpse-like perhaps, but not.

Oh, the body may have been bloodied a bit while I was away. It may have become the final resting place for an odd-shaped piece of rusty metal, but the old ticker that hunk of scrap iron nearly found was working just fine, thank you.

Yes, siree. Bloodied, but breathing and happy as hell!

Even decades after the fact (decades of repressing such thoughts), that precise moment—the words on the door, the realization of being alive—is tucked away, suspended animation of what amounts to hardly more than a heartbeat in time. It hangs there for instant replay. That, along with the crumbling sound of crushed limestone gnashing under the tires as the car rolled into the drive, lurching over a mounded gravel wake created by traffic at the farm exiting and entering more often to and from the west. I returned that day from the east.

Sight, sound, and motion, captured with the triumph of survival, the discovery of reaching life after death. Okay, okay. So maybe I knew I was alive all along, but then . . . who really knows for sure after combat?

Maybe it was just a malicious dream of some sort. Turning into the driveway, seeing the "Welcome Home," suddenly, I was awake and alive . . . truly awake . . . truly alive. Life was no longer a sleep-walking fantasy; it was real. I was home—*alive!*

1

It's curious how so many of the images, the sounds . . . *the emotions* . . . can once again be so vivid, so real, they are essentially part of the present, not the past. Other aspects of that period which should be stored away in the memory bank are nowhere to be found.

It's bizarre.

Like, what do you suppose happened to the plane ride (or was it rides?) from California to Wisconsin?

That should be a biggie, a major homecoming highlight, but it draws a total blank. There's not a hint . . . nothing . . . nada.

And why does my mental picture of the garage door "Welcome Home" consist of open, blue outlined letters on a white background, when, in fact, the artistically hand-crafted characters were solid, tinfoil-silver on flame red?

The size and shape of the letters are imprinted perfectly; the colors just don't match. Somewhere along the line my recalled vision went color blind.

Weird!

While there is no way of actually knowing, perhaps the basis for this "absolute recall—partial to total amnesia" conundrum had something to do with the stark contrasts being assimilated by a totally fatigued, bleary and wrung-out mind. Passing through the revolving door of a time machine, the carnage of war had been left behind in a blur. Then, in what seemed but an instant, the carefree life of a civilian was a mere step away . . . a characteristic of modern warfare, I guess.

Where's the opportunity to decompress when you fly home?

Even a month in the hospital, three months recuperating didn't do it for me.

In many ways, it was as though I had never left; nothing appeared outwardly changed. But, for some reason, the eyes through which I was viewing the people, the places, the things around me, no longer seemed to be mine. Lifelong images appeared vaguely out-of-focus . . . imprecise.

Somehow, returning from Vietnam was like rediscovering the "real world"— *home*—while squinting through the rotating ocular of a kaleidoscope: Familiar sights and remembrances coalescing as they emerged from the subconscious mind, picking up bits of data more recently stored, then flashing them into the realm of consciousness. The more striking the pictorial array, the clearer the recall, but the Vietnam lens altered every context and view. It was strange . . . *really* strange.

Looking back though, one recollection stands out over all the rest. And a stubborn S.O.B. it was too. Repeatedly, it would flash to the fore, an explicit realization that had mysteriously jumped out of the gray depths shortly after I landed back in the States.

Even now, the recycling revelation that occurred may seem totally illogical to some, but it wasn't really. Not if you'd been there, been where I had . . . face to face with death . . . mine likely . . . others actually.

Yes, indeed.

During that groggy, recovery from exhaustion phase after touching down in California, I was absolutely struck by an emphatic "mom and apple pie" sensation.

Odd, huh?

That slogan as a cause-to-fight-for from one of the earlier "Big Wars" was certainly not being bandied about as what we were up to in Vietnam.

NOT HARDLY!

Somehow though, during those first twenty-four hours back in the States, that analogy was dredged up from somewhere, and it made sense. I had been fighting for "mom and apple pie"—for freedom, liberty, justice—just like the guys during the world wars.

You bet!

And why would it be otherwise?

I had faced an armed enemy in combat, as they had, and I performed in a manner for which I was proud.

Yes, I felt PROUD . . . run-in-a-burning-building-and-save-the-children–type proud . . . a level of pride like no other. Laying it all out there when called upon by your country can do that; NO, *should* do that.

And there was no reason to suspect my situation was any different from almost everyone else's either. Not then, not now. In fact, I think it's likely—*highly likely*—that many of the feelings I experienced returning home from Vietnam were experienced by most of those who served there . . . those who've served in other wars as well.

Obviously, one would be happy and relieved to be back, to have survived. After hitting the States, but before actually getting home, there was the excitement and anticipation of seeing loved ones after what had been such a long, long time— almost a lifetime . . . *literally!*

Then there was the sadness for lost comrades and innumerable compatriots still serving . . . friends to whom my life had been entrusted—and saved by—day in, day out.

Would those friends survive?

During my first few hours back in the States, all those various feelings put me on an emotional roller coaster, rocketing from the heights of happiness to the pits of depression within minutes, then back again.

And I'm sure there was some "survivor's guilt" tucked in there as well. Had to be.

By sheer necessity, I had blocked out emotions entirely (or as close to 100 percent as achievable) while trying to stay alive—dodging bullets and shrapnel—in the swamps and jungles of Vietnam. Afterwards, laying in the hospital in Okinawa, I was afraid to let any real feelings creep back in.

Nope, not until I finally set foot on American soil.

What if by some black twist of fate, I don't get there?

Then, when I finally did, it was time to climb aboard the roller coaster while all those emotions, locked out for months, came rushing back in.

Soon, however, exhaustion took over (sleep being unfathomable during the long, trans-Pacific flight back), and all the intermingled, confused perceptions just bounced around inside. I didn't really know how to feel.

While my particular situation may have been somewhat unusual, since I was discharged from the Army the same day I arrived in California, I suspect this scenario was not all that uncommon.

3

I also presume that most who went to Vietnam returned with a feeling of pride mixed in with all those other emotions. This wouldn't have been universal, of course, but the majority . . . the *vast* majority of those who served . . . did so in a fashion for which they could feel proud.

No question about it!

They didn't abandon their country when called, and they performed with honor and pride. Recognizing that fact could lead to no other sentiment once back in the real world.

Not that everyone could look upon their tour of duty (whatever their job was) and feel proud of what they had done, however. I could think of at least one individual I served with who certainly wouldn't have experienced any feeling of self-esteem and pride. A lot of us could have died because of him. Fortunately, I don't think anybody did.

At least he represented the exception, not the rule.

Everyone else I could recall there *should* have felt proud . . . unquestionably! They served with distinction, in the same manner as those who took up arms in the big wars.

As a combat veteran, there was also something extra upon returning home, something beyond just pride. It was a bond or union with all those who ever fought—actually fought—to keep America free. Yes, that "mom and apple pie" feeling as it hit me; an undefined solidarity or togetherness, perchance, for others. It was a lifeline of sorts to the previous wars . . . the First World War, the Second World War, Korea.

For me, it was an eerie, yet comforting, feeling—a revelation of sorts. I had joined the brotherhood of war . . . past, present, and future.

The Second World War, particularly, crossed my mind that early morning in California; thinking about the combat vets, the guys who had been through it all, returning home. There I was walking down a quiet, deserted street in Oakland, and as I looked around, it was as if those Second World War infantry-types were walking with me.

Even though I knew I was alone, I really wasn't. They were there.

You talk about standing tall and walking proud!

It truly seemed as though I had fought beside them—for the same cause—to keep America free. What a way to be lifted up from my state of exhaustion, from the previous day's emotional roller coaster.

I felt absolutely great!

Then, totally alone in the crisp morning haze of that West Coast city, the real clincher came . . . a jolting recollection that genuinely put it all in perspective for me.

While in Nam, I had made peace with my maker: I was ready to *die* for my brothers and my country.

Holy crap!

Dredging that up from some hidden, unconscious crevice sent chills radiating from head to toe.

It wasn't an attempt to deal with a hypothetical situation, not when it happened. It was a *likely* reality.

READY TO DIE FOR MY COUNTRY!
Yes . . . indeed . . . HOLY CRAP!
I hadn't really thought much about it before that day in Oakland; accepting the commitment is one thing, spending time thinking about it is a *whole* different ball game.

Even laying in the hospital in Okinawa, I hadn't dwelled on what that affirmation really meant. Oh, I recognized that I shouldn't have lived through some of the situations I'd been in, but that's different than realizing, *if need be*, you're *ready* to die for your country.

That initiates one into a rather high-stakes club . . . joining all those who've ever accepted the ultimate sacrifice challenge when called. Most notably, it connected me to all those who've actually made that sacrifice.

When that realization struck, I suddenly felt like I had fought in *all* the previous wars, from the Revolutionary through the world wars and Korea. It was as if a piece of history of the country belonged to me. I was called by *my* country and I served her well, just as those who fought in the earlier wars.

That definitely clinched it.

The infusion with pride was complete . . . pride for the job I had done . . . pride for the commitment I'd made to my brothers and country . . . pride for the company it placed me in.

How could there be any doubt?

"Mom and apple pie" *were* the things I had fought for, the things I helped preserve. There was just no question about it; not that exhilarating early morning in Oakland, not catching the first glimpse of the garage door greeting at the farm.

Well, if that was true . . . and it *was* true, then . . . how could it be possible that in a blink of an eye I'd be characterized and treated as a criminal?

I fought with honor, my life on the line!

Who cares?

Within weeks, I'd be ridiculed in my own hometown. Beyond that, my country—her people—would just turn away.

Avert your eyes, children! Don't look at that vile, repulsive leper! We didn't support that war. Those who fought there are depraved.

Ignore him.

SPIT ON HIM!!! Maybe he'll go away.

Thus, my perceptions returning from war smashed headlong into the realities of 1969 . . . 1970 . . . 1971 . . . 1972 . . .

Welcome home!

COMBAT . . . THE "EASY" PART

Enduring Truth: *Pride serving honorably in war is timeless . . .*
valued by others or not.

Chapter 2

PATRIOTISM TO HELL AND BACK

Grasping the fundamentals . . . right or wrong.

Albert Einstein: *"Try not to become a man of success,
but rather try to become a man of value."*[1]

Perhaps the basis for how one feels coming home from war or even how one reacts to the perils of war is a result, in part, of one's experiences growing up. And of course, being an early member of the Baby Boom, I grew up during the patriotic post–Second World War era.

It was a time, when for a few cents and a Friday evening ride to town, I could see a movie, preferably starring Randolph Scott, Audie Murphy, or The Duke— John Wayne.

While these were often westerns, it was also an era when the latter two stars, especially, were fighting the forces of evil in a war movie . . . fighting for mom and apple pie, no doubt.

In the case of Audie Murphy, acting wasn't even required, since he had lived his most famous role in *To Hell and Back*, becoming the most decorated soldier in the Second World War. Remarkably, he still looked like a teenager when he was performing the part in the movie.

While the plots of the various movies differed somewhat, the message was always the same: Fighting for your country was an honor worth dying for. This was an absolute truth . . . no questions asked.

Proper behavior in war (war etiquette, so to speak) was also defined in these movies, and Murphy and Wayne were excellent teachers. Americans always fight fair, they taught us. American soldiers fight together. Every soldier looks out for his buddies, and he is willing to risk his life, instantly, to save his comrades. If wounded, a warrior fights on until no longer able. Giving up—surrender—is never, and should never be, considered.

If, in any of those movies, a soldier did not portray the very best American qualities, that soldier would likely recognize the error of his ways and give his life to save another. That's just the way it was.

Thus were the messages delivered and the childhood heroes of the time created. And powerful training it was. Projecting oneself into the images on the screen was part of growing up . . . part of solidifying future values and actions; ready to perform in a similar, Audie Murphy/John Wayne manner if called upon.

It's also likely that being raised on a dairy farm in Wisconsin contributed greatly to my own values and views of what America is all about. One is undoubtedly exposed to more conservative, fundamental issues and concepts when raised in an environment where neighbors helping neighbors is the norm, not the exception.

While they represent some of my earliest memories, I can remember the pre-tractor days (draft horses in the stalls in the barn) and all the neighbors being over for a "threshing party." That was quite a crew to be fed while the "party" was going on too. But then in time, they would move on to the next farm, and my father would do his part there. That's just the way things were done. "It encompasses the neighbors helping neighbors' approach of my parents' generation."[2, i]

As a result, old-fashioned American values, including pride in one's country, were things I took for granted, things I didn't question. Patriotism may have been more in vogue down on the farm, more so than in the big city.

But, then, I didn't live in the big C as a kid, so who knows?

However, one likely asked fewer questions concerning governmental decisions when growing up on a farm, except perhaps decisions affecting milk prices, corn prices, and the like. That may no longer be the case, what with the farm lobby and all, but fifty, sixty, seventy years ago, if actions by the government weren't just accepted at face value, they were certainly not scrutinized extensively. Farm folks back then tended to believe in the capabilities of officials involved in the decision-making process.

Naive?

Perhaps, but rural upbringing generally elicits a trusting nature, a significant likelihood that one will accept the expertise of others more knowledgeable about such things. You get used to trusting your neighbors, then people in general. If you shook hands on it (whatever it was), it was a contract.

In some ways, it's too bad we can't get back to that approach, back to more truthfulness on everyone's part. That heritage isn't bad.

One other aspect related to my early childhood years may have contributed to my feelings upon returning home from Vietnam as well. While my father didn't have to answer the call to military service (he served on the farm during the Second World War), a number of my uncles, my mother's brothers, did. In fact, between 1940 and 1953 there were only two years—'49 and '50—when at least one of the Zimmerman brothers wasn't in the military.

Em, Bob, Harry, Zip, and Gene all took their turns. Two fought in the Second World War: Em in the South Pacific with MacArthur; Bob in Europe. The youngest of my uncles, Gene, was in Korea for the first of our "police action" style military conflicts of modern times. It was a war to those who were there, but it wasn't "marketed" that way back home.

No specific discussions about my uncles' military service come to mind, but I can remember clearly many things that weren't said. Okay, so maybe that sounds a bit strange, but in some cases, the unspoken can leave the greatest impression. There was certainly quite a collection of military memorabilia around my grandparents' home, and there was an aura of pride surrounding it. When these items were handled or spoken of, it was obvious they were something special.

There was also something different about the respect given my uncles by the rest of the family. Having in later years seen some of the newspaper clippings and heard some of the stories, I can better understand the reasons.

My uncle Em was a private in the Wisconsin National Guard—the 32nd "Red Arrow" Division—when it was federalized on October 15, 1940. Two years later, the Red Arrow was the first division to take the fight to the Japanese in the Southwest Pacific . . . in the putrid swamps and sweltering jungles of New Guinea.

Em's outfit, the 127th Infantry, began shipping out from Brisbane, Australia for Port Moresby in mid-November of 1942. During their first major campaign in New Guinea—the ongoing Buna-Sananda Operation—the 127th started out with 2,734 men; they had 3,588 casualties before it was over three months later.[3] Not unexpectedly, malaria, dengue fever, tropical dysentery, and related swamp slime diseases extracted the greatest toll.

Not your typical stroll down Main Street in Sullivan or Oconomowoc, huh, Em?

Overall, the fighting in New Guinea was significantly more costly than on Guadalcanal; both were ongoing at about the same time. With one-third fewer troops engaged, the American and Australian allies had nearly twice the number killed in action . . . 3,095 compared to about 1,600 at Guadalcanal.[4] Another 5,451 were wounded, and there were the thousands upon thousands of disease-induced casualties. More than 200 died of typhus.

The conditions were ghastly. The warfare was incredibly fierce. There's a reason Lida Mayo—the Second World War historian—named her book about the carnage there *Bloody Buna*.[4]

The Company Em was in—Company G, 2nd Battalion—had its share of casualties, but those troops led by Captain Dames must have really "had their shit together," as the saying goes.

How could I know that, not having been born at the time?

Easy!

The corps commander, General Eichelberger, singled out five National Guard officers for special acclaim in New Guinea. After simply naming two colonels and two majors, he then referred to "the inimitable Captain W.H. Dames of Wisconsin, whose Company G, 127th Infantry, never made a wrong move in battle."[5] Having a three-star declare that any unit "never made a wrong move in battle" is incredibly high praise; generals don't usually notice such things at the company level. In fact, few generals have the ability to see that far down the military ladder, much less comment on what goes on there.

Of course, Lieutenant General Eichelberger must not have been your typical career soldier with star-laden shoulders. After his only three one- and two-star generals were wounded in action, "he took over direct command of the forward elements of the 32nd Division."[5]

I guess that might explain why he knew what Company G was up to in battle.

8

Yes, there's no question: Em must have been in some deep shit and in one hell-of-a unit . . . one to be damn proud of.

Then there was my uncle Bob. He's the only Zimmerman of that generation to make it back to the homeland from which his grandparents, my maternal great grandparents, emigrated a few decades earlier to escape the Kaiser. It was not exactly a holiday tour of Deutschland though; he did it as part of the Ardennes, Rhineland, and Central Europe campaigns with the Army's 9th Division.

Bob had to endure that frigid winter in the Ardennes during the last-ditch counter-offensive led by the Panzer divisions of the Wehrmacht—the Battle of the Bulge. Soon thereafter, he took part in the frantic dash across the Rhine's Ludendorff Bridge, the last bridge mistakenly left standing by the Nazis.

As a company wireman with the 60th Infantry Go Devils, laying wire "up front" so communications could be maintained was undoubtedly no picnic for Bob either. Not under intense enemy fire.

In the "small world" category, Bob's last C.O. with the 60th Infantry in Germany was a guy by the name of William C. Westmoreland, a colonel at the time. Somehow that name—at a slightly higher rank—has a familiar ring to it.

Bob may have achieved few successes after his discharge in 1946 . . . two failed engagements during the war apparently tearing the heart out of him, but he could never be denied his due for what he went through in Europe. Not only that, when he should have been relaxing on a leisurely cruise home, he wound up shipwrecked during a storm in the Bermuda Triangle.

The pictures I saw made it look like the ship had been bombed, the damage was so great. But Bob lived through that ordeal as well.

I guess it's no wonder my uncles were honored for their military service . . . for their contributions to maintaining freedom. Em and Bob both had Bronze Stars to show for their efforts, not that any medal or award can gauge the life and death commitments they, and others, made.

In addition, Harry, Zip, and Gene recited their oaths when called by old Unc Sammy as well. While they didn't see combat, they understood their duty . . . then, they did it.

With that sort of heritage, is it any wonder I would feel an extra measure of pride returning home from combat?

Having been raised to believe that fighting for one's country is proper, normal, and expected behavior, what else could result?

Nothing, if one fought honorably . . . which I did.

Furthermore, the patriotic post-Second World War era infused a clear-cut, "no questions asked" expectation as to how one would be treated coming home from war. A willingness to die for your country—for those you love and what you love—*MUST* be acknowledged by gratitude and respect. To do otherwise, would be incomprehensible.

I believed that absolutely. It was as true as "mom and apple pie."

Overall, in looking back, it would appear that I was indoctrinated to patriotism at a very early age . . . to always honor the flag and national anthem.[6, ii] During those childhood years when you first learn the values that will likely dictate how you live your life, I was definitely exposed to the concept of loyalty to America. With the lineup I had to look up to—Audie, The Duke, Em, Bob, Harry, Zip, and Gene—it was probably not unexpected that my response to serving my country favorably would have been so positive.

There's no question, however, that the actual combat experience in Southeast Asia contributed more than anything else to my feelings coming home. War can make or break your character and values—learned at a young age or not—faster than probably anything else.

Believe it! Facing off, M-16 to AK-47, will test your loyalties, capabilities, and every other damn thing in one hell of a big hurry!

You can perform—reacting *instantly*—or you can die.

Worse yet, a buddy can die. Simple choices . . . difficult solutions.

COMBAT . . . THE "EASY" PART

Enduring Truth: *Patriotism learned early inspires standards and expectations for life.*

Chapter 3

VIETNAM

The agony and the ecstasy . . . death and "dry" socks.

My situation was a bit different than the majority of the troops I served with in Vietnam, since I was four or five years older than most of them. I had done a fair amount of searching "to find myself" prior to getting drafted . . . studying accounting at a business school in Illinois, working as an accountant in a large corporate office in Milwaukee, then going to college back in my hometown in Wisconsin (switching from business to a biology major, chemistry minor after a semester). That was while helping to milk cows when my father had a heart attack. When he retired, I headed off to Hawaii to check out marine biology as a potential vocation.

That last inspiration hit while I was studying odd sea creatures in an invertebrates' course in Whitewater in 1964–1965, and it was solidified while trudging through monster snow drifts between classes in January and February . . . freezing my butt off. Fortunately, the University of Hawaii had no out-of-state tuition back then, so even a pay-your-own-way farm kid could manage to afford it—sort of—by working lots of odd jobs.

And, yes, my career search was rather circuitous and peculiar.

I had only one science course in high school though (biology as a sophomore), and I was basically a C+/B- student. My only A, as a senior in accounting, got me to the business school—a lofty aspiration at the time and a way to get cow shit out of my future.

But, when I actually "discovered" the sciences, the bug really bit me. Not only that, I was getting A after A without hardly trying . . . at least initially.

An A was tougher to come by in Hawaii, but I was managing by putting a little more try into it. However, after going from an honors student my first year at U of H to almost flunking out the second (when my mind wandered far too frequently with my heart to a distant time zone), I took a semester off to get my head on straight.

Well, good old Uncle Sam saw to it that I had a little more time.

How about a couple years, nephew?

Yes, after five and a half years in school—staying one step ahead of the draft board—my least favorite uncle at the time finally caught up. He managed to get even in his own less-than-subtle way too.

My "Order to Report for Induction" arrived two days before Christmas in 1967. *Two days*!

Greetings "and Merry Christmas" from the president. And while you're at it, have a *real* "Happy New Year" as well. You bet.

At least the ol' pres and his buddies at the draft board gave me plenty of time to get everything squared away before leaving. I didn't have to report until January 16 at 06:15.

Oh, thank you!

What was I going to do with all the extra time after giving two-week's notice to my two employers? There sure as hell wasn't enough time to sober up in between. Not even close.

Once the 16th arrived—and boy, that jumped out through the alcohol-induced fog quickly—it was off to Fort Campbell, Kentucky for basic training. Definitely not the location or method of choice for recovering from a hangover, although we weren't treated totally like dirt-bags the first couple days. They wanted to sweet talk the troops a bit before tearing us to pieces.

First, we draftees had to take a battery of tests, so the Army could figure out how to get the most out of all its newfound talent. Of course, as soon as the aptitude evaluations were completed, "we were given the opportunity to sign up for additional years of service—to enlist. Doing so would allow us to choose our military occupational specialty (MOS), our job assignment.

The downside was that our two-year active-duty obligation would increase to three years or more as a result. But as a plus, the dreaded infantry in Vietnam could be avoided.

An interesting approach; not bribery exactly, but close."[3, ii]

There weren't many takers though, and I too decided to take my chances.

"Fortuitously, I had scored highly on some of the tests, so the Army evaluator/recruiter reviewing the options with me thought it was likely—'ninety-eight percent certain,' were his exact words—that I wouldn't end up in the infantry anyhow. I'd probably be assigned to a medical or chemical lab technician specialty, since my scores for those were outstanding and both required months and months of specialized schooling.

My recruiter figured I could go to work immediately in either, or some office specialty as well, with minimal on-the-job training. He even suggested the Army would be 'nuts' to put me anywhere else based on all the money they'd save on training.

My undergraduate classes and labs in biology and chemistry were looking like lifesavers. So, at 'ninety-eight percent certain,' why sign up for an additional year or two?

That made no sense. Besides, I wanted to get back to college as soon as possible."[3]

Getting drafted gets your head on straight rather quickly, so two years was undoubtedly going to be enough time. In fact, those first two days had been enough and then some.

Well, surprise! "The test scores meant nothing, nor did the theory about the Army saving money. When the assignments came down toward the end of basic training, my MOS was 11B—INFANTRY! That's what graduating from a two-year business school and three-and-a-half years of college will do for you."[3]

NADA! ZILCH!

"Not only that, I was on my way to advance infantry training (AIT) at Tiger Land, a training area at Fort Polk, Louisiana. From there, the next stop was automatically Vietnam,"[3] unless your brother, mother, or some other blood kin was already in-country.

Since I didn't have a brother and couldn't talk my mother into it, there wasn't much doubt where I was heading at that point. The trip to Nam was still on down the road, however.

"First, there was a two-week leader preparation course at the Fort Polk Academy. That was followed by nine weeks of AIT in Tiger Land, an interesting place to say the least."[3]

Yeah, boy. It was different, training in the armpit of the south.

Running everywhere growling—*like a tiger*—was certainly novel for someone my age as was the field training at old "Fort Puke" as the trainees called it. But "you probably couldn't find a better place than the swamps of Louisiana to get ready for slogging in the Mekong Delta. The mucky, slimy terrain was certainly appropriate."[3]

The region actually boasts of being the only place in the country where one can find all the poisonous snakes indigenous to the United States. That's in addition to alligators, wild boar, and tarantula-like hairy spiders.

Pretty impressive, huh?

Considering that we managed to kill three coral snakes and a water moccasin inside the perimeter our first day on bivouac, I was impressed!

Can you imagine how closely one will inspect a sleeping bag and pup tent after that?

However, to prepare for the rice paddies in Nam, it was probably the place for AIT. You tended to learn good habits about staying alert.

Then, there was one other horizon-expanding opportunity prior to going to Nam—a chance to go to the infantry NCO school[iii] at Fort Benning, Georgia. It was the training ground for shake 'n' bake sergeants.

"Promotions of enlisted personnel into the sergeant ranks normally require years of on-the-job experience. However, Vietnam produced a massive shortage of squad leader and platoon sergeant NCOs, creating the need for shake 'n' bakes to fill the void."[3]

So, with real life-and-death combat lurking in my immediate future, I decided the more preparation, the better. That old 11Bravo can really tweak one's enthusiasm for "more training, drill sergeant!" And since the NCO school didn't add any time to my active-duty service (officer candidate school—my other option—would have tacked on a year), "I figured the additional training couldn't hurt.

But it hurt plenty. Army Rangers doled out lots of pain beginning with what seemed like endless physical training."[3]

The training was outstanding, though, for what it was intended to do. We were probably in the best physical condition possible, and a lot of the things that were supposedly taught in AIT finally made sense; they could be done.

Hand-to-hand combat as taught by the Rangers was a perfect example. It would have been a crime to use the rudimentary "skills" learned in AIT. They were a joke. Luckily, I never had to use those hammered home by the Rangers either, but they were workable. Hours and hours in the sawdust pit—beating the piss out of one another under the watchful eye of an E-5 with no neck—saw to that.

Of course, no one bothered to tell us until we were about finished with school that all the additional training and enhanced skills were going to *increase* our chances of *not* making it back from Vietnam unscathed. Recent statistics indicated it would increase that likelihood *significantly*. Four of five of us would be tagged WIA or KIA.

Say what?

Wounded-in-action or killed-in-action? Four of five?

How's that for cheery news?

That's what the "Follow Me" motto at Fort Benning will do for you. The guys up front tend to catch the "shit" first. So do those talking on the radio when a sniper Victor Charlie can pick and choose.

I still worked hard though, figuring the more I knew, the better the chances of staying alive, even up front or jawing on the radio. It sure wasn't easy, but "somehow, I managed to survive the twelve weeks, graduating as a staff sergeant, E-6, one of eight making that rank. The others who endured to the end of the marathon, roughly 160, came out as three-strip, E-5, sergeants.

Then, after pushing troops through AIT an additional nine weeks at Fort Ord, California and a thirty-day leave [half in Hawaii, half in Wisconsin], it was time to head out to apply the lessons learned."[3]

Did I learn enough to be the lucky, unscathed one in five?

The thing about having been through the NCO school—going to Vietnam as a staff sergeant—was that I was immediately responsible for the lives of others, not just my own. That also may have contributed to my feelings going home later, since in that position, there were fewer opportunities to be concerned with my own wellbeing.

When you're busy getting the job done—keeping track of everyone, getting orders, giving orders, and generally trying to maintain order during chaos—you don't have a hell of a lot of time to think about anything else. Especially not during a firefight, when live rounds are flying all directions. Live rounds tend to be a tad bit unforgiving.

Of course, everyone in the replacement detachment in Vietnam was jealous when my assignment came down; it equated to having it made. The unit I was going to—Company D, 2nd Battalion, 3rd Infantry, 199th Light Infantry Brigade—was operating air mobile out of Long Binh, the largest military base in the country. They were routinely spending three days in the field, then six back at the base guarding the perimeter. Rumor had it, they hadn't had a single casualty in over five months.

It was going to be "walk in the park" time.

Sure, it was. I never saw the inside of Long Binh again after going to the field. Delta Company got new orders . . . seemingly making us air mobile from just about anywhere in the boonies in Southeast Asia.

Into the Hueys! Out of the Hueys! Watch it—it might be a hot LZ!

For starters, we took a little jaunt up to Xuan Loc, northeast of Saigon, to break me in by busting my butt in the jungle for a few days. It was fun-with-machetes time; trail blazing, ten whacks per inch.

That was just to get a taste of the good life in the hills, however. Soon thereafter we were choppered back to the booby-trapped sauna region southwest of Saigon. Time for new fun: boiling in your own sweat followed by a quick dip in a refreshing pool of rice paddy sludge.

Then, it was on to visit the 25th Division, up the road, near Cu Chi.

Need some help up here, guys?

Unfortunately, someone forgot to tell us that we were expected to act as greeters for a bevy of vacationing Northerners hiking in from across the Cambodian border.

Yes, indeed. A mere three weeks after I arrived in country—two weeks after listening to Joe Willie Namath make good on his outlandish Super Bowl prediction—Delta Company's 1st Platoon was ambushed by what was later estimated as a battalion of North Vietnamese regulars; a far cry from the original assessment that they tangled with a VC squad. The whole damn bunch of them had burrowed underground, and 1st Platoon stumbled upon . . . almost into . . . their tunnel and bunker complex.

Checking for shadows on Groundhog Day, those creeping out of burrows, had a whole new meaning that February. *Shit really hit the fan!*

Morning entries in the 2nd Battalion's Combined Staff Journal barely touch on the grim realities in the field that day.

At 0831, 1st Platoon reported that they had been ambushed by what they thought was a VC squad. It wasn't noted until 0900 that they sustained five WIA and two KIA as a result. Orders for the remainder of Delta Company to move out in support of 1st Platoon came at 0840, and 2nd and 3rd Platoons departed our night defensive position (NDP) at 0902. I was 3rd Squad Leader in 2nd Platoon and we had seen no action since my arrival.

Our platoons arrived at 1st Platoon's position at 0925 when small arms fire erupted from the tree line to our right (unreported to battalion, apparently). Remarkably, we didn't take any casualties at that point.

At 0945, we received orders from the battalion C.O. to sweep the contact area and we were underway at 0957. By 1010, we had two WIA and added one KIA at 1015. Based on our expenditure of ammunition, it was already clear we would need to be resupplied, which was requested at 1025.

At 1100, we had a helicopter LFT on site blasting the hell out of the enemy positions inside the tree line, the second one to do so since 1st Platoon got hit. Between the first and the second LFT, artillery bombarded the tree line constantly.

None of it seemed to do squat.

By the time the dustoff arrived—also at 1100—we had five WIA in need of evacuation, not just the two called for earlier. The one bit of good news was our

DAILY STAFF JOURNAL OR DUTY OFFICER'S LOG				PAGE NO. 1	NO. OF PAGES 9		
(AR 220-346 & FM 101-5)							
ORGANIZATION OR INSTALLATION	LOCATION	PERIOD COVERED					
Combined Staff Journal	XT7120		FROM		TO		
2d Bn, 3d Inf		HOUR	DATE	HOUR	DATE		
199th Inf Bde (Sep)(Lt)	CONFIDENTIAL	0001	2 Feb 69	2400	2 Feb 69		
ITEM NO.	TIME IN	TIME OUT	INCIDENTS, MESSAGES, ORDERS, ETC.		ACTION TAKEN		INL
1	0001		(U) Journal Opened by Sgt E-5 Horcha DNCO		JSF		JH
2	0100		(U) Sitrep negative		2/25		JH

Item No.	Time in	Incidents, Messages, Orders, etc.
12	0831	(C) Co D #2 Eagle has contact with VC Sqd; Reported grid XT685218 for contact
14	0840	(C) Co D (-) ordered to move out into contact area
15	0900	(C) Requested urgent dustoff of 5 WIA, 2 KIA
17	0902	(C) Co D leaving NDP to assist in contact
31	0925	(C) Co D arrived at point of contact
41	0945	(C) Co D moving on sweep of contact area
46	0957	(C) Co D is sweeping area of contact
50	1010	(C) Co D sustained two frag wounds
51	1015	(C) Co D – 1 more KIA
53	1025	(C) Requested resupply bird from 2/25
63	1100	(C) LFT firing – Right on target
64	1100	(C) Dustoff complete – took 5 WIA
65	1100	(C) Resupply complete

resupply of ammunition arrived then as well, but our afternoon turned out to be worse than the morning . . . LOTS worse.

* * *

What an absolute bitch of a day that was. The temperature reached well over 100 degrees and too fuckin' much. It was like fighting in a furnace. To make things worse, we ran out of water by midday and didn't get any choppered in for what seemed like days. Try swallowing fire sometime. With your mouth and throat already exhibiting symptoms of Death Valley, that's about all swallowing burning air contributed.

Food?

None at all that day . . . not even C rations.

Hell, the closest I came to cleaning my M-16—something of significantly greater importance than food—was squirting some grease into it *one* time while two jets took turns screaming in overhead. They were delivering the mail to our hosts . . .

Air Mail Special.

As if it wasn't hot enough already, they spread a little napalm around the area. Just what the fuck we needed.

Those Airedales would make an abrupt U-turn at the last possible moment in their dive, releasing canisters that tumbled in slow motion, then spewed flames and molten incendiary waves along the ground . . . the inferno belching and pulsating . . . engulfing everything in its path.

Shit! Getting shot was the least of our worries. With all the extra Goddamn heat, we were just going to fry . . . or choke on the stench.

Wrong again.

As soon as the jets quit their bombing and strafing runs, Charlie popped right back out of the ground, bringin' smoke back our way.

Damn!

How in the fucking hell did he survive that?

Back at it: AK-47s . . . M-16s . . . 30 caliber machine-guns . . . M-60s . . . grenades . . .

Keep down! Move in!

The only time anyone under my command was killed was that day; a ghastly experience I won't ever forget! He wound up at the bottom of a hellish gully— *dead*—late that afternoon, but it wasn't possible to get him out until the next day. Oh, we got to him before dark . . . even got a rope under his arms, around his chest, but the ravine was just too deep, the walls too steep.

Our soon-to-be ex-battalion C.O. had already ordered most of Delta Company out—the ignorant asshole. Maybe if he'd been on the ground where the action was, rather than flying around out-of-range all day, he might have had a clue about what the fuck was going on.

He was definitely "Number 10," to use the local jargon in Nam.

There were only five of us left in there; three trying to keep Charlie pinned in his lair . . . that abscess in the earth being honeycombed with firing ports from a maze of intersecting tunnels. To top it off, somewhere along the line the Goddamn sun had sunken out of sight.

Son of a bitch! There was no choice.

Pull out!

* * *

"I put close to a thousand rounds through my M-16 and could have spit on Charlie when it all started. He was close."[3]

Welcome to Southeast Asia . . . the scenic view, gazing down the barrel of a Kalashnikov assault rifle—a Russian AK-47.

17

That little dawn-to-dusk fiasco near Cu Chi marked Delta Company's initiation into the '69 Tet Offensive; not as big as the one in 1968, but it certainly got *our* attention. We lost far too damn many of our company in one day . . . killed, wounded, heat exhaustion, dehydration.

The company commander was KIA merely trying to peek over the rim of a gully where we had been receiving intense fire from automatic weapons . . . the Gully of the Shadows of Death.[4, iv] Our platoon sergeant was shot through the kneecap by a machine gun burst, same gully.

With those two casualties late in the day, I moved from squad leader to platoon leader, my lieutenant taking over as company C.O.

It was truly baptism under fire: learn your job in one hell of a big hurry or don't even bother. You weren't going to be at it long enough to employ trial and error. Besides, most Charlie-induced errors weren't rectifiable, not without divine intervention.

Total U.S. casualties: twenty-seven WIA; seven KIA. Most were Deltas, but Bravo and Charlie Company joined the party just prior to midday. The latter made their share of dustoff requests to battalion headquarters as well.

* * *

Overall, the men performed exceptionally that day. For many, like me, it was the first exposure to combat, the first firefight. There would be more. Those of us who were left learned a lot about each other that day though. We learned quickly too . . . a necessity when a blink of the eye can represent a lifetime—and did.

Until the terrain explodes around you, no one can truly know how they'll react under fire; they just hope. But, from my experience that day, nearly everyone responded amazingly. Oh, one of our M-60 machine-gunners froze initially, but he stepped up the remainder of the day.

So, damn good, all in all.

In fact, the 2nd Platoon became almost unstoppable after that. Charlie may have gotten in the first licks in 1969, but we had the troops to turn it around.

Enyeart, Russell, Perry, and Petite. Cunningham, Hardison, and Rodriquez. Rogers, Martin, and Holmes. Those were just a few of my brothers in 2nd Platoon ol' Chuck had to reckon with in 1969.

Good soldiers?

Nope. THE BEST!

They were "Number 1" and then some. And there were a bunch more of equal quality.

As civilians, there probably wasn't one among them anyone would have thought looked like a combat soldier. Back in the real world they all would have been pretty much Average Joe. But, boy, if you wanted to surround yourself with people you could entrust your life to, there were none better.

Average Joe they were not.

Undoubtedly, the least likely soldier in the 2nd Platoon was Russell, our radio operator. The L.A. hippie, in a band . . . get this . . . called, "The Real Electric

Butterscotch Tractor." His family and friends expected him to stoke up and skip to Canada when his draft notice arrived.

He didn't.

Russell couldn't quite explain why not either (something nebulous about not letting his grandmother down), but no one minded. You could count on him for whatever was needed.

Russell had only been with us a day or two when he humped the radio along on my first "flying solo" command in the field. It was up at Cu Chi, while we were on perimeter guard at the 25th's base camp . . . prior to the gully escapade.

In the middle of the night, peering through a long-range starlight scope, someone on a nearby tower spotted lights flickering and bobbing along a couple thousand meters out. There wasn't supposed to be anyone out there, so I got to take a makeshift squad to check it out. Russell was one of the "volunteers" who went with me.

Except for some glowing embers in an old stump near a massive bomb crater, we didn't find anything that might explain the lights. However, we did find lots of footprints on an obscure trail running parallel to the base perimeter—boot prints and sandals; some barefoot—so Charlie might have been through there that night.

The tracks looked fresh too.

Why I thought that (and radioed it back to the base), I'm not sure. It wasn't like I was an experienced tracker . . . and it was night. But that's the way they looked in the moonlight.

Once I pointed them out, Russell saw the tracks as well. At least, I think he did, since he sure talked about it a lot afterward . . . indicating that he was going to stick close to anyone who could find footprints in the dark.

A few days later (during that daylong dance with the NVA in the gully), I was sure glad to have him there . . . close by. He was watching my backside so Charlie—the shadowy groundhog—wouldn't pop out of one of his many subterranean passages behind me. Russell was definitely covering my butt that afternoon—literally.

We were on the right flank during the last advance of the day . . . keeping the troops from getting too spread out.

Somehow, when we finally got in there, Russell and I were the only ones on the south side of that meandering bitch of a ditch. That was not the best place to be. With tunnel entrances hidden all over the place, you didn't know where the next AK burst might come from.

But Russell had me covered. I can still hear him back there: "Psst! Hey, Chief! Over here!"

Glancing back, there was Russell pointing his M-16 toward a spider hole or tunnel he'd found, waiting for me to join him. While he kept watch, I'd check it out, pull the pin on a hand grenade, pop the handle, and count to myself: "one thousand one, one thousand two, one thousand three, one thousand . . .;" drop it in and duck.

One or two grenades, depending on what Russell had found at that point, and it was back to business . . . inching in closer to the ravine to try to catch a glimpse of our man who had tumbled in there a short time earlier.

"Psst! Hey, Chief! Another one!"

More hand grenades, again and again. The radio was always there the instant I needed it as well.

Russell may have looked more like a librarian, with his big round glasses and bookworm face, but he was a damn good soldier. *Damn* good! Straight—no drugs—100 percent of the time too.

As he acknowledged, his *life* depended on it. Quite often, so did mine.

* * *

I bounced back and forth between platoon sergeant and platoon leader during the remainder of my time in Nam. That depended mainly on whether Lieutenant Enyeart, alias Lieutenant Rock, was acting as Delta Company C.O. or not . . . something that seemed to happen quite often.

The 2nd Platoon started gaining a real identity too. It became an exceedingly efficient, interactive team, and nothing could get the guys down.

Been in the field for days? Dehydrated? Exhausted? Up to your waist in mud? No sweat!

Out of food? Out of water?

The pain from seventy-plus pounds of gear on your shoulders is unbearable? No sweat!

Charlie is in the area? He kicked butt down the road?

No sweat!

We can handle it.

We did too.

We got lucky a few times, got into and out of a few things without losing *our* butts, and pretty soon the crusty "No Sweat Platoon" was being called upon whenever anything hairy would come up. Even Colonel Mess, our new battalion C.O., would ask for the laid-back, no-sweat eccentrics at crunch time, and somewhere along the line he fell in love with the number Two-Five . . . my call-sign at the time.

I'm not sure how that happened either.

There's no question Colonel Mess was convinced I had a few screws loose the first time he saw me. Or, to use the French/Vietnamese jargon of the time, he was certain I was "beaucoup *dien cau dau*" . . . totally nuts . . . big time.

The colonel's chopper had dropped him off in the toolies where Delta was slogging around in the muck soon after he took over as battalion commander. One of the first questions he asked our C.O. as he was trudging along with him was: "who's that crazy son-of-a-bitch out there, in mud damn near up to his chest, laughing and clowning around?"

Captain Davis told me later that he merely replied, "Oh, that's just Sergeant Trewyn. He's always like that."

With that feeble first impression, it was a bit surprising when he started asking for me specifically in potentially dicey situations.

One day, Colonel Mess radioed the C.O. with an intelligence report of *two-hundred-and-fifty* Russian-built Tiger tanks in the area.

His suggestion?

"Have Two-Five take six or eight guys and check it out."

EXCUSE ME?!

And just what the hell am I supposed to do if we find them?

Fortunately, we didn't, but we usually managed to find plenty of other stuff. We took care of whatever it was too.

The 2nd Platoon did one hell of a job!

* * *

Sometime early on during my tour of duty, soon after the Cu Chi debacle, I became absolutely convinced that the reason we were there—the cause we were fighting for—was worthwhile. Most importantly, I was convinced the South Vietnamese people were worth it.

I was in Vietnam for less than four months, but the Vietnamese I was exposed to—civilians and soldiers—were good people, committed to the fight. They wanted the North Vietnamese and Vietcong out.

The ARVN Rangers we teamed up with a few times were first-rate soldiers. They knew what they were doing, and they kicked Charlie's ass more than once.

The civilians wanted to be left alone; they didn't want to be visited at night and beaten by the VC tax collectors. But it wasn't like they could just pack up and leave. The ties to their hamlet, to their family, and the land where they were raised—to the ancestors who were buried there—were just too strong.

Leaving was not an option . . . EVER! Well, until *after* the war.

And, of course, we were in some areas where the civilian populace was on the other side, but that shouldn't have been unexpected. These were generally areas where the villagers had to deal with the VC each and every night. As a result, choices were not something they had the option to make . . . not if they wanted to live or wanted their family to live.

Survival: The option selected.

The two Vietnamese I knew best were the Kit Carson scouts with our company.[5] They had both been on the other side, so we were able to learn a great deal from them.

Chaum, a former VC, was the more dedicated of the two, so far as his willingness to fight. He "was always in the middle of the action, and there was no question he was fighting on the side he wanted to be on. He could have taken fewer chances with his life if that were not the case."[5, v]

Chaum was a good-looking kid, and now and then he'd have a chance to put on his civvies and head for some nearby hamlet to "socialize" a bit. "He always had a .45 caliber pistol under his shirt and you never knew who or what he might come back with the next day.

One morning, he returned with area VC tax collectors at gun point. Eight of them at once . . . all by himself."[5, v]

No, Chaum was in it by choice, although that was not always the case. He told of being beaten and dragged out of his village, unconscious, when barely in his teens, thus, "volunteering" for service with the Vietcong. Once he had the opportunity to repay his former benefactors, he certainly took advantage of it.

Our other scout, Long, was a little different story. He was from North Vietnam, from an area just outside Hanoi. Long was not a fighter though. "Had he been from the U.S., he likely would have qualified as a conscientious objector. Long couldn't seem to handle the concept of fighting in any way, shape, or form."[5, v] That's probably why he "chieu hoied," surrendered to our side, first chance he got.

What a neat guy though. You talk about funny. "Even though he spoke almost no English, Long could crack us up in nothing flat. It helped take the edge off at some very difficult times."[5, v]

The thing is, both Long and Chaum were worth fighting for. They helped us; we helped them. Politics had nothing to do with it. People were the issue.

What would happen to them if we weren't there?

Yes, the cause was worth fighting for and the people were worth fighting for. I was sufficiently convinced to be willing to put my life on the line for it. You can't go much further than that.

If the end came, I knew I'd be ready for it too. During some solitary moment, I thought briefly about having crammed a great deal of living into just a few years—traveling around the country, *partying a bunch* (much to my father's dismay), going to school in Hawaii.

I hoped my family wouldn't take it too badly if it happened; it would be worse for one of the younger guys to die—some of them hadn't really experienced life.

I had.

Although there is no telling exactly where we were when those quiet, inward conversations were conducted, the thoughts were imprinted indelibly. However, once that moment passed, I felt comfortable getting on with the difficult job at hand, more at ease.

In looking back, it makes me wonder if other members of 2nd Platoon didn't have similar thoughts; didn't come to some quiet resolutions themselves. Such things would never have been spoken of in the field, but the efficiency, camaraderie, and easy-going approach that developed suggest it may have been so.

Perhaps that's what made the "no sweat" philosophy work.

We were in other firefights after that initial one, and the 2nd Platoon came out on the long end each time. We avoided two or three other ambushes when we probably shouldn't have, and Charlie paid.

We found most booby traps before "they" found us. The 2nd Platoon just managed to do such things. We had the right attitude; we believed we could do whatever was necessary, and we did.

No sweat!

Somehow attitude seemed to be the key. While the 2nd Platoon was loose and confident, "3rd Platoon always thought they were going to get their butts kicked with whatever was assigned . . . and did."[6, vi]

The 3rd Platoon lost their Lieutenant and only two sergeants one day, and I had to take over as platoon leader. God, that was scary!

No matter what I did, they wouldn't loosen up. But I managed to survive the two to three weeks until they got a new second lieutenant and staff sergeant though, so it was back to the 2nd Platoon. What a relief.

But would you believe, in just a few days, the new second "Louie" and sergeant in 3rd Platoon both joined the Delta Company casualty club along with another NCO that had joined them only a couple days before?

Shit!

I told Captain Davis it was a bad idea to send me back, but he did anyhow.

The *next day*, I got hit.

"Third Platoon was pushing point on a teargas mission outside Binh Chan, South Vietnam, a mission intended to deny Charlie access to our base from that direction. Bags of powdered CS gas were being wrapped with detonation cord to be blown once the bags had been strung out in the dense vegetation along the river. Since the dry season was in full force, the nasty, irritating residue would likely stay on the overgrowth for a long, long time, discouraging Vietcong from sneaking in that way.

At least, that was the theory.

Clearing the path, we had gotten a bit ahead of the troops hauling the bags, so we held up on a patch of high ground to take a break while keeping alert up front.

I had already dropped my helmet when one of the guys found what might have been a cache of some sort next to a big tree. Since digging into it with entrenching tools would take forever, dropping a hand grenade into a fist-size opening that had been located seemed like a much better idea."[6, vi]

"I was kneeling down in front of the mound of dirt, grenade in my right hand, index finger on my left hand through the ring, ready to pull the pin.

Then my plans changed . . . abruptly."[6]

"A chemical and radiation expert major—a 'first-timer' in the field after seven months in country—tripped a booby-trap behind me"[6] . . . what may have been one of our "dud" mortar rounds that hit there. "Two of my PFC squad leaders and a sergeant accompanying the major caught some of the shrapnel at the same time."[6]

How's that for good luck?

Unbelievable, but SOP for the 3rd Platoon.

Since Delta was strung out so damn far and the muck and mire were not allowing much help to get to us quickly, I was scrambling around trying to collect bandages for all the wounds. There were lots of them.

Captain Davis and his radio operator got to us first, and they started working on the major who had the most serious injuries. But it wasn't until Captain Davis yelled at me to put a tourniquet on the sergeant's leg that he figured out I had gotten hit as well.

I was helping to get a bandage on one of my squad leaders and yelled back at the C.O. that applying a tourniquet would be tough to do, since I couldn't use my right arm. After his surprised query, asking if I'd been hit (I answered in the affirmative), he decided that one of the other guys would have to take care of the sergeant.

Of course, my helping out . . . with much of anything . . . ended a few seconds later.

In reaching across to grab another dressing with my left hand, I hit my right sleeve. It felt really weird.

"What the hell?"

Because some of the bags of powdered CS leaked, we all had our fatigues tucked and buttoned up tight, sleeves rolled down. Not only that, we had rubber bands around the sleeves at our wrists to keep any of the powder from getting on our arms. And although I realized I couldn't move my right arm, I hadn't thought about it bleeding. The thought never crossed my mind—not at all—even though I knew the top of my head was oozing a bit from where a piece of shrapnel had bounced off my thick skull. The blood running into my eyes was damn annoying.

But, being perplexed by the spongy sleeve (and obviously still not thinking . . . the arm didn't really hurt; I just couldn't straighten it out), I stood up, slipped my left index finger inside the rubber band, and pulled.

Dumb! *Really* dumb! It looked like someone was pouring tomato juice from a pitcher.

Whoa!

The old knees certainly quaked at that point.

Time to sit down before you fall down . . . *you dumb shit!*

"Hey, could someone put a bandage on this thing?"

Well, all of us who got kissed by "Mort" that day survived. The major—riddled with holes from his neck to his ankles—probably wouldn't have, except for the fact that a medevac chopper got us to 3rd Field Hospital in Saigon amazingly fast. Surgeons were scrambling to plug all the major's leaks less than an hour after it happened.

Lucky, damn lucky.

The call for a dustoff went to battalion that morning at 11:54. The guy was "on station" at 11:56. *Two minutes!*

How often did that happen?

We were loaded and airborne at 12:02.

"Totally by chance, the medevac was almost directly overhead with one casualty on board when he got the word,"[6] but I'll never know how he managed to get into, then out of, the place where we got hit. There sure as hell wasn't a big enough opening in the trees, but those dustoff/medevac pilots could manage the impossible.

We were all thankful many different times for that.

During the chopper ride, thinking about the situation, there seemed little doubt I'd be back in the field in three to four weeks. As one of two ambulatory stowaways, what did I have to worry about?

The head wound, while aggravating due to the blood running in my eyes, was obviously superficial, and the arm wound would undoubtedly heal quickly and the arm regain mobility once the shrapnel was removed.

Of course, it sure wasn't worth a shit the way it was, though.

Instantly when the shrapnel ripped into the upper portion of my right arm, lodging against the bone, the muscles in the whole arm locked up, my elbow frozen in place at about a right angle. That was going to be a real pain-in-the-ass for someone who was right-handed. It cost me my mustache (about a quarter of it with the first swipe) trying to shave with the wrong hand a couple days later.

That seemed painful at the time.

The only other noticeable annoyance during that short Huey trek to the hospital was a stinging sensation on my back; something akin to a floor burn I could recall from my basketball playing days. Hmmm. I must have scraped it against a tree at some point.

Oh well, having not felt anything back there before, it couldn't amount to much.

And it certainly made no sense when we touched down at 3rd Field in Saigon and the triage doc insisted that I needed to be second in line behind the major. I walked on and off the chopper for Christ's sake.

Our two other litter casualties—the sergeant accompanying the major and one of my squad leaders—were clearly in greater need of treatment than I was. I don't get it.

It wasn't until the surgeon working on my arm in the hospital told me I'd be heading to Japan the next day (it turned out to be Okinawa) that the revelation of the floor burn being an entry wound occurred. The guy was using local anesthetics, so I was able to carry on a conversation with him while he was digging around.

After making a few less than complimentary suggestions when he muttered "oops" at one point, I commented, "you would have thought if I was going to get hit, I could have at least done a good enough job at it to get shipped out of country."

That's when he informed me that X-rays showed a piece of metal in the middle of my left lung, about 2 inches from my heart.

Say what?!

Since they were expecting my lung to collapse and didn't want to crack open my chest in Nam, I was being shipped out. The surgeon explained that it had to do with infections being "slightly problematic" in Vietnam.

Oh, yeah! I had heard all about such infections. They were "slightly problematic" in about the same way as being run over by a two-ton truck tended to be.

But what the hell, I had "lucked out" and was on my way out of country.

Why worry about a little infection or some spare tin next to my heart?

No sweat!

Of course, at that point, I fully expected to be back in the scenic South in the not-too-distant future anyhow. The little bit of damage I sustained had hardly even hurt . . . YET!

COMBAT . . . THE "EASY" PART

Enduring Truth: *Pay attention! Lessons about death might really be lessons about life.*

25

Chapter 4

OKINAWA

Recovering from the wounds; reflecting on the battles.

Initially, by far the biggest thing about being in the hospital was the fact that it allowed me to get some much-needed rest. During my few months in Nam, I probably averaged two to four hours' sleep a night, and we were in the field essentially the whole time.

Even when operating out of a base camp (generally a small, company-size fire support base) the platoon either had perimeter guard or was split up for ambush patrols at night. Neither of those activities was particularly conducive to catching up on one's sleep. Not when "shit could hit the fan" at a moment's notice and often did.

Of course, some of the missions we went on lasted seven to ten days, so then the "luxury" of a fire support base wasn't even available.

Time in the field was definitely a bitch.

When operating in the Mekong Delta, resting at night generally meant rolling up in a poncho liner, wet from head to toe. In the morning . . . after a stint or two on guard, peering out into pitch blackness, straining to see or hear any sign of movement . . . it was back into the paddies, still wet.

Laying in the hospital in Okinawa, I could remember how great it felt some days just having a minute or two to take off my boots and wring out my socks. Putting those "dry" socks back on was a real highlight; we're talking close to a religious experience.

Hallelujah and pass the ammunition. That was as good as things got, and then the next step was likely to be in mud above the knee.

Yes, I must have been a tad bit tired if such things rated as fond memories while lollygagging around in bed in the hospital.

I could remember one mission in particular, one that kept getting extended every time we thought we were heading back in. We were wet continuously for more than a week, and that was during the *dry* season in Nam.

Dishpan hands?

No, we're talking dishpan bodies here. That doesn't exactly conjure up a pretty picture, and in thinking about it, it wasn't.

However, on that particular mission, fatigue and excruciating pain everywhere that moved (and most places that didn't) were much bigger problems. We lost twelve of roughly seventy in the company, including the company commander, just from heat exhaustion. They were hauled out, one or two at a time, by chopper.

It was one "Number 10" nut buster.

With the shoulder straps on my rucksack feeling like razor-wire being ratcheted tighter and tighter, day after day—cutting into muscle and bone—I swore I'd never pack anything on my back again if I made it back to the real world.

The medics couldn't keep up with the demand for Darvon or salt tablets on that mission, since those had to be rationed along with everything else. Guys would try to keep going, straining to pull one foot out of the muck, then the other, until they'd just lose consciousness. Down they'd go, out cold, so to speak, in the mud.

By chance, I saw it happen with one of my guys. He didn't stagger; his knees didn't buckle. He was struggling along at the same comatose pace as everyone else . . . then, the lights went out. His forward momentum kept his upper body heading in the same direction, but his feet stopped moving.

Over he went like a chopped-off lodge-pole pine. His hands didn't so much as twitch to break the fall.

And there he was, face down in the muck . . . unconscious.

"Call in a dustoff!"

I almost joined the Delta Dustoffs on that mission as well. I stepped in a hole, fell, and had cramps in my legs so bad I couldn't even begin to get up.

I was sprawled out on my back, across a large dike adjacent to a stream; my right foot hooked under a root in the hole and my head and shoulders down almost in the water. All I was able to do was thrash around for a time, until a couple of the troops managed to get me up. After a few salt tablets and a lot of arguing with the lieutenant then acting as C.O., it was agreed that I wouldn't be medevaced out . . . at the moment.

While such things were just a fact of life in the field, it didn't take long in the hospital to recognize I really did need some time to recover from the overall physical toll. Those typical days at the office near the Cambodian border had me a bit wrung out.

Of course, maybe I should have been hospitalized for an identity crisis as well.

During my last six weeks in Nam, I bounced from job to job so often it was hard to keep track of who or what I was supposed to be. It started with my move from platoon sergeant with the 2nd Platoon to company first sergeant (being the ranking NCO in Delta at the time with all of two-plus months in country). One perk of that assignment was that it allowed me to trade in my M-16 for the previous first sergeant's sexier CAR-15, a little, chopped-off version of the M-16.

Then I moved to platoon leader with the 3rd Platoon—doing a lieutenant's job again (while keeping my new toy, the CAR-15). After a couple weeks or so it was back to 2nd Platoon as platoon sergeant, followed by platoon leader, then platoon sergeant again . . . the latter for less than a day.

27

Why such a short time? Because the C.O. had me go back to playing platoon leader with the 3rd Platoon one more time, that also for less than a day as it turned out.

Hello, Sybil? I've heard of split personalities, but Holy Christ!

What else could have been thrown in there?

Oh, yeah, there was also a stint as "command liaison" at an ARVN Ranger base seven straight nights somewhere along the line. That was while performing one or more of the other jobs during the day.

What fun!

The job as command liaison was a real trip too. At least it gave me a chuckle or two in the hospital while thinking about it.

The purpose of that esteemed position was to coordinate our ambush patrols, so Delta Company wouldn't be mixing it up with the ARVN troops by mistake. It almost happened a couple nights that week, but there were other, more compelling highlights I could recall.

Since I was the ranking American going across the river to the Ranger base every night, protocol dictated that I dine—have soup and green tea—with the ARVN commander. Most nights that was no big deal . . . the vegetarian soup was quite palatable.

However, the only time I've ever eaten dog (that I know of) was the fourth or fifth night over there. It wasn't bad. But, figuring out what it was took more than a little arm waving and hand signals. With the ARVN commander knowing, at most, ten less-than-understandable English words and my minuscule—"ti ti"—knowledge of Vietnamese, our ability to converse wasn't all that easy.

He finally got the message across though. And I was just happy to figure out that the meat I was chewing on in the soup that night wasn't rat; that's the only four-legged source of flesh I'd seen running around the camp.

I wouldn't have believed that rats would fight you for food until those seven nights at the ARVN base. We're talking sizable vermin too . . . ten, fifteen pounds, some more than that. Big city sewer rats would have nothing on these brutes.

The first night at dusk up on the roof of the ARVN command post, 2nd Platoon's Tennessee knife-throwing aficionado pitched his toad-sticker at one of those small dog-sized critters just as the first three or four were slinking up onto the roof. He skewered it mid-body from about 15 feet. Of course, our knife-tosser then had to jump off the roof and chase the rat and his favorite blade all the way across the compound before the damn thing finally keeled over.

It took one hell of a big club for the guy on radio watch to keep those aggressive bastards off the other two guys *trying* to sleep.

What a way to live. The hospital bed in Okinawa sure seemed cozy and peaceful by comparison.

It turned out that the time in the hospital in Okinawa was probably needed to recover from the overall mental exhaustion imposed down south as well. During my brief three-and-a-half months in Nam, having never been off duty, I had no chance to relax mentally either.

That included while sleeping too. In fact, I don't know if I was ever *really* asleep.

Oh, four-deuce mortars were sometimes being fired twenty to thirty feet from where I was "dozing," and I wouldn't hear them. There was constant chatter on the field radio maybe a foot or two from my head, and I wouldn't hear that either. But, let an enemy sighting be *whispered* as part of that chatter (with or without the nearby din of mortar fire), and I was wide awake. It was a matter of all the senses operating at 100-percent-plus efficiency 100 percent of the time.

On one occasion in the field, I was catching some late night Zs on an ambush patrol north of Long Binh while "friendly" artillery rounds were thundering overhead, as they had been most of the night. All at once, I sat straight up, totally awake—scaring the shit out of the guy on guard next to me, I might add.

What?

For a moment, I didn't know why I woke up. Then it hit me: Two rounds had gone over the opposite way.

Again, these weren't things I thought about in Nam, it was just the way of life there. At least it was, if you wanted to have a life to live. However, in Okinawa, I was finally able to let all the systems shut down. You talk about "crash and burn" time. I felt totally drained. The rest was really needed.

Not that everything about the R&R in the hospital was what I would call positive, however. Taking a shower, for instance. There was one rather disconcerting episode the very first time I was able to lather up. That was a few days after getting to Okinawa though, since enough bandages had to be removed so I could get at least partially wet.

Well, after being dry for a few days, my feet basically started to disintegrate once they were reintroduced to water. Layers and layers of skin . . . in patches and granular pieces . . . began to just peel off.

Not a clear enough picture?

Visualize dropping an oatmeal cookie into a glass of water. That's the only good way I've ever been able to describe the phenomenon.

Jungle rot.

Who says we didn't get to bring home any souvenirs?

Something to occupy one's spare time for the next few years: a mandatory foot fetish. Get a case of athlete's foot as a future civilian, and it's back to jungle rot-induced, oatmeal cookie time.

Of course, this particular affliction would have been more aptly named "paddy rot," but that doesn't quite have the same ring to it.

Can you imagine Uncle Sam with paddy rot?

Nah! Jungle rot is definitely better, and there I was, fortunate enough to have it. Lucky me.

Jungle rot wasn't the biggest aggravation during the early phase of my hospital stay in Okinawa though, the shrapnel damage was. My head wound had been stitched up in Saigon, but the two entry wounds, the one in my arm and the one in my back, were kept open. It was a precautionary measure required because of those "slightly problematic" infections one could contract in Southeast Asia.

Twice a day the medics would come by with wooden swabs and hydrogen peroxide, supposedly, to clean the wounds. I truly believe their goal was to see if they could push those damn sticks out the other side. You talk about a real thrill.

Jesus!

For about the first week, the pain from those innocent-looking little cotton-tipped wooden bastards was *orders of magnitude* worse than getting hit by the shrapnel!

Imagine a stick being *pushed* into a dime-size hole in your upper arm until it hits the bone, then twisted a few times to make sure you're paying attention. That's what I had to look forward to twice a day.

With the puncture wound in my back, there was nothing solid to hit, so the medics would just wedge the swab in between the two ribs as far as they could. I fully expected to look down and see that one coming out the front sometime.

Whoa!

I must have been white as a ghost when the medics showed up the first few days. I never passed out during that lovely procedure, but I'm not sure why not. It hurt enough.

After about a week though, the nerves were deadened to the point where I was able to work on my arm myself. In fact, I then sometimes wandered around the ward with the swab pushed in as far as it would go, with the remainder sticking straight out of my arm.

What can I say?

Hospital humor has a tendency to get a little weird. M*A*S*H wasn't totally off base about life in an Army hospital, even if it was only a fictional account of that earlier "ignore it, maybe it'll go away" police action.

As one might suspect though, "fun" was not the sort of thing that is likely to last too long in the Army during wartime, even if you weren't in the actual combat zone. Just as I was starting to get used to that lazy, laid-back hospital life, I got thrown out . . . days earlier than I was supposed to, as a matter of fact.

The hole in my back had nearly healed shut, but the larger one in my arm still made a nice home for the working end of one of those cotton-tipped swabs. As a result, the doctor had planned to keep me around a few more days.

Unfortunately, things had gotten busy down south, so the "walking wounded" had to give up their beds to the host of new arrivals. Therefore, a bunch of us got sent to a patient casual detachment where for every three or four guys we probably could have built one reasonably functional soldier.

A sorry-looking lot, but we managed . . . with a great amount of teamwork.

I started my outpatient activities (such as they were) on a thirty-day "profile," a term in Army jargon that meant I was "medically qualified for duty with (physical) profile limitations." Those limitations (Codes C, D, and G on your standard, household variety DA Form 3349) included: "No crawling, stooping, running, jumping, prolonged standing or marching; no strenuous physical activity; and no assignment requiring prolonged handling of heavy materials including weapons."

That didn't leave too many options for an infantry soldier, and I was in better shape than many of my bunkmates; my only "defects" according to Form 3349 being "multiple wounds arm and back" and "shrapnel in lung." However, those were enough to get a Code U typed on the profile in all capital letters: "IS NOT FIT FOR COMBAT TO INCLUDE RVN" (the Republic of Vietnam).

That certainly seemed reasonable to me.

In any event, I was still expecting to end up back in Nam, but as I wrote my sister, Butch, the day after leaving the hospital, "(at least) I managed to squeeze a two-month paid vacation out of them." The vacation turned out to somewhat longer though, since the profile was extended a couple of times by the good doctor.

Thanks, Doc!

Kicked back on light duty in Okinawa for what turned out to be slightly over three months did give me ample opportunity to think back, to reflect on my whole Vietnam experience. It probably gave me too much time really.

Yes, indeed.

The one thing that gradually became clearer . . . then slammed into me like a freight train . . . was the realization that I should have been dead!

Not could have. *Should* have!

That assessment had nothing to do with the time I got hit either.

Why would it?

That wasn't even close to the hairiest situation I was in, although any of the three pieces of shrapnel could easily have done the job had their trajectory been slightly different.

In fact, had I not heard a barely audible click behind me and twisted around into the face of that gray cloud rushing toward me . . . I never did hear the explosion . . . I more than likely would have had an entry wound in both lungs. Not a healthy condition. Contorted slightly, my arm caught the VC present addressed to my right lung.

No matter. Considering the big picture, it was still trivial by comparison. There were a number of other times—during ambushes, fire fights, and the like—where there was just *no way* I should have survived. It shouldn't have been possible for anyone to get into, then out of, some of the things I managed to without getting killed.

Charlie wasn't that bad a shot!

Hell, there were at least a half-dozen times just during that initial Groundhog Day melee when I could have "bought the farm" . . . easily, no money down. There were the Second World War–style on-line assaults our flying-overhead out-of-range battalion commander had us doing against the tunnel and bunker complex. When Charlie started firing rockets at the tanks brought in to provide support, the dumb shit ordered the tanks to retreat, but made us keep going.

Hey, losing a tank would have looked bad on his combat record.

At the time in Nam, I was too damn busy to worry much about it . . . or other equally fun situations. However, mulling over the details four or five months later sure scared the crap out of me.

31

Boy, did it ever.

Come to think of it though, there was one occasion—for just a few seconds near nightfall—there on the rim of that rotten fuckin' gully when I wasn't too busy.

I *did* worry about it . . . BIG TIME!

It was at the end of our last-gasp assault of the day, the final time when we reached the brink of that cratered cavity. A short time earlier . . . minutes earlier, another member of Delta Company and I had crawled to the very same spot to drag the C.O. away.

What a God-awful, gruesome task that was. As I tugged at the captain's shoulders, trying to keep as flat to the ground as he was, his head flopped over toward me, his eye, as if dangling on a bungee cord, nearly slapping the side of my face.

Damn!

The C.O. bought it merely trying to sneak a peek into the gully at our guy down below. His head inched ever so slowly above the edge when an enemy machine-gunner let go with a perfectly aimed, skull-shattering burst.

I was about to snake, headfirst, over the edge—unarmed—with Russell hanging onto my ankles.

Yep, I did worry then. The captain and our 3rd Squad brother below were dead. Every other member of Delta that was seen by the enemy at that end of the gully—100 percent—had been shot.

Not great odds!

Yes, the moment my life-sustaining M-16 left my hand, the Grim Reaper took a strangle hold on my Adam's apple, whispering perceptively, "you're gonna *DIE* doin' this DUMMY!"

NO SHIT!

The "pucker factor"—heart in my throat, unable to breathe—was a bit intense there for a few. But once the earth started rotating again, I was able to choke old Adam back down and snake over the edge with one end of a rope, hopefully, to get around Larry.

AND Russell didn't let go.

With all the time in Okinawa to think about such mirthful incidents, there was certainly *no way* I wanted to go back. Especially, not when I had been privy to intelligence information prior to getting wounded indicating, among other things, that over 150 NVA troops had managed to sneak out of my favorite ravine *after* I had dropped in for a visit. There was an underground hospital down there big enough to park a two-ton truck or two inside.

Yes, indeed, indeed, indeed.

Five of us left in there against 150 of them . . . maybe more. The odds would have to catch up with me at some point. Had to, considering I really should have been dead already.

Of course, looking back wasn't the only cause for concern that summer, not by any means. At some point after my discharge from the hospital (late June, early July, as recollection serves me), I was all but embalmed by an overpowering awareness of impending death—my death.

Take one I.V. bolus of embalming fluid, don't see anyone in the morning. Satan's taxi is waiting for you back down south, son.

Hurry back!

That morbid shroud hung over me for only a day or two there in the Casual Company, but the lifeless impression was scorched into my mind like a searing brand into tender flesh.

Two decades later, learning of a Delta Company blood-bath near Xuan Loc, July 3, 1969, I wish I could remember the precise date those visions of death came calling in Okinawa.

Were they forewarning the grisly, pre-Independence Day events to come? Events in which I'd participate if I returned?

Were they but lucid premonitions of the ongoing carnage?

I guess I'll never know for sure.

Unfortunately, though, I now know of nine KIA counted out from the Delta Company ranks that July 3. NINE!

The posthumous Congressional Medal of Honor was awarded to the company commander's radio operator . . . not Russell, although I feared at first it might have been. The company's field strength dropped to barely more than twenty that day. Another war-induced bloodbath like I'd experienced first-hand, only worse this time.

Although I may not have known the realities of Delta's circumstance while I was recuperating in Okinawa in 1969, there was one thing I understood perfectly back then. I knew—UNEQUIVOCALLY—I would die if I returned to Vietnam.

I could see it clearly. The corpse peering back at me in the mirror left no doubt, none whatsoever. To return meant certain death.

I could bet my life on it . . . and I'd lose next time around.

Feeling that way, who would have thought that in less than six months—as an A student civilian again—I'd come within an eyelash of volunteering to go back to Nam?

Give me a break!

Not possible! I was returning to the "make love, not war" life of a college student for Christ's sake.

How could that be more agonizing than what I'd just been through?

It couldn't!

Could dying in combat somehow look enticing to me?

NOT A FUCKING CHANCE IN HELL!

NONE!!!

I've done my, "yea, though I walk through the valley of the shadow of death"[3] stint slogging the Mekong Delta, thank you. Worse than that, the gully of the shadows of death too!

I'm finished . . . KAPUT.

Not unexpectedly, in the summer of 1969 in Okinawa, all I wanted was to get back home, get to school, and get on with my life . . . my real life in the real world. With close to three months on light duty after a month in the hospital, I had plenty of time to make plans for the future, or at least, better define plans I had been thinking about for some time.

First, I would complete my undergraduate studies, probably where I started college in Wisconsin. Then, it would be on to graduate school for a Ph.D. in some area of the life sciences where I could pursue a career in research. I hadn't yet made a final decision about the exact area. The latter goal, though, was assuming I hadn't trashed my grade point so badly that last year in Hawaii that I couldn't get it back to a respectable level.

However, with my newfound motivation, I didn't think that would be a problem.

* * *

Finally, after what seemed just slightly longer than forever, it was time to hijack some wings for home. And what an emotional drain that was . . . hanging on as the moment crept near.

It seemed like I'd been away for decades.

In July, sitting in the day room of the 257th Replacement Company, I was watching Neil Armstrong take "a small step for man, a giant step for mankind." In August, I was looking to take "a giant step" of my own and, somehow, the distance seemed equally as far as the earth to the moon . . . maybe farther.

For a while it had looked like I was going to be sent to Korea to finish out my two years of active duty, but because of the length and timing of my profile limitations, it was decided I qualified for an "early out." So, it was off to Oakland to be discharged —August 18, 1969.

After a couple quick detours—to San Francisco to see an old college buddy and to Fort Ord to see Steve, my best friend from the NCO school—it was time to head for the homestead in Wisconsin.

It's hard to describe the elation, the relief, the *PRIDE*, and the overall great feeling upon returning home, but it was sure all there. Boy, was it ever. And that sign on the garage door was certainly a welcome sight; it looked absolutely beautiful.

WELCOME HOME!

COMBAT . . . THE "EASY" PART

Enduring Truth: *Valley of the shadow memories can beckon more fear than the walk.*

Chapter 5

REINCARNATION

The first weeks at home. A dead man gets a reprieve.

My initial—levitating-off-the-floor—return to America's Dairyland was certainly what I expected and then some. Obviously, my family and friends were happy I made it back, that I had survived.

The response by some bordered on euphoric and, I'd have to admit, I was a tad bit euphoric myself. Life was good.

Linda, a hometown girl I had met just a few days before heading to Southeast Asia, picked me up at the airport in Milwaukee. At least, I've been told it was Milwaukee, and that sorta rings a bell.

Linda and I had gone out a couple times and then corresponded regularly while I was slogging around in the paddies and after I was knocked out of action. Whatever the basis for the relationship that developed, she offered to serve as taxi driver upon my return. She had also delivered me to the airport—into the hands of the Almighty—seven and a half months earlier, so it was a much-appreciated reciprocal action—especially, the return trip . . . back out of His hands.

Nothing personal, folks, but somehow, female companionship rated as a priority at the time.

Now there's a surprise.

From all indications, the first few days after returning to the old homestead in Wisconsin were spent interacting primarily with Linda and my immediate family—my mother and father, my two sisters, Sis and Butch, and their families. I have to admit, however, those first days are little more than a blur for the most part. Brain drain must have set in because I recall almost nothing of that period . . . it evaporated somehow.

While there is little doubt that I imbibed to excess—consuming my share and a few other people's while I was at it—I really don't think I could have been totally zonked morning to night, each and every day. Something should register.

But who knows?

Maybe I was that bombed all the time, although some quirky, psychoanalytical explanation seems much more likely.

I do know that my birthday—number twenty-six—was just a couple days after I got home, and the family threw a surprise party for me at a local night spot . . . more as a "welcome home" I guess, but the two momentous events did correspond quite closely in time. The supper club, Riolo's, was where I had worked as a bartender prior to getting the call from Uncle Sam, during my hiatus from higher education.

I remember seeing my Uncle Pete's car in the parking lot that night when Linda and I arrived, and it was curious that he wasn't at the bar when we strolled in . . . must have been in having dinner already. However, I became somewhat more suspicious when Rio, the owner, wanted to show me a newly remodeled party room downstairs. Hey, walking into ambushes was not something I was accustomed to doing back in those days. And sure enough, I was greeted down there by a whole host of friends and relatives (some I hadn't seen for years) along with that great sign from the folks' garage door; the "Welcome Home" crafted by my artistic niece, Lori.

The remainder of my recollections from the first three weeks back home, prior to school starting, is little more than a blender-like mishmash of disjointed activities . . . viewed through a kaleidoscope again . . . nothing connecting. I do recall catching some good-natured crap the night of the party concerning the fact that I was growing my beard back already.

My previous go at such facial locks were sacrificed the morning I left to be sworn in . . . and sworn at. About 05:00, there I was, first with scissors, then razor, hacking away. I wasn't going to give the damn military-types a shot at it.

Of course, my mustache in Vietnam had also bitten the dust along the way, a sacrifice to ol' Lefty. As a result, the "stache" had to be jump-started again as well.

By the night of the party though, there was already some annoying stubble to show for my efforts since being discharged. So much for the long harped-on military bearing but, hey, I was a civilian again! No more dry shaving for the Kid, thank you.

A day or two after the party, as recollection serves, I went with my sister and brother-in-law to look at a horse; a Palomino they ultimately bought. Now that's certainly worth remembering.

Geez!

Then, Sis and her best friend Donna took me along to Milwaukee one day. We had champagne that morning with an interior decorator in Waukesha, and I had a Reuben sandwich for lunch.

Memorable stuff, huh?

And don't ask me why I remember a sandwich I ate in August of 1969. I don't have the foggiest, but that memory is utterly fixed in the gray matter. I can still see the grilled rye bread creation there on the heavy white plate; the corned beef, sauerkraut, and melted Swiss bulging all around. Flying home was lost; a sandwich was saved.

Buying a Triumph Spitfire from a former girlfriend, now that at least makes sense. I should remember that rather significant event, and I do.

Absolutely! Drop the top and let the good times roll.

And while I don't recall them asking, my nephew Ryan and his buddy Scott apparently suggested I should camp out with them one night.

I didn't.

"Thanks—NO!"

That major piece of "stop the presses" news was in the *Milwaukee Sentinel* shortly after my return to civilization, so I know it must have occurred.

God, the *Milwaukee Sentinel*? A slow news day, perchance?

Not that those first three weeks back in the real world were devoid of better things to report. There was Governor Knowles proclaiming September as Operation Patriotism month for the State of Wisconsin.

Now, that turned out to be a sure-fire winner, what with Ho Chi Minh dying on the 3rd of the month. He ended up being eulogized by ever flake in the state thereafter . . . especially after Lieutenant Calley was charged with premeditated murder on September 5.

My Lai, you say?

Yes, indeed. September was a resounding triumph for patriotism all right.

So, why can't I remember any of that stuff?

Damn!

Memories of war remain; peace coming home . . . gone.

* * *

While I may have missed the boat with regard to the big-time news events of late August and early September, there were a couple other minor league highlights of memorable significance. Take, for instance, the inhalation of clean country air back in the Dairy State. That was actually something of an awe-inspiring, nasal nirvana-type experience; especially when compared to the overpowering, pungent odor of smoke and fish that permeated everything everywhere in Okinawa.

And fish and smoke were trivial by comparison to the choke-a-horse stench of burning shit in Vietnam. Stepping off the TWA charter at Bien Hoa just after the Christmas holidays, now that was something. The foulness of human excrement being torched with kerosene in cut-in-two fifty-gallon drums was enough to knock one into an instant gag response and right back into the plane.

Yuck!

Try that as a replacement for "chestnuts roasting" at your next Yuletide festivities with family and friends. See which way Santa, his elves, and all the other virgin nostrils head . . . at double-time.

But the clean air back in Wisconsin wasn't the only primo experience that stands out. Tasting *real* food in the *real* world was another delight and a half for one so recently reincarnated. What heavenly fare it was.

Not that the fried rice in Okinawa was anything to complain about. I opted for that on the menu in various non-military, out-of-the-way eating spots whenever possible. Good stuff.

37

The chow we got in Vietnam though, that was a totally different matter. What garbage!

There were the tubs of reconstituted, *green* scrambled eggs when we were "treated" to a warm breakfast in the field. From all appearances, those pseudo-eggs were warm because someone had upchucked in the container after eating pickled eggs and drinking green beer . . . a post St. Paddy's Day gag-and-puke-a-thon.

Tasty?

Ah, not exactly.

Admittedly, we did get pretty innovative in Nam with the 1940s vintage C rations, and at the time, certain items—ham and lima beans sautéed over a pinch of flaming C-4 explosive, then blended with a melted cheddar sauce and sprinkled with crushed saltines—tasted mighty good; particularly if one of the locals had contributed a blazing hot pepper for dicing and spicing. Compared to my mother's cooking, though? Well . . . maybe it wasn't all that good, come to think of it.

And, somehow, the dog soup didn't hold up all that well either.

God, it was good to be home! The tastes, the sights, the sounds . . . perfection personified.

To coin a phrase from the past, I was "floating on cloud nine." Unconscious most of the time, perhaps, but on cloud nine nonetheless. I had the world by the old cojones (one of the tactically more important Spanish slang terms in my vocabulary), only the world didn't know it yet.

How much better off could anyone be?

It was an ideal—number 1, GI—situation.

I was lovin' life . . . every minute of it . . . at least, I was during those minutes I remember. And the view from my private cumulus cushion was positively sensational.

Float on, float on.

Disregard those storm clouds on the horizon. They're nothing to worry about; forget about them.

COMBAT . . . THE "EASY" PART

Enduring Truth: *Soldier to civilian should be easy—"no sweat!"*
Bet on it, you'll lose.

Chapter 6

BACK TO SCHOOL

Walk-in-the-park student life . . . where the grisly carnage really begins.

Going back to college in Wisconsin, rather than Hawaii (my more recent academic home), undoubtedly represented the easy way out. My higher education had drifted appreciably lower during those sophomore and junior years at the University of Hawaii . . . especially my junior year, prior to taking the educational sabbatical that got my butt drafted.

The precipitous drop in the ever-important GPA—grade point average—had to be turned around if graduate school was ever to be in my future. Therefore, Wisconsin seemed like a much safer bet, heading back to where the GPA was built on a foundation more stable than Waikiki quicksand.

Furthermore, Wisconsin State University—where I had launched my undergraduate efforts—was actually in my hometown . . . the major Wisconsin metropolis of Whitewater (population 10,000 plus or minus; College Cowtown, U.S.A.). As a result, there's no way I could find a more supportive, welcoming environment to readjust to civilian life.

What could happen in Whitewater?

Besides, I had continued to think of myself as a temporarily derailed civilian the whole time I was in the Army anyhow. They landed no "lifer" when they set the hook in this draftee, so readjustment shouldn't be a problem.

How could it be? It was my turf.

I knew Old Main, the mammoth, centerpiece building on the Wisconsin State campus, like I knew the back of my hand. When I was growing up, there was a grade school, junior high, and high school housed in that imposing landmark structure.

I started my education there—literally, kindergarten—and continued through my sophomore year of high school, when it was decided the high school portion of the education mill should be closed. The students were deemed to have too great an advantage using college facilities and equipment . . . with college professors as teachers.

How much more familiar could any place be?

There were even a few of my old instructors from those formative years still on the faculty. My eighth-grade teacher, Mac McGraw, was dean of the graduate school.

I was going home . . . to peace and tranquility.

Unfortunately, with only three weeks from discharge to degree program, there wasn't enough time to get copies of my records from the University of Hawaii before school started. Therefore, I could only attend part-time that first semester back.

In thinking about it though, perhaps that was actually a plus. After all, it would give me some time to ease back into the study routine. Studying was certainly not the way I had been spending my leisure hours, what there were of them, the last couple years.

No question, part-time should help.

It also seemed plausible that a less hectic transition period might assist on the social side of civilian life as well. Somehow, the social graces have a penchant for taking a hike rather abruptly in the military.

A good friend of mine from AIT, Bulldog Williams, told of verbally tomahawking Emily Post while spending a couple days with his parents in Missouri just after basic training. His family was very religious, and four-letter words were unquestionably taboo. He had never so much as heard anyone curse in his parents' home, much less doing it himself, at least, within earshot of the folks. So wouldn't you know it, the first night at the dinner table—employing conventional mess hall etiquette—he blurted out to his dear, loving mother, "Pass the fuckin' salt!"

Nice move, big guy.

But didn't you forget the magic word? You know, please?

Please pass the fuckin' salt, mother dear.

Fortunately, Bulldog's father had been in the service (during the Second World War, I think), and he almost fell off his chair laughing. Good old dad recognized that swearing was the only way to communicate in the military—at least for the enlisted personnel—so it becomes second nature, a verbal reflex action.

Yes, slowing down those trigger-quick reflexes could take a little time. So, easing into school—rather than jumping in with both feet—might help.

After all, if Bulldog had a problem after only nine weeks of basic training, what would it be like for me after almost a full hitch?

As a well-trained NCO, I was capable of inserting a four-letter expletive between every word in a sentence, so getting away from that habit might be a good idea. Hell, I could slip the little pearls between syllables of words if need be to make a point with the troops.

My professors and classmates at Wisconsin State might appreciate some absolution from that "exo-fucking-lent" military elocution. So too, might the occasional stray bystander with as yet undefiled, cherry ears.

If I could take things slow and easy, there might be a little more time to think before speaking. Using that time is another story, of course. Reflex actions, verbal or otherwise, are difficult to short circuit . . . *very* difficult.

Since I was limited to taking a maximum of eight credit hours that first semester, I figured two courses in my old major, biology, would be the way to go. And, as luck would have it, there were two four-credit laboratory courses offered, so when registration rolled around on September 5, I signed up.

Laboratory courses can eat up lots of time and be fairly demanding, but anything involving lab work sounded great at that point. Compared to what I'd been up to recently, it was sheer heaven.

Again, it was the easy way out (research being what I wanted to do in the future), but why not? I'd earned an easy road for a while.

It turned out, however, that by only being able to take two courses, graduation wouldn't be possible until the following summer instead of spring. At least, that's what one of the admissions' counselors told me.

So?

At that point, I wasn't in any huge-type hurry. Considering that I should have been planted a few months back, why would I worry about something taking a little extra time? Merely having time . . . breathing, in and of itself, was awfully damn nice. Just let me make progress toward graduation, graduate school, and a research career. That, while enjoying every step along the way.

Damned right! I deserved it.

Enjoying every step was going to involve some work though . . . some tap dancing through the academic tulips, as it were. Once classes started on September 8 it became uncomfortably obvious that studying would require more than a little getting used to.

In fact, studying in the library proved to be abso-God-damn-lutely im-fucking-possible, i.e., "hard," in civilian terms. It was too quiet. Not totally quiet, just *too* quiet.

Whenever there was any little noise . . . someone whispering, a pencil hitting the floor, knuckles cracking . . . I found myself straining to hear more, to create a mental image of what was going on.

What was that?

Did something move?

Who's there?

Funny, I used to play those little games in Nam too, out of necessity. Picking up sounds, especially in the dead of night, was the only way to survive . . . to not become "the dead of night."

With only seven or eight guys out on squad-size ambushes most evenings, set up in a circle, not knowing where the enemy might appear, your auditory capabilities sure got a workout on far too many pitch-black nights.

Is that an animal causing the sporadic, barely discernable rustling out there?

Is Charlie sneaking in?

Try to block out every other sound.

Focus!

Move your weapon . . . ever so slowly . . . until it's pointing toward where you think you heard the grass move.

Did it? Was that a twig cracking?

Get ready to slip the safety off . . . to nudge the guy sleeping next to you . . . just in case.

Who would have thought that stuff would have carried over?

I was back in the real world, a carefree, loving-life civilian once again. There's certainly nothing to worry about in a *library* for Christ's sake. A little creaking and whispering here and there shouldn't bother me.

Oh well, no big deal. There was always the student union as a place to study. Not really quiet, just a fairly constant noise level. Somehow that seemed to work out much better.

I'd get a table in the back of the old part of the union, and studying there was perfect. With the expanse of the room before me, my backside to the wall, I could concentrate on what I was doing, savoring a pot or two of coffee along the way. And, all in all, there were very few distractions.

So, I'd gotten back in school and found a place to study. I had a steady girl.

What else could one ask for at that point?

MONEY!

Since I had blown most of my military savings on the sports car . . . the "wow the coeds" Spitfire, it was time to look for a job, a source of green. The GI bill was nice, but somehow $60 a month didn't seem to go too far.

Moreover, the V.A. disability payments that eventually kicked in—$23 per month for "shell fragment wound residuals of the back"—didn't quite do it either.

Some additional cash was definitely in order.

Initially, the only job I could land was one at the local foundry. Not exactly the sought-after Park Avenue position. However, compared to life in the Delta, it wasn't so bad. At least, the filth and funk could be washed off without having to dodge human feces floating down a grunge-colored river where we bathed at times. Villages on the "Grunge" typically had a hole cut in a dock over the river—two sides screened—to use as their public toilet.

What ultimately turned out to be a much better job solution was getting my old bartending position back at Riolo's; the perfect option for a student in need of cash. Not that some changes weren't in order though.

The place had been remodeled while I was gone, so it was no longer as rowdy as before. That meant I had to clean up my act a bit, and it pretty well put an end to my on-stage singing career, since the improved, higher-class establishment no longer had a band on Friday and Saturday nights.

Working in a better class saloon did have some advantages though, like serving drinks to the chief of police and the president of the university. They certainly offered some interesting perspectives on current events that year, and it never hurts to be on good terms with the cop at the top.

It was also a real trip to be asked to have coffee in the student union with President Carter (the WSU-W version . . . not the peanut variety that stumbled into the White House later on).

Boy, I got some strange looks from the longhairs when that happened.

* * *

Somehow, I never really expected that making the transition from the regimented lifestyle of military to the somewhat less regimented lifestyle of a student would be too tough. Having spent twenty-four years of my life as a civilian (with over seventeen of those as a student) and less than two in the Army, it should have been easy enough . . . a "walk in the park."

No sweat!

Well, it didn't take long to figure out that it wasn't going to be that effortless. There was something different about the whole atmosphere on campus.

Funny how things could change so much from the spring of '67 to the fall of '69. It sure had though, and it was a lot more than the difference between Hawaii and Wisconsin.

Everything was so damned negative. Being a student just wasn't the same. It wasn't fun.

By the end of September, the twice-a-week student newspaper, the *Royal Purple*, was filled with antiwar articles, front to back. The headlines were antiwar. The editorials were antiwar. There appeared to be no other news worth reporting.

Almost every issue had stories about the faculty-sponsored Draft Information Club. Yep, that's right: the omnipotent big DIC at WSU-W. Let's be sure we know how to avoid the draft, boys and girls.

Oops, make that, boys . . . only. There's a distinction back here in the real world. Unlike Vietnam, girls don't normally kill you here . . . or at least, not as often.

Then there was the constant hammering at the fact that my school, "WSU-W is one of the 500 colleges planning to participate in the nationwide Vietnam Moratorium October 15."[3]

Oh, good.

And for what purpose are they doing this?

"To raise public opinion within the University and Whitewater community against the Vietnam War,"[3] you say?

Not to discuss the war? Not to look at the issues involved? Not to assess what's best for the South Vietnamese people?

Just "to raise public opinion . . . against?"

Terrific! That's certainly why kids go to college, to hear just one viewpoint, one perspective.

Not that one could do any better looking for answers—some sort of balanced opinion—outside the walls of the ivory tower. The TV screen was filled with the very same garbage, day in, day out.

Protests! Protests! Protests!

When anything came on concerning the war itself, it had no resemblance—none whatsoever—to the war I'd been involved in.

Why?

I just left there. Things couldn't be that much different. They could NOT!

God, it makes no sense.

If anything, the news off campus was as bad as or even worse than that on campus.

Fortunately, life in the lab offered an escape. I could get away . . . run off and hide if need be.

It was sure no picnic elsewhere, however.

One thing that probably didn't help my particular situation on campus was the fact that I openly displayed my pride in having served my country. From the very beginning of the school year, I wore my Army fatigue jacket quite often. I sensed early on that it wasn't received very well, even though it was just a plain fatigue jacket, the insignia having been removed as required by Army "regs."

What was the big deal?

Later on, when I added a small American flag pin, that really seemed to turn off some of my fellow students. I didn't understand the reason either.

Why should I be viewed negatively for having served my country?

That was totally contrary to everything I'd been raised to expect.

Why?

It didn't make any sense.

How could risking my life for my country . . . and damn near losing it in the process . . . result in being treated like shit?

That couldn't happen in America, not the America I'd been raised to believe in—not the America of Audie Murphy and John Wayne.

Not possible. No way!

COMING HOME . . . HOSTILE AND DEADLY

Enduring Truth: *Wounds suffered in war heal. Wounds inflicted at home persevere.*

Chapter 7

HIDING OUT

Ducking incoming rounds. Where's the Goddamn DMZ?

Edwin Louis Cole: *"You don't drown by falling in water; you drown by staying there."*[1]

Even tromping around in the boonies in Vietnam, the troops all knew there were problems with the war back home. We weren't fighting on the far side of the moon, although at times, it may have seemed like it. Somehow, though, I never really considered what impact the antiwar bombardment might have once I got home; the tourniquet that would be placed around my chest . . . gradually being twisted tighter and tighter . . . making it harder and harder to breathe, crushing my heart.

Hey, I'd seen an antiwar demonstration in 1967 while I was in school in Hawaii. It was no big deal.

In fact, that afternoon featurette was almost comical.

It was apparent, even to a rally novice like me, that the individuals up on the stage were the protesters. They were the ones running their mouths all the time. But with almost everyone else looking like they were on their way to or from the beach, it was a challenge (more like impossible actually) to tell who was siding with whom.

Picture it: A robust flock of tan young lasses standing around in bikinis, "hanging out" at the rally, so to speak.

Were they for or against the war? How could you tell?

It's not like they were displaying placards, pro or con. But either way, there were those among them it would have been easy to side with given a call for allegiance. Some of the non-placard displays were noteworthy-plus . . . a D+ beating an A+ on this honor roll.

It was *not* difficult to identify those in the crowd that were "plain clothes" cops though. Hawaii probably has (or, at least, had in 1967) the largest, per officer, police force in the country. As a result, looking around and seeing a few Hawaiians looming a foot or two above everyone else was a dead give-away. In addition, these covert Clydes were wearing their usual camouflage outfits—bright, flowery aloha shirts (requiring yards and yards of material) and white pants.

Yes, they were real inconspicuous in a crowd of students.

No one was stupid enough to get out of control in the presence of the "incredible hulks" though, so the protest didn't amount to much. The only incident of the day was when a girl in the audience—one whose father was serving in Vietnam at that time—got up on the stage and tried to tear up a VC flag. She didn't have much luck. Of course, that got the in-uniform, "motorcycle hulks" called in, but little else.

All in all, it was not what one would describe as a major event. But that was the extent of what I knew about protest rallies first-hand.

Things had changed in two years. The antiwar activity I was seeing on the Wisconsin State campus was much more intense. And as the school year proceeded, the demonstrations began to get more and more vocal. It was increasingly difficult to avoid them.

And from all indications, the situation at WSU-W merely mimicked what was happening elsewhere in the country at the time. The TV, newspapers, *Time*, and *Newsweek* were filled with Vietnam negatives almost exclusively. Oh, the civil rights movement was also in full force, so black versus white was thrown in as part of the mix as well.

What a strange time.

A mere few months earlier I was entrusting my life—no questions asked—to the person next to me, behind me. We were all brothers; "black, white, pink, purple—TOTALLY irrelevant."[2, i] Everyone was equal.

With but one exception (a white exception, I might add), each person could be trusted—unequivocally—to do everything humanly possible to keep you alive.

Almost daily, I saw individuals risking their lives to protect the life of a comrade nearby. It's just the way things were done.

Your brother's life was more important than your own. And your brother was the guy next to you trying to keep you alive . . . color be damned.

So, what went wrong?

What happened?

God, what a mess.

With the antiwar activity picking up on campus, I found it necessary to stay out of earshot of all the bullshit. Although the protests were not all that intense to start with, at times they were sufficiently vocal that I found them agitating and troublesome . . . they were gnawing at me inside more than a little bit.

In response, I found myself becoming more reclusive, staying out of the newer, snack bar end of the student union. A lot of the creepy looking troublemakers spent their time there, and it was not difficult to overhear the conversations emanating from that crowd. They weren't exactly whispering most of the time.

As a result, I started spending even more time in the older, quieter section, whether I had studying to do or not. Somehow, socializing seemed less important than peace and tranquility.

Besides, a significant portion of the humanity milling around at the other end of the union didn't quite fit my vision of the "in" crowd I wanted to hang out with. Anything social they had to offer, I didn't want to contract, thank you.

Something was strange about the whole situation though. Even hearing or seeing only small portions of what was going on around campus, I found myself becoming *very* uneasy. I might be sitting quietly, having a cup of coffee, when I'd realize my muscles were taut . . . straining against an unseen force.

In addition, there were times (often, relatively nondescript times in the union) when I'd find myself shaking slightly—mild tremors—but discernible. It was thoroughly bizarre, and I couldn't begin to comprehend why such a thing would be happening.

I had no similar problems in Vietnam. It didn't make any sense that I should be tense or nervous back home, but I was.

That led me to spend more and more of my free time in the biology department, even if I didn't have anything to do there. It just felt more peaceful, more like I belonged.

* * *

A phone call from an old Army buddy in California then added to the hellish, gut-wrenching uncertainty I was facing.

Steve was the friend from NCO school I had stopped to see at Fort Ord just after being discharged, his future wife Karen having given me a ride down there. Steve and I were also the two crazies who opted to pair off for hand-to-hand combat training with the Rangers—to beat the piss out of one another in the sawdust pit—as best friends in the military are wont to do.

Hey, what are friends for?

Steve had been severely wounded a mere three weeks after arriving in Nam . . . another "welcome to my digs" from Chuck.

The fireworks from that booby trap gala necessitated reconstructive surgery on Steve's leg—skin grafts and all. After a period of recuperation, stateside duty was all that remained for him, pushing new troops through their training at Fort Ord.

It was there, reading the "obits" in *Stars and Stripes* one day, he learned that a close, mutual acquaintance of ours, Chris, had been killed in Vietnam. That had happened back on August 12, six days before I was discharged.

Shit!

Just what I needed to hear.

Steve, Chris, and I had bunked near one another in the 4th Platoon at the NCO school, and we quickly became the best of friends. When we had finally been there long enough to get some time off, we always hung around together, Steve and I looking out for the youngest member of the group, Chris.

The three musketeers.

For some reason, the military seems to forge such bonds in a hurry.

We all wound up going to Fort Ord after graduation, so the friendship continued. The three of us definitely had some great times together, on base and off.

Then, after nine weeks of pushing troops through AIT, we went our separate ways on leave for thirty days prior to meeting at Steve's house in Sacramento.

We all had to report to Oakland at the same time for processing to our next duty station—Vietnam.

The car ride from Sacramento was not the most enjoyable road trip I've ever taken. Steve, Chris, and I all recognized (more or less) the realities of the situation. We had all gotten the word about what the extra stripes from the NCO school would likely get us—our *butts* handed to us!

Not exactly what you'd describe as a car full of "happy campers." Two draftees—Steve and me—and a volunteer—Chris—heading to a place none of us really wanted to go.

Well, I probably shouldn't say that . . . at least not for Chris. He had enlisted, so presumably, the infantry was what he had picked. And in the late '60s, there wasn't much question about where you were heading with an infantry MOS—to Vietnam.

Maybe Chris was going where he wanted.

However, I doubt that any of us really considered the possibility that one of the group might be killed. Wounded maybe, but killed?

No siree. Not one of the musketeers.

Damn! I had sure looked forward to the day when Chris would return, so we could all get together to tip a few.

Damn, damn, damn!

You couldn't find a more happy-go-lucky, everything's right with world person than Chris. He always seemed to be smiling . . . Steve was more likely scowling about something. They were both built like fireplugs, but with diametrically opposed personalities. Nonetheless, we were inseparable best friends—or had been.

And the more I considered Chris' effervescent slant on life, he probably was where he wanted to be . . . in Vietnam, serving his country.

Mulling over the fact that Chris had been killed though, I remember thinking that as soldiers in Vietnam, we didn't ask for much. Oh, we used to wish out loud that they'd get the damn politics out of it and let us do our jobs. That didn't seem too unreasonable.

There were times it was like fighting with one hand tied behind your back. We might see the enemy (fully armed and ready to kick our ass somewhere), but if we were in a designated "No Fire Zone," we couldn't do diddly shit about it.

Does that make any sense?

Not to me. There's no question, that was probably the biggest hang up. Quit the political bullshit, and let us get on with our jobs.

I was in Nam during the change in administration in 1969—Johnson out, Nixon in—and that was something we talked about openly; hoping it would finally happen.

It *didn't*!

However, I never asked (and I never knew anyone while I was there who asked . . . draftee or not) to be pulled out of Nam. We just wanted to get the necessary support to get the job done. Then we could ALL go home.

Somehow, I was certain Chris had felt the same way, out there cruising with the 11th Armored Cav.

Just give us some damn support!
Was that too much to ask?

* * *

Apparently, support was too much to ask that autumn at WSU-W. Less than two months after my return to the real world—on October 15, 1969 to be exact—Whitewater took part in the nationwide Vietnam War Moratorium.

Even with all the press buildup ahead of time, I wasn't prepared for that Wednesday onslaught. And while I was not among the nearly 2,000 spectators at the rally featuring former Wisconsin Attorney General Bronson Lafollette, dodging the thousand or so students who participated in the parade that day was not so easy. They seemed to be milling around everywhere.

You better hit the dirt and low-crawl out of here.

With all the shit going on around campus, I took up refuge in my first-line of defense, the old end of the student union. I was doing pretty well there too until some longhaired freak came running through the back door and yelled to one of his filthy twins:

"Hey, you should see it out there! We just took down the American
flag, and ran it back up the pole upside down. Not only that, we've
got a North Vietnamese flag! It's great!"

I couldn't have exploded out of my chair any faster if an AK-47 round had just cracked overhead. I was on my feet in a shot, but then, every muscle in my body went rigid instantly; rigor mortis set in.

Fists clenched. I was locked and loaded, but couldn't pull the trigger.

In fact, I couldn't move.

They were spouting treason!

They were condoning the killing of American soldiers—the killing of my friend Chris!

How in the fuck could they be allowed to get away with it?

I wanted to climb over the table right then and there, but my muscles were absolutely frozen.

And the more those treasonous statements echoed over and over in my head, the madder I got. My breathing got heavier, my jaws locked, and my eyes were burning, shooting daggers around the room, looking for more of the filth.

The sleazy pukes were gone, but the one's comments continued to echo: "A NORTH VIETNAMESE FLAG!"

Jesus H. Fucking Christ!

What the hell was going on? How could this be happening here . . . in the United States? In my hometown?

It makes no sense!

With those thoughts bouncing around upstairs, the rest of my body—all those locked up muscles—started first to tremble slightly, then to quake uncontrollably. I couldn't stop shaking from head to toe.

What the fuck?

Nothing like this had ever happened to me in Vietnam.

Why now? Why here?

Son-of-a-God-damn-mother-fucking-bitch!

WHY?

I was absolutely shattered at that point . . . disoriented, dazed, bewildered. I didn't have the foggiest notion what to do.

Assuming I could manage to put one foot in front of the other, should I go outside?

Should I stay put?

What if I go out and actually see that shit going on?

I'd most certainly have to wade into the middle of it. There's no way in hell I could watch anyone mess with the American flag; not having just heard what happened to Chris, not having served that flag so recently.

Then if there really is a North Vietnamese flag out there, heads will definitely roll. No way . . . no way in hell could I let that pass.

It was one of the most agonizing quandaries I've ever had to deal with in my life. I really, *really* wanted to go out there and bust some heads—for Chris's sake . . . for my own even more.

Part of my dilemma at that point is very difficult to explain though. At least, it is without sounding like one of those crazed killers Vietnam veterans are all too often portrayed to be. While I may have relished the opportunity to try to knock some sense into those worthless, treasonous fuckheads, I didn't want to go out there and kill someone. Not really.

The problem was that I would have willingly taken on any and all involved. As a result, I would likely have taken a good beating myself.

And, no, I wasn't afraid of that happening. I really didn't give a shit whatsoever.

However, I *was* afraid that under those circumstances, "involuntary" reflexes would take over, and those hours and hours of training in the saw-dust pit at Fort Benning had instilled the reactions and techniques necessary to do someone in quickly and efficiently. And my reflexes were still sharp enough at that point . . . I knew if I got pummeled, those reactions could very well take over out of self-defense.

There in the student union, finally sitting but still quaking, I recalled one occasion while I was home on leave prior to going to Nam when a friend of mine unexpectedly grabbed me in a bear hug from behind. Since Piep had me by a good fifty pounds back then and was strong as an ox—no one got loose from that hold—we were probably both surprised that day in his father's body shop when I instantly broke free and started into a counterattack.

It was an Army Ranger-induced reflex action. Totally automatic—no thinking required.

In that particular situation, I caught myself prior to executing the offensive move. If I were knocked a little groggy or was in a really threatening, hostile environment, who knows?

It was a tough dilemma to wrestle with that day in the union, since the offensive moves the Rangers taught us to execute in NCO school *were* intended for *executing*. Somehow, I suspected that was an on-campus activity that might be frowned on just a tad.

In or out?

Kick ass or hide?

A genuine—screwed if you do, screwed if you don't—no-win situation.

Not surprisingly, the solution I came up with was the same one I employed often that semester: hiding out in the biology department. That particular day it was in an open area by some large windows and a group of display-type specimen cases. It was my version of the demilitarized zone, a place where I would encounter only "friendlies."

The first friendly I encountered that day was Dr. Brady, my favorite biology professor . . . the one who inspired me to switch from business to biology as a major. My first semester at Whitewater, he taught an absolutely superb botany course that tweaked my interest in exploring the scientific frontiers. The exhilaration of delving into research unknowns had never occurred to me before.

When you couple the Dr. Brady inspiration factor with my first business course that semester being an absolute abomination, that about did it. Why would anyone memorize the net profit of Sears Roebuck and Company in 1957 . . . one of the questions on the first test?

Well, Dr. B and Cliff, an older graduate student in one of my biology labs, found me that October 15 pacing back and forth among the display cases—ranting and raving. They spent a great deal of time trying to calm me down. And while I honestly can't remember the specifics of those discussions, I do recall that they spent a fair amount of time at it.

Finally, I was shaking somewhat less and only intermittently when another of the professors I knew quite well came up behind me and as a joke said: "Hey, Trewyn, why aren't you out there protesting with the rest of the bearded weirdoes?"

Whaaat?

Not today, *Asshole!*

If I wouldn't have had my back to him, there is no way Dr. B and Cliff would have gotten to me before my fist got to the prof's face, but those two old guys moved pretty damn quick. Knowing the explosive state I was in, they both lunged instantly, grabbing for my arms as I spun around.

Somehow, they managed to prevent the impact, my itchy knuckles on the guy's deserving jaw.

Then, while both were still holding on, Dr. Brady suggested to the other prof that he get the hell out of there. He did too, and a good thing. I really didn't need it that particular day.

Damn! The whole business was turning me into an absolute wreck . . . a basket case and a half.

So much for tranquility in the DMZ. So much for peace on the home front.

The damn campus was becoming a war zone.

I could handle the out-of-vogue conflagration in Vietnam. You could count on people there, entrusting your life to them daily . . . moment-by-moment . . . footstep-after-footstep.

I couldn't handle this shit; not at all.

COMING HOME . . . HOSTILE AND DEADLY

Enduring Truth: *Antiwar rants ravage the hearts and souls of patriots who've served.*

Chapter 8

SURROUNDED BY TRAITORS

Time to reenlist; time to go back to the Delta.

Gary C. Peters, Carlisle, PA: *"A Vietnam vet could take being spat on by one person. What broke our hearts was being spat upon by our country."*[1]

There's no question about it: the 1969–1970 school year was the toughest time in my life, the worst year ever . . . by orders of magnitude. By comparison, the stretch in Vietnam *was* "a walk in the park."

Hard to believe, but undeniably true.

While I certainly didn't expect to be treated like a hero when I returned, I did anticipate some level of respect for risking my life when called by my country . . . a draftee not running and hiding like so many did. Serving one's country in combat deserves respect.

And why did people who knew nothing about what was going on in Vietnam expect me to be ashamed of serving there?

And, ashamed of what?

It made no sense, and it wasn't just the protesters.

Even "Jo(e) Public" didn't seem to know if she or he should have any respect for those who had served; probably due to the fact that only the aberrations were being "glorified" by the media. How could anyone learn anything about what was going on in Vietnam based on seeing only blood and gore in Nam and protests and riots at home? It's just not possible. Yet, that's all I ever saw on the tube when I got back.

People I knew would make patronizing comments like, "What *a shame* you had to go to Vietnam. Are you all right now?"

Damn!

I wonder how many proud servicemen and women were finally convinced that it was *A SHAME*. The whole damn business was really wearing me down.

Then, just when things seemed to be at their worst on campus, additional salt was ground into my festering wounds. Along with the news about Chris and the insanity around me, it nearly pushed my pen to the dotted line on an Army (re) enlistment form.

Funny what a simple letter from a "friend" can do.

In this case, the letter was from a girl, another Linda, I knew from school in Hawaii. My sister Butch and her husband, Tom, had vacationed in Hawaii in September, and they had talked to Linda while there, informing her of my brush with death in Nam. Apparently, that was the impetus for the letter, "to cheer me up."

Back during the 1966–1967 school year, Linny and I had become the best of friends. We were both engaged, but the loves of our lives were oceans away. Thus, we provided mutual support whenever "bummed out" came calling . . . purely platonic, just count-on-each-other best friends.

Tragically, Linda's soulmate was killed in Vietnam. Then my engagement went belly up for less traumatic reasons—distance and my inability to cope with the distance primarily. Hawaii stressed the bond; my juvenile behavior fractured it irreversibly. So, Linny and I had a go at something more than platonic for a few days while I was on leave prior to going downrange to the shooting gallery in Southeast Asia myself. Considering where I was headed, the odds for success of that effort should have been obvious from day one.

Zilch.

In any event, I still had Linda assigned to my "best friend" category, and I must have expected the few people I ever placed there—the *very* few—to know intuitively how and when to offer support during personal crises. And, damn, was I ever in the middle of a personal crisis where I needed some support.

Well, the letter I received was *EXCEEDINGLY* antiwar. It was filled with down-with-the-military proclamations and edicts, treasonous commentary and newspaper clippings about "great" protests and riots; the whole nine yards. It was definitely *not* what I needed at that point.

On top of everything else, that letter of "non-support" was like driving a stake in my heart.

Take that, dirt bag!

God, what a time for a "fuck you, you patriotic jerk" letter to arrive.

In thinking about it, though, the biggest problem was probably not the letter per se as much as the realization it drove home—that I was battling for my life totally, irrefutably *ALONE*.

Why?

I didn't have to fight any battles alone with the 199th in Vietnam. My brothers were *always* right there.

Why this one?

I was being torn to shreds inside by all the shit going on. The former love of my life was married—gone; trusted friends sold me out, defecting to the enemy. I felt abandoned. The letter from Hawaii just brought into focus the fact that *I had been*. I was entirely, 100 percent alone in an alien wasteland . . . deserted and forsaken on a hostile battleground.

My hometown?

Ha! What a fucking joke.

I'm not sure whether my family or the Linda I was dating at the time even knew this particular battle was raging, but even if they did, what could they say?

Cheer up?

Right! I'm sure they must have seen the consequences though. It probably wasn't too pleasant for them either, just having me around.

Of course, the problem was really more than people at that point. I felt abandoned by my ideals. Everything I'd been raised to believe in had gone south . . . or sour . . . or in the shitter . . . or something. The whole concept of patriotism—what America is all about—no longer seemed to be true.

What happened? What went wrong?

At that point, I just didn't know.

All that training on how to live one's life, on how to perform if called upon by your country—the childhood messages from Audie and the Duke; from Em, Bob, Harry, Zip, and Gene—were they lies?

I had performed up to my expectations in Vietnam and well beyond. The cause, saving South Vietnam, was worthy; I committed to dying for that cause if need be. As a result, I returned home feeling a consummate level of pride, a level unattainable ever again—no question about it.

Yet, for all the pride I felt coming home, I was being scorned and condemned; openly by people I didn't even know, more quietly and condescendingly by people I did.

"How terrible you had to be there," acquaintances would say. "It must have been awful."

Well, maybe it was, but there was more to it than that. I don't recall anyone ever asking me if the cause was worth fighting for, if the South Vietnamese people were worth dying for. Apparently, they didn't have to ask. They knew just by watching TV.

Like hell they knew.

They knew SHIT!

* * *

According to the university newspaper, the *Royal Purple*, President Nixon must not have liked the way things were going either, since he gave a major speech on November 3 defending his handling of the war effort. I missed his address to the nation, television having attained a high ranking on my "lost cause" list by that time. However, excerpts in the *RP* from newspapers around the country suggested that I hadn't missed much.

With the exception of the *Cleveland Plain Dealer*, which seemed fairly neutral, the statements from the *New York Times*, the *Madison Capital Times*, and the *Minneapolis Tribune* were all intensely critical:[2] "President Nixon disappointed the nation's hope. . .;" "The President is not telling the truth;" "In appealing to the American people for their trust . . ., President Nixon did little last night to dispel the doubts so many Americans have about the war."

Hmmm.

Apparently, the pres wasn't all that convincing in his arguments.

The armed forces were really starting to take a hit on campus as well.

In an article about the "great social value" of dissent, one of Wisconsin State's English professors stated, "The ideals and the aims of the military are foreign to the humanitarian objectives of the university."[3]

What? Are you shitting me?

What the hell does that idiot think we're doing in Vietnam?

Damn. We're over there to save the lives of the South Vietnamese people, for Christ's sake.

How much more humanitarian can you get?

Of course, this statement came out of the same department where another professor was quoted earlier as saying he came to Whitewater because, "at the time, there were no openings in the Communist party."[4]

Oh, how cute. And this was the same guy who as a hobby likes "to blow up things."[4] Just what we needed on the WSU-W campus.

WSU-W also contributed a sizable contingent to the November Peace Moratorium in Washington, D.C. that year. Hey, our students had to keep their priorities straight.

What were they in school for, anyhow?

Unfortunately, as Christ's birthday approached, the heat was turned up even more . . . indoctrination to carry us through the holidays, I guess. There was an advertising blitz in the *Royal Purple* for the showing on campus of the movie, *In the Year of the Pig*. The director was quoted as saying that he made the movie to depict "the utter immorality of our involvement."[5] VC atrocities were overlooked in the film, because "Americans need to see the ugly face of our actions, not the other sides."

Terrific.

Let's go for balance here, folks.

Then, the last week of school before Christmas vacation, there was a big anti-ROTC demonstration. Another march with students carrying enlightening placards: "ROTC Kills" . . . "Ruck Fotsie."[6] What a great time it must have been for the young kids going to college on that federal program.

So much for patriotism.

Christmas vacation did offer a bit of a respite that year, but little else.

I was really close to the end of the line. There was no sign of anything getting better, and in fact, things just seemed to get worse day by day. The torture and agony were unrelenting.

What was there to look forward to?

NOTHING!

My long-term career goals seemed unimportant. What was the sense of continuing in school just to be miserable all the time?

I couldn't come up with any good answers.

It had been absolutely clear to me in 1969 that the cause and the people in Vietnam were worth fighting for . . . worth dying for. By January 1970, it was even clearer to me that the cause and the people in the States *were not*.

NO FUCKIN' WAY!

They were carrying North Vietnamese flags. They were supporting the *killing* of American soldiers . . . the killing of my friend Chris. They were filth! They were the lowest scum on the face of the earth!

It was all too much to take.

Every day I became more and more convinced that there was only one solution—to go back in the Army. Not just to reenlist, but to volunteer to go back to Vietnam. My efforts and abilities were appreciated there.

When I got hit in Nam, Colonel Mess, the battalion commander, was in the hospital to see me within an hour and a half. He walked the full length of the ward, past eight or nine other guys from the 2nd Battalion (including two lieutenants), to see how I was doing and if I needed anything. Colonels don't normally do that for sergeants, but that's how much he appreciated my efforts and abilities.

And, yes, I WAS *that good.*

For whatever the reason, I was in my realm . . . every synapse focused on the task at hand and all the senses honed to a level I would have thought impossible. I don't know how it happened either.

It was as if I had spent the past twenty-plus years preparing for this one purpose—even though I hadn't. Everything—every muscle, every nerve, every reflex, every instinct—seemed to be revved to the max and functioning in perfect unison in Vietnam. Basic life and death survival skills, I guess, just took over.

On one occasion as the platoon sergeant bringing up the rear on a company sweep, I found a VC base camp everyone else in Delta—about seventy guys—had trudged past. Something didn't look quite right with two nipa palm fronds among thousands; they were bent down ever so slightly, across one another . . . maybe even turned out just a touch, making the broad top surfaces obstruct the view a bit more than they should.

Nothing major, but for some reason, it caught my eye.

Like spotting a hidden image in a painting, once I noticed it, a frond X jumped out at me. So, I radioed ahead to hold everyone up while I thrashed through the tangle of vegetation and muck to see what was back there . . . a steel-reinforced concrete building for one thing.

Charlie had been eating American freeze-dried LRRP rations (something we couldn't get) and booked out the other side of the camp when I waltzed in. Some papers they tried to burn in the small building were still smoldering.

Finding stuff was what I did—tracks, caches, booby traps, base camps—while keeping my guys from getting caught in any crossfires. Colonel Mess didn't ask for ol' Two-Five just for the hell of it. And unlike his predecessor, he spent time on the ground—not just flying around overhead—so he knew what the hell was going on.

No question, if one should do in life what it is they are best at, then the best solution for me was Vietnam. I've never done anything better than I did my job in Vietnam . . . a fact I was proud of back then and still am.

So, by early 1970, I was ready to "chieu hoi"—to give up and head back to Nam. What the hell, maybe the odds wouldn't catch up with me.

Maybe I would survive. If I didn't, so what?

At least, the cause *and* the people would be worth fighting for, worth dying for, and it would be easier than what I was going through in Wisconsin. *Anything* would be easier.

I was dying a little each day in Wisconsin.

Why not make it for a worthy cause?

Such was the nature of the battle occupying my time day after day, week after week.

Go? Give up my goals, quite likely my life?

Stay? Be tortured, torn apart, and miserable every day?

What to do?

Damned if I knew, but a decision was close. It had to be. The end of the line was fast approaching. I couldn't take much more.

Funny thing, I was about to . . . the whole town was, like it or not.

COMING HOME . . . HOSTILE AND DEADLY

Enduring Truth: *Life or death? Unrelenting hate can turn the latter into the chosen path.*

Chapter 9

MOLOTOV COCKTAILS, DINNER & DANCING

Weathermen torch the campus. Police guard the dance.

FIRE! Fire at Old Main!

That alarm raced through the town Saturday night, February 7, 1970, faster than the kerosene-fed flames raced through that huge old building on the Wisconsin State campus. The final indignity, gang rape of a university—a whole community—was underway.[2, i]

Who would have thought it possible?

Arson, big time, in "Backwater," Wisconsin.

Of course, it was probably only a coincidence that a group of militants from Milwaukee were in town that night; that suspected members of the Weathermen, Black Panthers, and SDS radical groups out of Chicago were there as well. They were undoubtedly all in Whitewater to take advantage of the greater social and cultural opportunities. They certainly couldn't have been any of the individuals seen pouring kerosene around in Old Main just prior to the fire starting . . . or the guys with Molotov cocktails the next night.

Heavens no!

I'm sure they had nothing to do with any of the other mysterious fires that kept popping up in the area either.

It was never proven though, so who knows?

Maybe Whitewater just offered more interesting late night "entertainment" than Milwaukee or Chicago for H. "Rap" Brown and his anarchist friends. Neither of those cities probably had any colleges with the same appeal for non-students as Wisconsin State.

Or perhaps those colleges just didn't have as many willing student trainees to help out.

Some help.

Prior to that night in 1970, Old Main *was* the university for all intents and purposes. Oh, there were a few other buildings around, but none the size of the original, sandstone-colored brick monster on the hill—Old Main.

59

The tall, three-story central portion of the building had a sloping roof rising to the height of a fourth story. It was topped by a picturesque four-sided tower with short spires at each corner, a narrow walkway around it, and a steep roof with a tall flag pole at the peak.

Definitely an impressive sight.

The tower on Old Main was undoubtedly the most noted landmark in the area, being visible for miles around. As a matter of fact, it could be seen easily from our farm, a couple of miles north of town.

Three other wings, east, west, and north (the latter not visible from the front of the building), were added to the original central portion, the east and west connected to it by enclosed "bridges" above the first floor. Similar brick construction was utilized for each of the wings and the bridges, so the final structure—"Old Main" as we all knew it—was a massive, imposing sight there on the hill.

Driving down Main Street, lined with beautiful, mature elm trees, and looking up the long circular drive bounded by two entry pillars, Old Main was not a sight to soon be forgotten. I certainly haven't.

What a loss.

The fire alarm for Old Main was sounded at 10:18 p.m. By midnight, it appeared that the whole town had turned out to watch the desecration; the after-dinner light show.

Linda and I got there early, when only the west wing of the building was involved. Standing at the bottom of the hill on Main Street, looking up the few hundred feet at that Goliath-like structure, one-third of the visible portion of the building in flame, it was a devastating sight.

I had truly started my academic career there, the very beginning—kindergarten. In the front entrance of the west wing, first room on the left. That's where the classroom was.

Staring blankly at the flames, all floors ablaze, memories of each of the subsequent grades attended there—first, second, third, fourth, fifth, and sixth— passed through my mind. You talk about watching your life pass before your eyes.

I didn't say a word for the longest time. I just stared, watching my childhood ablaze . . . being reduced to ashes.

I could remember when Old Main was essentially the only building on campus except for the ancient field house across Graham Street—now the Walker D. Wyman pedestrian mall. While in grade school, some of us would occasionally sneak around the back of the east wing at recess to watch the construction workers excavating for the "new" library, completed in 1953. A lot of my early life was visible in those flames that night.

As we all stood there in the bone-chilling night air watching the inferno rage in the west wing, soft reflections of the flames—a melding of oranges, reds, and yellows—could be seen in the windows of the central portion of the building. We all knew that the fire would be stopped at the bridge though.

People standing in the area were discussing that fact openly.

60

The Whitewater Fire Department, although strictly volunteer, was exceptional, and they had been well trained at Old Main. Plus, they had lots of help from around the area.

Therefore, everyone agreed—*no question*—the fire would be confined to the west wing.

Of course, we didn't know about the kerosene. We also didn't have long to wait to discover our mistake.

All at once, someone close by screamed: "Oh, my God, it's spread to the middle part!"

As all eyes focused there, scanning the reflections in the windows, I hoped beyond all hope that the pronouncement was wrong. However, it became clear in an instant that no longer were all the dancing colors merely reflections in the glass; some were now originating behind it.

Son of a bitch!

They didn't stop it.

From our vantage point at the bottom of the hill in front of the building, we had no idea what was happening out back. Soon, however, someone making the long trek around the whole fire scene came by and passed the word that the north wing was burning too. It had been destroyed by fire once before, in 1891,[3] but this time the destruction would be *permanent* as well as complete.

There went my junior high years, and from where I was standing, I could watch my freshman and sophomore years of high school go up in smoke, those years having been spent mainly in the central portion of the building. The doors of old College High were really being closed forever this time.

What a horrendous night.

With all the noise emanating from up on the hill and around the area, it's amazing how quiet everyone became as the fire engulfed the floors beneath the tower and, finally, the tower itself. While only the west wing was burning, it seemed like everyone crowding around on Main Street was talking at once, offering an opinion.

What an abrupt change. It was as if someone came by and stuffed gags in everyone's mouths.

Personally, I didn't feel a hell of a lot like talking at that point either. I just stood there listening to the hissing roar of the fire and the chaos on the hill . . . listening to the sporadic sirens here, there, and everywhere.

I could see a fireman, perhaps two, on the roof of the bridge to the east wing, but the smoke was getting worse, making it hard to see. The smell of smoke seemed to be getting stronger too.

That must have been what was making my eyes burn, causing them to water. Rubbing them didn't seem to help a lot though.

Damn!

We maintained the vigil until "the pinnacle of the Old Main tower started to fall, [then] I turned and walked away. I couldn't watch the end, or the impact."[4, ii] Even though the east wing was saved, the tower signaled the end for me.

Without closing my eyes, "I can still see the top of the flaming tower—frozen at a 45-degree angle—on its terminal plunge,"[4] like video stop-action. It's as if my mind won't (or can't) let it finish its journey.

Odd how the mind works sometimes.

At least no one was killed in the fire that night. It could easily have happened, though. One of the professors was in his office in the basement of the west wing when the fire started. Fortunately, a police officer first on the scene saw his light before it was too late to get him out.

There were also a few students in the building; some working on art projects, others "on the air" with WSU radio. One of those students actually directed the police officer to the professor's basement office in the west wing.

With as rapidly as the fire spread, it would have been easy for those individuals to be trapped inside.

Damn lucky!

Some of the fire fighters were damn lucky as well. Two of those responding from a neighboring community to the six-alarm blaze fell forty feet from a ladder, but both survived. One did suffer severe head injuries however, and was in critical condition for some time.

There were also a few other "minor" injuries—broken legs and such. And having seen some of those volunteer firemen climbing around on the roof of that mini "towering inferno," it could have been a lot worse.

I wonder if the intellects with the kerosene had weighed the possibilities of lives being lost. I doubt it. Or more likely, they just didn't give a shit.

FUCKING WORTHLESS ASSHOLES!

At least it turned out to be "only" a building that vanished into oblivion—bricks and mortar, wood and plaster.

Who would miss it?

Who, indeed?

It turns out a lot of people probably miss that antiquated edifice. Old Main had been more than a landmark in Whitewater. It really embodied the heart and soul of the community.

The tower served as a focal point, a source of pride, for everyone who lived there. A truly inspiring sight, and the sort of thing the town had gotten used to looking at after a hundred years—an old friend you could always count on being there.

The fire may have resulted in the loss of physical facilities at the university . . . 107,000 square feet of floor space, but it was much, much more to the community.[5] When driving down Main Street now, it's clear that the east wing should have burned as well. It just serves as an ugly reminder of what once was. It's like rubbing salt in the wound, year after year after year.

The Alumni Building they put up on the hill sure as hell doesn't help either. Yes, they used brick from Old Main when it was built, but the wooden "tower" at the top of that one-story brick shed looks like it belongs on an oversized outhouse. And the damn building isn't even centered at the top of the oval drive.

What a fucking joke. It sure makes me proud to be an "alum" looking up there. God!

Then when you consider what Dutch elm disease did to Whitewater, almost denuding the landscape, there's very little left to take pride in. On the occasions when I go back, the difference is clear.

It used to be someplace special. Now the old pride is gone.

I guess being raped can do that.

While other towns in the area—Fort Atkinson, Jefferson—prospered in the years since the fire, Whitewater still had the look of a ravaged and battered victim the last time I was there. If not for the university (which continued to struggle forward), the city fathers might well have rolled up the sidewalks by now.

But the patient still shows some signs of life . . . a Wal-Mart store and a few other businesses in the midst of what used to be a west-end ghost town must mean something.

Unfortunately, lots of old, unanswered questions about the fire still remain.

Like, who did it? Who were the *specific* individuals involved?

The police figured they knew back in 1970, but they never quite had enough evidence to press the issue.

And who were the three hippie-types in the Student Union who reported seeing the "perps" pouring kerosene around in Old Main? The ones mentioned in the police reports filed that night?

Why did the two Whitewater police officers on duty at the dance in the union not get their names?

Mightn't the names of eyewitnesses be worth noting?

Apparently the two cops "guarding" the dance didn't think so . . . until after the fact, when they couldn't find the guy and two girls again.

So much for being able to press the issue.

Of even more relevance, why didn't one or both of those watchdogs of law-and-order haul ass up the hill to Old Main rather than just staying at the dance and calling the report in to the police station?

They were perhaps a hundred yards away from Old Main, max.

Were police procedures in Whitewater so stringent back then that the senior officer "guarding" the dance couldn't have made such a decision?

Might they have gotten to Old Main before it was actually torched, catching those involved?

Considering that officers arriving at the scene from downtown almost got there in time, it makes one wonder. Could the fire have been contained at least?

It's only conjecture, of course.

Things that went on in Whitewater on subsequent, post–Old Main nights can also make one wonder as well. The bastards with Molotov cocktails the police spotted, for example . . . the ones trying to take out the library and administration building.

Should the cops staked out in the area have been allowed to blow their asses away?

No?

Well, why the fuck not?

Explain that one.

Dumb!

What a waste . . . the whole stupid business.

But, then again, maybe everything wasn't a waste. Some potentially life-saving questions were answered, or were at least starting to be answered.

Personally, it was a turning point, a subtle one perhaps, but a turning point nonetheless. Although standing there watching my childhood go up in smoke could have been the final straw that sent me packing for Vietnam, it was not. Instead, a hint of anger was starting to smolder . . . the first sign of fighting back.

I know almost exactly when it happened too. It was a few moments after realizing that the fire had reached the central portion of Old Main. While I had been beaten down watching the west wing burn . . . the site of the old grade school . . . suddenly I realized what had happened.

The fucking protesters had started it. There may have been no way of knowing for sure at that point, but still, I *knew*!

Well, they had gone too far this time, and for some reason, that realization diminished my urge to re-enlist.

The questions from within were beginning to be answered—I had to fight back. One additional question put forth by a trio of idiots contributed to settling the issue . . . once and for all.

ANTI-AMERICA AMERICANS . . . LADY LIBERTY'S ACHILLES' HEEL

—Antimilitary/Antiauthority Zealots—

Enduring Truth: *The flames of anarchy cannot burn free
lest the free soon won't be.*

Chapter 10

SCREW THE BASTARDS

Enough is enough; the rotten bastards don't have the right.

"Do you have any idea what war is all about?"

That question, or one very, very similar, was asked of me three different times during my first year back from Vietnam. Three different coeds asked the question.

Weird, huh?

I guess it must have been my fatigue jacket with the tiny American flag on it that elicited such brilliance.

The first time the question was asked, early in the school year, I was caught so off guard . . . I was so flabbergasted . . . I just stood there shaking my head, wondering to myself, "who is this fucking idiot?" Then, of all things, she decided to educate me about the realities of war and explain why I shouldn't be wearing the American flag.

Good luck, lady.

Would you believe I didn't learn much from that Phi Beta Kappa of military warfare?

My employment as a bartender had taught me that bar room arguments accomplish nothing, so even on nights when I was on the drinking side of the bar, I tended to stay out of provocative "what war is all about" type discussions. Not always, but most of the time.

Although I would wear the American flag for all to see, trying to convince non-believers of its value was futile—especially a bunch of stoned, half-drunk Benedict Arnolds who weren't worth a shit anyhow—so why try?

Perhaps the reason I wore it was as much to announce my allegiance as anything else; most who didn't like it stayed away from me. Unfortunately, some of them had the I.Q. of a demented warthog . . . or a banana. As a result, I would have to listen to the babbling of idiots.

It really is amazing how people with absolutely no first-hand knowledge of a subject can be such "experts." Of course, that never seems to change. Around a university one can face that predicament every day . . . only the topics have changed.

And while I managed to maintain my composure, nodding quietly, while the first two young ladies tried to explain what war is all about, by the third, I could no longer bite my lip and remain silent. It was significantly later in the school year and too much had happened—riots, arson, and treason; loves, friends, and friendships dying.

I had been dumped on enough. I was also sipping suds in the Hawk's Nest at the time, one of the college crowd hangouts, so the brew may have oiled my tongue a bit.

"Excuse me?"

"Do I have any idea what war is all about?"

Well, I informed the pseudo-military historian as politely as possible under the circumstances, that "having a piece of shrapnel residing in my left lung" . . . [I thought] "my up close and personal experience in combat last year might give me a reasonably good idea 'what war is all about.'"[2, i]

Based on her shocked expression and noticeable lurch backward, I thought the conversation was over and looked forward to drinking in peace among the friendlier drunks. Unfortunately, that was not the case, and this sweet young lass (who at a distance had appeared quite attractive, but now—with hatred raging in her eyes—was far from it) had to ask one last, sneering question:

"What does it take for someone like YOU to *kill* somebody?"

Well, that was it! That was absolutely the last fucking straw. I had finally taken all I could take from those miserable, ignorant, *fucking bastards* without retaliating.

But, mind you, I didn't overreact. At least, *I* didn't think so.

I carefully put my beer down on the bar and very slowly moved my right hand up in front of my face, about a foot away, palm facing me, fingers extended. Looking at my hand, I closed the middle, ring, and little fingers; keeping the index finger pointed straight up, thumb straight out.

I then looked the inquisitive young lady in the eye, and *very, very* slowly moved my hand down, extending my arm slightly, so my index finger was pointing straight at her. Sighting down it, glaring directly into her hate-filled eyes, I gradually closed my index finger, in a manner indicative of *squeeeezing* a trigger.

The only thing I said at that point was, "*About that much!*"

Well, would you believe, I didn't see much more of that sugar-lipped self-righteous charmer?

I'm not sure if she had an accident right there on the spot or what, but she sure booked out in one hell of a hurry.

"*Didi mau*, BITCH!" And make it FAST!

God! What did she expect?

When the situation actually presents itself . . . when you catch a glimpse of the business end of an AK-47 aimed your way (a privilege I experienced on the rim of that fucking gully while Russell was covering my backside), it sure as hell better not take any more than "*about that much*" to get the job done. The one major difference being, of course, that the response had better not be in slow motion.

Hesitating for an *instant* in that situation will get you one thing; it will get you instantly DEAD!

Moments after I got to the edge of the ravine where I could sneak a peek at our guy down below at the west end—with machine gun and AK fire coming out of multiple firing ports just below me—I caught some movement out of the corner of my eye in the shadows of a tunnel entrance across the way. In the split second I had after seeing the tip of a rifle barrel being pointed my direction, I instinctively flipped the lever on my faithful M-16 from automatic to single shot and proceeded to empty most of the clip—one shot at a time—into the tunnel.

I'd sure like to see Miss Congeniality or any of the other holier-than-thou creeps try to face up to it sometime. You pull the trigger—or you're dead. PERIOD!

You don't think about it. You don't debate the pros and cons.

You pull the trigger . . . *again* . . . *and again* . . . *and again!*

But I suppose if *she* would have been around in 1941, she would have proposed that we ask the Japanese to *please* not bomb any more of our harbors.

Perhaps we should have reasoned with Hitler. Please don't gas any more of those people. Pretty please.

You bet! Pull your head out of your ass . . . *you ass*!

In retrospect, though, I probably shouldn't have been so hard on that lovable sweetheart. In fact, I probably should have kissed her. She sealed the deal for winning my battle, for not taking the "easy" way out and going back in the Army.

And, in truth, she probably saved my life by finally making me mad enough to stand up to any and all comers.

SCREW THE BASTARDS!

Got a problem with where I've been or what I've done?

Sin loi MF . . . tough crap.

You can *eat shit and die*! I really don't give a rusty fuck.

In early 1970, it was a big step on the road back. It was still pretty much all inside, but the corner had been turned.

Strange as it may seem, Wisconsin State may have turned the corner as well. Just as the burning of Old Main nudged me on to the road to recovery, it appeared to instill some degree of sanity back into the students on campus also.

The metamorphosis was subtle, perhaps, but noticeable just the same. The number of protest rallies, as well as their intensity, dropped precipitously.

The *Royal Purple*, which had been "wall to wall" with antiwar articles all year, reduced such stories markedly. Coverage of the fire occupied the student journalists most of February, and once that tapered off, it's as if they recognized the consequences of their actions. Gosh, stoking the flames of anarchy can have catastrophic consequences.

Who'd a thunk it?

Whitewater paid the price, BIG TIME.

While the rest of the country continued to heat up over the war in Vietnam, the *Royal Purple* focused on environmental issues and Kenny Rogers. Pollution became the enemy; Kenny, a would-be friend. Mr. Rogers and the First Edition were scheduled to give a concert in Whitewater, and as part of the new, "light and airy" overkill, the *RP* publicized that upcoming event ad nauseam.

That probably had a lot to do with the disappointment surrounding the performance itself: "Monday's Edition Was Roger's Worst."[3]

Oops.

In that same issue was a picture of two American flags on a flagpole; one with a peace symbol replacing the stars flying below a normal flag. Beneath the picture was the caption: "In memoriam: Allison Krause, Sandy Scheuer, Jeffrey Miller, William Schroeder; Died Monday, May 4, 1970, Kent State University."[4]

That was the *only* reference to Kent State; an event that touched off riots and media firestorms elsewhere in the country.

Boy, the *RP* staff and WSU-W students must have been racked with more guilt than I imagined. Either that or the university leadership—my buddy President Carter—tightened the clamps down.

Not that the war and associated campus turmoil were without coverage, however. It's just that they no longer appeared to be the *only* news from a student reporting perspective.

After the fire, it was predominantly the Wisconsin State faculty that pushed for continued chaos.[5, ii] The department of English, especially, created the daily news.

A mere two weeks after Old Main was torched, the faculty member who liked to "blow up things" was forecasting significant antiwar activities for spring.[6] A couple days later, his boss was "relieved of administrative duties as chairman,"[7] and a week after that, the "blower upper" and three of his colleagues were suspended by WSU-W President Carter.[8]

Whoa! English takes a hit.

It was alleged that the "Whitewater 4," as they soon became known, had supported a student boycott of classes, the "Out to Lunch" program. The president didn't seem to find humor in that and wrote to the four noting, "harm to this University may result if you are continued in your present position."[8]

Adios, mothers!

Of course, Judge Doyle quickly overturned the suspensions, but shit was hitting the fan fast and furious there for a while.[9] And soon thereafter, most of the faculty members in the department of English joined Janesville Local 579 of the International Brotherhood of Teamsters, Chauffeurs, Warehouseman, and Helpers of America.[10]

Yes, indeed, the burly teamsters.

Can you picture an assistant professor of English . . . a tie dyed, sandal shuffler . . . as a teamster union steward?

We had one at WSU-W.

The *Royal Purple* had lots of coverage of the teamsters that spring. They were picketing on campus. They were arguing about the future of academic freedom.

I wonder if that was common practice for most teamsters of the era; sitting in a "shot and a beer" bar contemplating the future of academic freedom. There's a scene to visualize.

"Wha da ya think, Hacksaw? Might academic freedom be unpropitiously impacted perchance?"

Strange, strange times.

At least by the end of spring semester, my sense of humor was recovering to the point where I could appreciate certain things associated with the antiwar protests—those that there were of them—as being funny.

There was one day when I was standing in the hallway of the student union talking to the WSU-W president and some of the other administrators, when one of the big dog antiwar types came walking past. When President Carter said, "Hello John," and asked him how things were going, I thought the guy was going to fall down and give himself whiplash all at the same time.

You talk about someone not knowing "whether to shit or go blind."

It was obvious that John was in shock that the president knew his name, and all he could do was stutter in response, "Oh, o . . . o . . . okay!"

At the same time, his head was snapping around in all directions, apparently looking to see if any of his "classy" friends were around. I suppose if any of them had been close enough to hear, they might have suspected a mole in their midst. When he finally stumbled into the snack bar area, still stunned and looking around, we all cracked up.

What a sight.

The poor, dumb son-of-a-bitch actually thought he could go around inciting riots on campus, and no one would know his name.

Jesus!

Nobody ever said college students were necessarily smart. And, in fact, some can be downright stupid; lacking the common sense God gave a goose . . . or goose shit, for that matter.

There was also one other absolute classic that occurred in the student union that semester.

Pete, a friend of mine with the sheriff's department, was doing "his thing" undercover on campus. He had been a student there a short time before, so he looked like he belonged, wearing grubby tennis shoes, cutoff shorts, and a baggy fraternity sweatshirt with no sleeves.

Well, Pete wandered into the student union one day and found a table in the midst of a bunch of the troublemakers.

No problem.

Unfortunately, the tables in the union had captain's chairs around them.

Colossal problem . . . for Pete!

As he sat down, Big Bertha, the .357 magnum he had under that baggy sweatshirt, hooked on the arm of the chair. Eyewitness accounts indicate that Bertha did a half-gainer before she bounced and skidded across the floor.

GUESS WHO?!

I suppose since she didn't "go off," Big Bertha's dive—blowing his cover—could have been worse. But it certainly gave a lot of us who needed a laugh that semester just what the doctor ordered.

I wasn't even in the union when it happened, and I still got a hell of a laugh out of it. Word travels fast in a small town.

* * *

By the time summer school rolled around, I was actually speaking out somewhat . . . making my own anti-antiwar statements.

In the non-verbal category, I changed fatigue jackets. Not as in putting on a clean one; I did that often enough. However, the fatigue jacket I had been wearing had all the insignia removed as required by military regulations. I had merely added the small American flag pin.

It wasn't very showy. It didn't make much of a statement.

I switched to a fatigue jacket with ALL the insignia left on. Staff sergeant stripes (three stripes and a rocker) in full living color on both sleeves made a statement: "I took my job seriously and I was damn good at it."

The combat infantry badge (CIB) above the left pocket made a statement: "I was in the heavy 'shit' while I was in Vietnam. I was shot at, assholes, and I know how to shoot back."

The overall message being delivered?

"FUCK WITH ME AND I'LL HAVE YOU FOR LUNCH!"

I was going to take no more crap from anyone. I was proud of the stripes. I was proud of the CIB. I was proud of my unit patch—the 199th Light Infantry Brigade—the Redcatchers.

Bottom line?

I was proud of the whole damn uniform.

I *earned* that pride, and I was going to display it. *NO ONE* was going to take that away from me again . . . ever.

My uncle Em had earned his staff sergeant strips and CIB in the muck and mire of the South Pacific during the Second World War. He was damn proud of his service.

I earned mine in the muck and mire of South Vietnam. I was damn proud of my service.

As the saying for that would have gone in Vietnamese street jargon: "All same, same, GI."

Yes, the fully adorned fatigue jacket helped. I felt much better wearing it, being able to recapture the esprit de corps that had been stolen from me.

Putting that fatigue jacket on was like getting an instant infusion of military bearing—head up, chest out, stance erect. I'm not sure if those around me noticed the difference, but it was certainly an uplifting, rejuvenating experience from my perspective. I could once again "stand tall and walk proud."

It felt great!

I felt great . . . again . . . finally!

The other portion of my anti-antiwar statement was not all encompassing by any means, but it was a start.

Somehow, I had managed to put off three non-major, pain-in-the-butt courses to the bitter end—the *very* bitter end—and all of them were in the arts and humanities . . . *protester central, ground zero*. Taking Art Contacts, Speech, and Advanced Composition could be interesting.

Fortunately, none of my teachers seemed to be foam-at-the-mouth-type antiwar lunatics. That helped. So, I decided to take the leap.

After writing a few off-the-wall papers in the only English course I ever halfway enjoyed—one using the senses to describe a 2-D blued lath nail, another about an egg—I tested the anti-antiwar waters with an intimate perspective of the first moments of Army basic training.

The assignment was to write about "a memorable experience with an institution."

What could be more memorable than basic training, day one?

Surprisingly, no firestorm erupted.

With that one data point—an A accompanied by Mr. Ellis's scrawled critique: "a graphic evocation with interesting allegoric overtones"—I decided to jump into the really deep end with my last oration in Speech. It was clear by then that my Speech classmates were not rabid protesters, but none of them were advocating the bombing of Hanoi either.

In any case, it seemed like a good place to unload a bit. So, my last speech was entitled, "What War Is All About."

In the few minutes I had, I described the basis for the topic—my three favorite coeds—what it was like "living" in Vietnam as a combat infantry soldier, and what it was like watching people die. The second of the three coeds had tried to explain to me what that was like in war . . . as if she had any idea.

I didn't need the explanation, thank you . . . you prissy, sanctimonious jerk!

I also didn't pull any punches in my speech about seeing people die. It's not the sort of thing one can take lightly, or explain unemotionally, having been in the middle of it.

However, I opted not to get into the whole issue of whether the cause was worth fighting for. I even overlooked the issue of pride felt by returning soldiers; one I knew quite well.

I only tried to make the point that the soldiers who were there were the only ones truly capable of assessing "what war is all about" . . . the *ONLY* ones! They were also the ones in a position to judge the merits of the cause. People who wanted to know about such things should consider asking those who had been there.

It was an interesting endeavor, and my point to the students in the class was simple: Just ask people who have been there, friends or acquaintances, for their opinions. Obviously, not all those opinions would be the same, but at least, they would be hearing them from knowledgeable people . . . for a change.

I don't know if it would "sell in Peoria," but it didn't do too badly in Speech 101. The overall response by the class was certainly much more positive than I had expected—not that I really worried about it anymore. A couple people were almost apologetic, saying they hadn't realized many of the things I'd pointed out.

It was even suggested by some in attendance that I should let people know; that I should speak out. I don't know why I never did after that.

Well, yes, maybe I do.

It was a matter of first things first. Having taken my pride and self-esteem back from those who wished to rob me of them, I could focus, once again, on my career goals.

71

Nothing would be allowed to stand in the way. I had come too close to losing them . . . to losing everything.

Besides, convincing a few students in speech class is one thing. There were still too many idiots spouting treason—siding with the enemy, supporting the killing of American soldiers—for anyone to hear my voice even if there were a few who might be willing to listen.

Nope, it just couldn't be done.

Impossible!

ANTI-AMERICA AMERICANS . . . LADY LIBERTY'S ACHILLES' HEEL

—Sanctimonious Amoral Moralists—

Enduring Truth: *Only the war fighters truly know*
"what war is all about" . . . ASK!

Chapter 11

DECADES DEFIED ... 1970 TO 1987-88

Shutting the door on the war; closing out the world.

Career goals aren't reached overnight, so once I closed out the world around me—put on a flak jacket and blinders to deflect the vitriolic fusillades targeting Vietnam vets—there was time for little else. I had come too close to missing the chance for a research career to dedicate anything less than total effort to that cause.

I had to prove I could do it . . . to myself if no one else.

Defeat was never a consideration for the "No Sweat Platoon" in Nam. It sure as hell wasn't going to be for me back in the real world either—not after the bloody war I had just gone through.

Fortunately, in the midst of the hometown warfare that year, I at least managed to figure out the direction my research career would head . . . more or less.

And, again, Dr. Brady at WSU-W gets full credit. Just as the first course I took from him—botany—got me into biology from business, the last one—microbiology—determined my future scientific focus.

My graduate studies (if I made it that far) would also be in micro—research at the cellular and sub-cellular level. The chemistry minor had tweaked my interest in how things work at the molecular level as well.

Then, getting sufficiently pissed to fight back when Old Main got torched, I managed to eke out just enough time in the library examining graduate programs to get one—*and only one*—application shipped off prior to the deadline for school the next fall . . . to the department of microbiology at Oregon State University.

Remarkably, I got accepted.

So, finally, in August of 1970, I had pretty well put things back on track. I was able to get on with my life.

I graduated from Wisconsin State on the 7th of the month and got married on the 8th . . . to a knock-out, "she's the one" young lady I'd met all of four weeks earlier. A week after that, Marcy, our just-turned-7-year-old daughter Lorna, and I left for Oregon. It was off to graduate school and that long sought-after career in research.

A year late—but better late than never—I finally felt like a bona fide civilian again. And for the most part, I perceived of myself as being relatively unchanged by all the skirmishes of the recent past.

Through my eyes, I was once again a normal, perhaps slightly scared and callused, civilian. Everything seemed A-OK once my pride and self-worth had been recaptured from the scum-sucking antiwar bastards. With that and my new family, I could face any obstacle, no matter how great.

Graduate school?

Piece o' cake.

Well, sort of. I went to work for probably the toughest faculty member in the microbiology department, but for my money, he was the best as well. Dr. Parks—Leo—had a reputation as being a real crack-the-whip slave driver with graduate students. And, well, that would be tough to argue.

The students in his lab put in some unbelievably long hours—Kenji, Gunnard, Rich, and me—but we blew off lots of "don't talk back" steam along the way. The practical jokes and water fights with other labs late night on the fourth floor—long after Leo went home—were something else.

I'm not so sure we didn't come close to pushing Leo over the edge at times though. However, he had loosened up a whole bunch by the time Rich and I graduated four years later, and he got plenty of work out of us along the way as well.

It wasn't all work though.

I managed to get back into a few spare-time recreational activities I had enjoyed during my previous lifetime in the U.S. of A., prior to Nam. For one thing, there was playing softball with the department of microbiology "Micro Mets."

Even though my arthritic throwing arm wasn't going to contribute all that many outs, I was immediately deemed *the* person to play third base. The hot corner was more than a little tricky, what with the plowed fields we played on, but the grizzled old combat vet would keep his nose in there when others would clutch and bail.

What the hell, being smashed in the kisser by a bad hop isn't any big deal.

No sweat!

Besides, there was usually plenty of pain killer available—beer most often, then the 40 liters of handpicked elderberry-blackberry wine we concocted in the lab while Leo was on sabbatical in France. The postdoc in the lab, Ed (a.k.a. "P.D."), was left in charge, and he had a real knack for such things. So, working in a yeast lab turned out to have some definite advantages.

P.D. was the Micro Mets' shortstop, and he and I usually covered our side of the infield better when half in the bag anyhow. One day, swilling home-brew between innings, we damn near got our pitcher a no-hitter—in *slow* pitch. We pulled a whole bunch out of some orifice that day, totally unconscious.

And there were other extracurriculars to fill in the occasional spare moment or two while navigating the graduate school minefields as well. My sisters—Sis and Butch—and their families made the long drive out from Wisconsin, as did a few friends . . . Joe and Corrine who were responsible for Marcy and me connecting, then Lou, one of my old bartending compatriots at Riolo's.

My parents flew out the second year we were in Corvallis, Marcy's folks the third. Obviously, such visits necessitated ditching the books and lab coat for a time, so we could go exploring.

Want to see the Northwest sights?

Join R&M tours.

Living in the pristine state of Oregon even cured my Southeast Asia-induced aversion to camping out. But *car* camping only; there was *no* backpacking involved.

Although we never had much extra money, Marcy and I managed to scrape together enough bucks to purchase a tent at Sears. That allowed us to pack up Lorna and our dog Mai Tai to experience the Northwest up close; hiking the ground we were sleeping on . . . Beverly Beach, McKenzie Pass, Mount Hood, Crater Lake.

There's no place like Oregon to immerse oneself in outdoor activities—an ocean, mountains, forests, desert. Oregon has it all; a great place to recover from life-threatening combat, foreign *and* domestic.

Seafood at the seashore likely contributed to my overall recovery as well. There was Mo's clam chowder . . . the best in the world for our money. An infusion of that elixir could fix almost anything. Hell, it was so good at recharging spent batteries, the local fishermen in Newport used to have it for breakfast.

What a way to jump-start the day.

Then, for a done-in student, there was always smoked salmon or fish jerky to gnaw on while strolling on the beach—blasted by wind and rain—scouting for agates.

Nourishment for the body *and* the soul; it was great.

P.D. also had a 14-foot boat available for a time. That got me back into fishing, another R&R activity I had enjoyed prior to being transformed into a no leisure-time GI. Getting out of the harbor, across the breakers at Newport, wasn't always the most pleasurable task in that dinky little boat, however. But we came back with some great fish caught off the reef—mainly cod and a few bass.

If the waves were too towering to make it out of the harbor, Ed would just break out the crab pots. And settling for Dungeness crab was not exactly a tragedy. More like, salvation unlimited.

Yep, fishing I could manage, hunting . . . well, that was a, uh, somewhat different matter.

I used to enjoy the challenge of the hunt prior to my stint in the shooting gallery. Somehow, though, that primal urge had waned. When the "big game" shoots back and you've been on too many big game hunts, such interests must dissipate, I guess. Something in the depths of the psyche undergoes a metamorphosis; at least, it did for me.

The thought of shooting a deer or any other free-spirited wild being just didn't compute . . . it didn't compute at all. I couldn't comprehend doing such a thing again.

It wasn't that the sound of guns ever bothered me as it did so many others who spent time ducking incoming rounds in Nam. That was no big deal from my perspective. It was the killing part.

However, there was one military sound that did cause some problems, an all-too-common audible provocation . . . the resonating echo of a Huey helicopter somewhere close by. No other model, only a Huey—your standard UH-1B military variety.

Boy, there were a bunch of those flying around back then.

It took years and years before that noise didn't automatically kick my senses into the 100 percent alert mode. Early on it happened every time one came within earshot; gradually though—very gradually—it dissipated.

The last time I recall having a Huey-induced flashback was one evening in Ohio, eleven or twelve years after leaving Vietnam. I was walking past a small, Civil War-vintage cemetery near where we lived. Dusk was gradually melting into darkness.

All at once, my eyes were darting hither and yon; I was straining to hear every infinitesimal sound around me. Some raw nerve had been exposed; the synapse ready to fire. I had been propelled backward in time . . . back to the Delta.

Did something move behind that gravestone?!

Then I heard it, *way* off in the distance, a Huey.

Shit!

I guess I spent so much time jumping in and out of those damn things—deafened by the pulsating roar—that the distinctive, thumping reverberation resonating from their engines could trigger reactions and instincts of years gone by, no matter how old and rusty.

Ring a bell and Pavlov's dogs salivate. Fire up a Huey and the old Sarge agitates.

Red alert! Survey the surroundings for any sign of movement, any unusual sound, anything out of the ordinary. Coiled and ready to strike.

Weird.

Of course, not all the reminders of Southeast Asia over the years—the aggravations—originated from external sources. One veritable dandy was definitely internal.

For some reason, that hunk of metal I'd been carrying around in my left lung, my buddy "Mort," moved. After a dozen years of behaving himself and staying put (so told the occasional chest X-ray), Mort decided to take a hike. The new location was not appreciated either.

For about a year and a half, it felt like I was being gouged in the back with an ice pick every time I inhaled. Cough or sneeze, and it was like someone was trying to brute-force the damn thing all the way through the left side of my chest, from back to front.

Mort and I definitely had some interesting conversations there for a while, with lots of invective punctuation emanating from my side.

"Fuckin' A . . . Goddamn it!"

It's tough to get much accomplished without inhaling, and coughing or sneezing can't always be helped. Shallow breathing definitely became the norm; to hell with taking a deep breath.

And, God, don't let that be a sneeze building up!

The prescription painkiller Zomax helped, and a shot or two of José . . . Señor Cuervo . . . could always boost it a tad bit extra if need be.

So, what if Zomax did in a few people?

Eventually, though, when nothing the doctor suggested did crap, I decided to try something drastic—exercise. The only lifestyle change I could figure out prior to Mort's move and after was exercise. I had gotten rather lax in that department once I took the faculty job and quit playing softball a couple years earlier, so I decided to start running in the morning.

I had to try something . . . hurt like hell or not. I couldn't stay Zomaxed to the max all the time. Being clear-headed was required job-wise.

The V.A. doc figured the extra strain would only make things worse . . . and worse . . . then worse yet. But I'll be damned if that old shit Mort didn't move back to his previous, innocuous position in a few months.

* * *

It also proved impossible to avoid all news of Southeast Asia over the years, even though I was making a concerted effort to do so. I managed to miss a lot of it, but not all.

Hey, we weren't living in a total vacuum after 1970, so major political news—big-time antiwar debacles—were sometimes noted, even if they weren't particularly noteworthy.

At least at Oregon State, there were few protests, so I didn't have to contend with those face-to-face. In fact, I can't remember any. Those all seemed to take place at the University of Oregon—Fighting Duck-land . . . home to flocks of militant fowl (and flocking foul militants) in the 1970s.

Oddly, though, even after all the shit that went on at Wisconsin State, I never did have a problem with those antiwar types who were willing to pay their dues. If they accepted the consequences of their beliefs and actions, so be it.

Ali stood behind his religious views, giving up his heavyweight title and going to prison. I admired him for that.

Those who skipped to Canada, willing to give up their citizenship for what they believed in, that was fine with me too.

Coming back?

NO! Chris can't come back, so forget it.

They gave up that right. Well, maybe to *visit* after the war; that might be alright, but not as U.S. citizens.

But, of course, Benedict Arnold Carter—Peanut Jimmy—took care of that in 1977; within minutes, it seemed, after his White House inauguration.

Nice. Why not just spit in our faces, asshole?

Oh, excuse me: Mr. President . . . Asshole!

Then, of course, there were those jerks who committed treason—Jane and her shitbird chums. That's a little different story.

While most of her bud John Kerry's 1971 war crimes bullshit bounced off, Jane's trip to Hanoi in '72 managed to penetrate the facade. And don't give me any antiwar cock-and-bull about what she was up to.

Providing aid and comfort to the enemy during wartime, declared or not, is *not* antiwar. Ditto communist propaganda photos on an anti-aircraft gun. It's called *treason*; not something to be pardoned . . . EVER!

American soldiers most assuredly *died* because of it!

Yes, Jane, that's what you and your fuckhead traitor friends did; John and others. That's a fact to those of us who served.

You pulled the trigger on American servicemen, my comrades-in-arms. You should have been charged and tried for the seditious, treasonous acts you committed. When found guilty, *executed!*

Back then, I might have been convinced to serve on the firing squad, to accommodate my country once again. Killing four-legged creatures I couldn't do. Killing a vile, immoral traitor; a rabid jackal bitch. . .

Okay, why not?

She did it to us . . . to members of my family . . . my brothers-in-arms who would have died for me. Yes, I could live with that.

Now you want to what? Apologize?

Ha! No fuckin' way. Not to me.

Go to the families of the 58,000 killed—face to face—and apologize to them, one by one. Apologize for killing their husband, their father, their son . . . for squeezing off the round that did it . . . for torturing them to death in a POW camp. Yes, Jane, those POW camps where you did photo ops.

See what their families have to say.

But, a few decades after the fact, I guess I've mellowed a bit. A firing squad no longer seems compulsory—too compassionate actually.

Eternal damnation, though?

Who knows? Justice may yet be served.

Back when The Wall was dedicated in 1982, I heard that the names were recounted, one by one, at the National Cathedral. So perhaps Jane can spend the hereafter in front of an ebony monolith modeled after that pseudo-memorial on the Mall, reciting the KIAs in order, knowing some are there because of what she did . . . the trip to Hanoi, all her other cheer-for-the-enemy activities.

What an appropriate thought.

Truly an aesthetically pleasing apparition; black granite surrounded by a raging inferno. Jane, at her favorite post, center stage, narrating.

What do you think, Jane?

Not knowing for sure which names you etched in the stone, somehow that seems appropriate as well.

Apologize?

I'll tell you where you can put your apology. And it can reside there for eternity as well.

Yes, the flak jacket and blinders weren't totally impenetrable. An exposed nerve could be hit.

Clearly, there were times over the years when I had to face the consequences of Vietnam, one way or another. However, considering that the time frame was measured in decades, such issues weren't dealt with all that often. Posttraumatic stress disorder–inducing they were not.

In addition, I took a small, positive step in 1980 by joining the Veterans of Foreign Wars—the VFW—not that the positive features were obvious immediately. Another Vietnam vet and I decided to check out some veterans' posts one Saturday afternoon, but we weren't exactly made to feel at home in some. In fact, we damn near had to fight our way out of one of them. The Upper Arlington Second World War crowd there didn't want any Vietnam losers in their midst. However, the down-to-earth members of Post 4931 in the blue-collar community of Hilliard decided Jim and I weren't all that bad, so we signed up.

Participating in a number of VFW activities in the early '80s at least got me associated with individuals who understood pride in serving the flag. It was a start. And dealing with "real people" at the post periodically was certainly an enjoyable change of pace.

Then Lorna, our daughter, joined the Ohio Air National Guard, becoming a jet engine mechanic. She managed to get on at Rickenbacker, south of Columbus, as a full-time civilian employee, working with an air-refueling group. Our occasional visits down there were reinvigorating as well.

There was also one other military veteran-related matter that presented itself, quite unexpectedly, in early October in 1981. Marcy and I had taken our first "by ourselves" vacation that year, a 16-day, few-thousand-mile camping marathon in the Four Corners region—Colorado, Utah, Arizona, and New Mexico.

It was in that remote, enchanting part of the country where the unanticipated encounter occurred . . . while we were navigating the Enchanted Circle, as a matter of fact.

We were on the tail end of our amateur geological expedition, in the high elevations of northern New Mexico, just prior to making the long dash for home. We'd already cruised among the majestic mountain peaks of Colorado. We'd visited Arches National Park, Dead Horse Point State Park, Lake Powell, and the Goosenecks in Utah . . . all masterful works of art that Remington, Russell, or others of their ilk would have been hard-pressed to recreate.

And in Arizona, we'd camped out on the north rim of the spectacular Grand Canyon, sped through the regal, yet mysterious, Monument Valley, and traversed Oak Creek Canyon, Sunset Crater National Monument, and Petrified Forest National Park. We'd gotten "up close and personal" with most of the natural wonders Mother Nature has to offer in that part of the world.

Nevertheless, nothing we'd experienced anywhere on that trip could compare to the profoundly moving and thought-provoking location we happened upon, purely by accident, on the Enchanted Circle . . . a small chapel honoring Vietnam veterans, nestled on a peaceful rise in the Moreno Valley.

What a place!

The day had been a long and tiring one, and Marcy and I were quietly contemplating our return to the campsite in Taos, some 30-plus miles away. We'd just blown through Eagle Nest and were almost to the turnoff to Angel Fire when Marcy spotted a small, hand-painted sign by the side of the road—a sign denoting a Vietnam veteran's chapel and pointing up a narrow gravel track to the right.

In my nearly comatose state, I did little more than mumble and nod in response to her announced sighting and kept the gas pedal of the El Camino pushed to the floor. I was too exhausted to even think about lifting my foot to the brake.

Upon clearing the hillside obstructing our view, however, the situation abruptly changed.

A striking swept-wing edifice appeared out of nowhere, and instantly, I slammed on the brakes. A mere five or six weeks earlier, I'd seen that very same structure on TV, on the program *Real People.* Sarah Purcell, if memory serves, did an absolutely compelling piece about the inspirational site that stood above us.

An about-face was executed at the double-time, and in but a minute or two, we were parked in the lot overlooking a structure most assuredly sculpted by heavenly hands. The exhaustion of the day had dissipated, and we were immediately drawn forward, cradled in the tranquility of a sacred place.

Beside each circular step on the path leading down to the chapel was a name, a name of a comrade lost in service to the nation in Vietnam. Chills shot up my spine with every lingering stride, as I silently—reverently—recited each roster of one. Marcy and I were speechless; not a word was uttered during our mesmerized descent.

Amidst an otherwise placid setting, an October, mountain gale was howling mightily, buffeting our every move. And when we reached our destination, it became clear that the west wind was standing guard at the chapel door, denying entry to those of this world.

A two-fisted tussle ensued as we tried to wedge our way in, and finally, Marcy, then I, managed to squeeze through, the glass door slamming shut behind us . . . closing us in.

Whoa!

Words can't even begin to describe the eerie, yet serene feeling upon entering that triangularly shaped shrine. We transcended the present into a spiritual-like realm beyond words. Almost tiptoeing forward, the sound of soft music became barely discernible over the haunting serenade of the wind, as a magnificent sanctuary opened before us.

On our left, photographs of servicemen—images to go with the faceless names by the trail—adorned the concave, rough stuccoed back wall. Similarly constructed sidewalls swept inward and upward, merging artistically at the front of the small chapel, the left wall wrapping into the right. At the point where they joined, a narrow band of louvered windows reached up from the glossy-white concrete floor toward the heavens.

Six shallow steps—traversing three landings with seat cushions scattered about—led down to a tall, white metal cross, just to the left of a dancing beam of light streaming in. A few flowers rested and, from all appearances, wept sadly at the base of the cross, heads bowed.

It was a stark world we'd stepped into, yet inspiringly beautiful.

There was a presence, an aura of life after death, within these hallowed walls like nowhere I've ever been. Chris was there, among a host of others. I could feel him reach out and gently touch me.

Instantly, a feeling of sadness for those lost overwhelmed me, but there was something more present as well. There was a pride in this place . . . a pride in the sacrifices made . . . a pride that was totally lacking when I visited The Wall a few months later. I felt only grief and regret at The Wall. In the chapel, however, it seemed clear, the sacrifices made were not all in vain.

Marcy will say to this day that the most awe-inspiring experience of our whole trip that year was that brief afternoon stop at the chapel. She hadn't been in Vietnam . . . she didn't even know me when I was there, but we shared the same feelings, the same exhilaration and spiritual presence, being there in the chapel.

With the impact of that visit, it's hard to believe it took us seven years to get back there. But I had a career to pursue.

The brief respite in the west was merely a bend in the trail on that long, arduous journey. Nothing could be allowed to stand in the way . . . or to slow the progress, for that matter. Sixteen days camping was about it.

* * *

Career-wise after 1970, it had been basically onward and upward in the express lane only, with few detours along the way.

There was graduate school for a Ph.D. with Dr. Parks, majoring in microbial physiology, with minors in biochemistry and genetics. That occupied the better part of four years . . . full-time, over-time, all the time . . . except for the occasional Oregon day-trip as a diversion.

That was followed by postdoctoral research in biochemical oncology at the University of Colorado Health Sciences Center with my new research adviser Sylvia and her husband Ernie—four more years.

Same-same, hour-wise, plus.

I recall boarding a plane in mid-April of 1978, on my way to a national scientific meeting, and realized it was the first day since Christmas I hadn't been in the lab. Going back in on Christmas Eve had allowed me to cheat and take the next day off.

Yes, it was a full-time job, I guess. Forget the diversions. We left those behind in Oregon.

Then a faculty position in the medical school at Ohio State . . . assistant professor.

No time to stop at that point. It was time to write grants, do cancer research, and publish. Twenty-four hours a day, seven days a week. At least, it seemed that way. Lots of accrued vacation time was lost back then, including the year I ditched work for sixteen days for our camping extravaganza in the west.

Associate professor with tenure . . . five years to that hurdle.

Secure, but still no time to stop. Success at a university isn't measured at the associate professor level.

So?

Write grants and publish.

By that time, the students and technicians in the lab were doing most of the research. Write more grants and publish. Teach. Do committee work.

God, the committee work . . . academe's way of spreading the blame. The university administrators' credo: Don't make a decision, form a committee.

Then, between endless committee meetings, write grants and publish.

Over and over.

Professor of physiological chemistry (modernized to medical biochemistry later on), yet another five years.

Write grants, pub . . .

Do re . . . No!

Whoa!

Top of the ladder. Eighteen years in all since closing out the world and charging headlong down the academic path—unwavering.

1988: Time to remove my flak jacket and blinders—the protective armor. Time to take a look around the campus and beyond . . . outside the sheltered environs of the research lab.

Damn!

Things may be better—a few university types may have some compassion for those who served—but there's a whole shit bag load still out there that can't keep from spitting if a Vietnam veteran gets too close. They're just less obvious about it, so I didn't see it coming . . . most don't.

Of course, those spitting on vets are no longer grubby, long-haired students in filthy jeans, tie-dyed tee-shirts, and Jesus sandals bellowing antiestablishment threats. Nowadays, they *are* the establishment on campus . . . supposedly "respectable" administrators, faculty, and staff.

Regardless, their message to the lepers they've reviled since their old protester days is clear: "Stay off in the shadows to hide your shame."

Son-of-a-bitch!

What fucking shame?

Unbelievable!

Welcome home . . . back to 1969 . . . AGAIN!!!

ANTI-AMERICA AMERICANS . . . LADY LIBERTY'S ACHILLES' HEEL

— Antimilitary/Antiauthority Zealots —

Enduring Truth: *Antipatriot hatred can't be seen when the spitting isn't snot-obvious.*

82

Chapter 12

SOS

Platoon: Served by Lee Iacocca with shit-on-a-shingle.

Helen Keller: *"The only thing worse than being blind is having sight but no vision."*[1]

Human nature . . . being human nature, most people undoubtedly like to think of themselves as perceptive. I'm no different. I'd like to believe that if I were zapped by lightning, I'd be able to look at the charred remains in the mirror and figure out what inflicted the damage.

Unfortunately, being perceptive doesn't always equate to being struck by a bolt of lightning out of the blue. More often, it's something akin to a summer storm meandering across the far reaches of the Great Plains.

The first discernible forewarning could be nothing more than a slightly darkening hue off in the western sky or, perhaps, a barely audible rumble somewhere in the distance. The developing crescendo—methodical or nearly instantaneous—might then culminate in a soft, gentle shower contributing to a bountiful harvest, or it could spew forth a savage, destructive deluge rending virgin crops from the soil.

Oft times, however, the storm merely passes by, the impact, pro or con, being felt on down the road.

Somehow, my recognition of some long enduring, '60's antiwar-related prejudices and loathing . . . the "stay off in the shadows and hide your shame" and, at times, overt hatred leveled at Vietnam veterans . . . had many similarities to one of those unpredictable, August, Kansas squalls. And unfortunately, the nature of the ghosts and ghouls from the past that were ripped loose from a previously bruised and tattered psyche dictated that a gentle shower was not in the offing.

The timing of these less-than-appreciated revelations correlated, superficially at least, to my promotion to full professor. However, by no means was it a case of instantaneous awareness, an all-inclusive realization of truth. The genesis— that initial, barely perceptible clap of thunder—occurred, more or less, when the paperwork recommending the final step of academic advancement left my home department, around October or November 1987.

The promotion didn't become effective until months later, July 1988.

However, with the aid of 20-20 hindsight, it's clear that late autumn, early winter of '87 is when some of those issues I had closed the door on eons before began to creep back to the fore . . . subtly at first.

Then, when my recommendation for promotion cleared the College of Medicine, the last real hurdle, it was as though some monstrous, unseen burden had been cast aside. The emancipation was palpable.

It was similar, in many ways, to one of those multiple Darvon-and-salt-tablet-requiring missions in Vietnam (those extended time and time again), when we'd finally make it back to the fire support base. Dropping your flak jacket, steel pot, clips and belts of ammo, grenades, canteens, etc., etc., was an indescribable feeling. After pushing yourself to the limits of your endurance, then beyond, the weight of the world was suddenly off your shoulders.

Somehow, that's the way it felt at the end of 1987 as well.

After nearly two decades of slogging toward one single goal . . . an extended mission and then some, the end was in sight. As a result, I was looking forward to kicking back a tad. A little base camp R&R, once again, seemed like just what the doctor ordered.

So, as a change of pace during the Christmas holidays that year, I put the lab work on the shelf and began outlining some sketchy concepts for a book about my first year back from Vietnam. I had been declaring for years that I would compose such a beast someday, and quite unexpectedly, the time had come to do a bit more than think about it. Not that I was planning to write the book at that point, but generating an outline . . . somehow it just seemed appropriate.

For well over a decade and a half, it had been clear to me—crystal clear—that my first months back in the States were *infinitely* worse than the time I spent in combat in the Mekong Delta. People I'd mention that to couldn't seem to comprehend, even vaguely, the basis for such a bizarre assessment.

How could that be?

You were clinging to life by a thread in a senseless, apocalyptic lost cause, and you returned to the safe confines of your hometown.

Wake up, for God's sake!

Well, believe it or not, the hometown carnage—the welcome home—was worse. It was *orders of magnitude* worse.

Believe it!

What's more, I was convinced my situation wasn't all that unique. Others returning from battle must have experienced something comparable . . . an unexpected kick in the groin after laying their life on the line for their country.

They had to.

That part of the story—the part nobody could seem to understand—had to be told. As a result, I plodded alone, roughing out the skeleton on which, hopefully, my story would come to life someday.

Then, just after the first of the year, in an effort to reacquaint myself with the realities of the Vietnam era and the war itself, I rented the home video of *Platoon*.

Marcy and I had heard all the propaganda about that particular movie's therapeutic properties; the healing founded on truth.

Somehow though, we hadn't gotten around to catching the multiple Academy Award winner in a theater even though numerous acquaintances had recommended it as a superbly accurate portrayal of the war in Vietnam. Of course, had any of those individuals actually been in Vietnam, I, for one, might have been more convinced of the film's intrinsic values.

Watching it at home though? Who knows?

Maybe it was as good as everyone said.

What a surprise it was that Saturday afternoon when we popped the video into the VCR and Lee Iacocca, of all people, came sauntering across the screen. A pleasant surprise as it turned out . . . at least, initially. He gave an absolutely compelling introduction to *Platoon*.

Even though it was nothing more than a covert advertisement for Jeep—enacted beside a prototypic Battle of the Bulge-type four-wheeling "relic of war" (his words)—Mr. Iacocca was poignant and introspective in his lead in to the movie. He described it as "a memorial, not to war, but to all the men and women who fought in a time and in a place nobody really understood."

Holy crap!

Somehow, to me, Lee Iacocca projected an image of trust back then, a compassionate standard-bearer of American values. As a result, I was ensnared by his perceptive understanding of the soldiers who served in Southeast Asia, as he described their linkage to those who served the country all the way back to the Revolutionary War, at Concord.

Déjà vu.

He was describing those very same "mom and apple pie" emotions I had experienced in California in 1969 . . . walking side-by-side with those soldiers of bygone eras.

He went on: "They were called and they went. That, in the truest sense, is the spirit of America. The more we understand it, the more we honor those who kept it alive."

Wow! There *is* somebody out there—someone of national stature—who understands. I was psyched, genuinely psyched.

I was about to watch a "memorial" to those who served . . . my countrymen . . . my comrades-in-arms, fallen and still alive . . . me.

Fantastic!

Ha! Horseshit is more like it; it was an appalling piece of crap.

Two hours after that treatise about honor, I was nauseous with dishonor. There was nothing, nothing whatsoever, to honor in the whole damn flick. It was an abomination . . . an insult to those who served, to those who perished answering the call.

God, veterans of the 25th Division, especially, must be sick . . . their shoulder patch flashing repeatedly across the screen. *Platoon* depicted them as total misfits, military "incomps."

Perhaps if the film had been intended to depict what went on in the early '70s, just before the final pull out . . . a time when the term "fragging" had actually come into vogue. Maybe then I might have believed what I was seeing.

Who knows?

By then, maybe the morale had dropped to the level depicted.

But, 1967, 1968?

No, sir! That was *before* my tour.

Not only that, the battalion I was with, the *Old Guard's* 2nd of the 3rd, was assigned to the 25th Division (OPCONED, in military jargon) just after I got to Nam. That's why we were near Cu Chi—the 25th's home base—when we got ambushed by the NVA Battalion on Groundhog Day . . . that damn Gully of the Shadows of Death. So, I had a brief opportunity to get acquainted with the 25th, the Hawaii-based Pineapple Division. There's just no way in hell I can believe they were that screwed up a year earlier.

Not a fucking chance!

Would they have put some "cherry" on point three times during his first week in country as described in the film?

Hell, NO! That would have been a good way to get your whole damn platoon wiped out, including the stupid asshole giving the orders.

It didn't exactly take career military intellect or experience to figure that one out either. A tad of common sense was needed, perhaps, something marginally above that exhibited by your standard, backyard-variety garden slug.

You wanted your *best* walking point . . . someone who wouldn't stumble into an ambush or a tripwire-rigged Chinese claymore . . . someone who wouldn't get the platoon's butt handed to them.

My top guys walked point.

I walked point! Not often, but I did it because I was *damned* good at it. Plus, I never asked my guys to do something I wouldn't do myself.

Then, what about having the troops cluster-fucked on top of each other in the boonies at night while a sergeant rips butt regarding the need to keep their "shit wired tight at all times?"

Another real beauty in the film.

That would have been common, right? Performing that close-order tirade just after getting shot up on ambush?

God, I don't think so. Not unless you really wanted to get your ass stomped. Chuck would have been damn accommodating under those circumstances.

No, Sergeants in the 25th couldn't have been that blatantly dimwitted. They would have pulled the zipper on their own body bags long before that had they been in the habit of screwing up that badly.

But, how about the standard, E-nothing snuffy, you might wonder?

Would he not have been standing around in the field having a smoke, paying no attention to what's going on, as depicted at one point in the film? That, when he was *alone*, 50 meters out, guarding the flank, the platoon having just found a VC/NVA bunker complex? One where Charlie was still in the immediate vicinity?

Jesus!

Any simple-minded S.O.B. that unremittingly moronic would have deserved the fate depicted in the movie. He should have died . . . to spare the world from self-propagation.

Of course, in *Platoon*, said dummy getting killed gave a fitting excuse for a "My Lai Syndrome" scene, a big seller in such flicks. Hey, if one accepts the premise that most of the troops in Nam were deranged psychopaths, similar atrocities would likely have occurred routinely. It's only reasonable. Then *Platoon* rhetoric like "let's 'do' the whole fuckin' village" would represent the norm.

Spot on, right?

LIKE HELL!

Marcy posed an interesting question about the American soldiers brutalizing South Vietnamese civilians in that scene and others in the movie. She asked: "If that went on all the time, why do so many Vietnamese want to come to this country?"

Hmmm.

Good question.

Why do you suppose hundreds of thousands of them would risk their lives at sea to escape their beloved homeland? Why an exodus like never before in history? With most of them trying to get here?

Odd, isn't it?

Let us not forget the pot scenes in *Platoon* either; that was another characteristic of the fighting man in Vietnam, right?

Everyone knows the troops in the field were getting stoned all the time. That's just the way it was.

Yeah, there we were wandering around with our M-16 in one hand and a joint or bottle of booze in the other.

What a crock of shit! Anyone who believes such crap should have the barren wasteland just to the left of his or her right ear examined.

Hello! Is anyone home in there?

During my few months in Vietnam, I only knew of *one* guy in 2nd or 3rd Platoon who smoked pot when I was platoon sergeant or platoon leader. He would have been court-martialed if I could have proven it, just like the NCOs and officers in the 25th Division would have done.

That worthless bastard could have gotten a lot of us killed.

On one occasion, he was smoking dope and fell asleep on guard. That word eventually filtered back to me from the guys he was with . . . the ones who pointed out to him what the consequences would be if it ever happened again.

Adios MF. He might not survive the next firefight.

The time that son-of-a-bitch tripped off to La La Land was on a night when Delta Company was the early warning unit outside Long Binh for an expected attack by two or more battalions of NVA reported to be in the area. We were spread out so unbelievably thin, Ho Chi Minh and the Hanoi Marching Band could have paraded through unseen had they probed that unguarded position.

The point is, except for a few rare exceptions, essentially everyone recognized the realities of the situation. Smoke pot—you die!

It doesn't take a great degree of intellect to figure that out when you're in the field. You had to be alert at *all* times.

So, smoking dope? Drinking booze?

It just wasn't done by the vast, vast majority.

Wake up America . . . try to understand.

IT WASN'T DONE! We weren't that damn stupid.

Unfortunately, the few infantry-types who were that retarded—and lived—probably got some of their buddies killed because of it. As a result, they most likely have to be very vocal about "everyone" doing it just to live with themselves.

Of course, that concept is undoubtedly endorsed by the protesters of the era. They must eat it up. It proves they were right all along.

BULLSHIT!

And that's exactly the term I used in correspondence to Mr. Iacocca on February 7, 1988 to describe "80 to 90 percent" of the film he had blessed.

In a letter I wrote the day after watching *Platoon*, I pointed out: "The average infantry soldiers during the era illustrated in the movie were not the uneducated, pot-head, drunken killers and otherwise 'screwed up' individuals that the movie made them out to be. They were just average young men of the time doing a very difficult job."

Then, for Mr. Iacocca's edification, I concluded: "Therefore, dedicating *Platoon* to those of us who lived and, more importantly, to the memory of those who didn't, is a severe injustice."

I suppose I shouldn't have been surprised, but old Lee didn't bother to respond. Somehow, I thought he might, since my letter made it a clear question of integrity—*HIS!*

Oh, well.

A few months later in an effort to ensure that my original response to *Platoon* had not been unduly critical—that it hadn't just caught me on a bad day—I rented the video one more time. And to be totally honest, my first impression wasn't as accurate as it could have been . . . as perhaps it should have been.

During the first viewing, I must have gotten rather upset early on and not watched as analytically thereafter. As a scientist, I was not being particularly scientific in my data collection. The second time around though, I worked hard at keeping my emotions in check, and as a result, my opinion did change somewhat.

Yes, the movie was *worse* than I first thought.

Granted, some of the combat scenes in *Platoon* did portray the chaos of battle quite effectively and accurately. That's true.

And the depiction of "burning shit" back in the base camp and the new guy's, the cherry's, ass being busted the first few times in the field were also done pretty well. Not that the nasal sensory pleasures of the former—YUK—or the "I think I'm going to die" pain of the latter could ever be recreated altogether believably . . . but not bad.

The bunker complex stumbled upon in *Platoon* also elicited a few déjà vu-type pangs on my part as well, what with the tunnels, underground hospital, and all. Somehow, that struck home as I flashed back to the Gully of the Shadows of Death blood bath we were immersed in on Groundhog Day, 1969; up near Cu Chi with the 25th.

Yes, there were certain attention-getters in the film an old Vietnam grunt could reminisce about.

And the movie actually did depict the potheads as being in the minority in the infantry in Nam. That too was as it should have been.

However, something that became clear only during the second viewing was that the dopers came out as the compassionate good guys. The less than subtle take-home message was that they smoked dope only to escape the unprecedented brutality of the Vietnam War . . . that inflicted by the warmonger majority.

Ah, ha! You bet, Sherlock.

So, why had I never seen any warmongers over there?

Not with the 199th. Not with the 25th Division.

Zero! Zip! Nada!

Oh, I suppose there may have been some around . . . somewhere, but they sure as shit didn't represent the majority. For that matter, not even a detectable, "where the hell are they" minority.

Somehow though, I suspect our one pot-smoking asshole—the one who could have tagged a bunch of us with the initials KIA—probably thought *Platoon* was a great flick. He likely owns a copy or two, so he can show it to his friends, to demonstrate what an insightful, enlightened person he was.

Well, no, that's not really very likely. Someone like that jerk wouldn't have any friends . . . he'd sell them down the river; just like the cowardly *Mother* did his brothers in the Mekong Delta.

He could always watch the movie himself, though, for the same purpose . . . to prove what a clairvoyant, great person he was, and is. That way he'd have an audience that might believe it.

Damn!

Of course, it probably says something about Oliver's motives as well . . . 100 percent. He and our Nam pothead—with no pride within—probably justify it by blaming their proud brothers . . . the guys who had the guts to perform under fire.

Were those guys deranged warmongers?

NO!

Honorable warfighters?

YES!

Why is it, do you suppose, that essentially all the movies about Vietnam deal only with the bizarre, the aberrations in war?

Sure, some of them are based on real events. But aberrant behavior—abhorrent actions by individuals or sporadic, isolated groups—has occurred in all wars, not just Vietnam. Hell, it occurs on Main Street, U.S.A. Read a newspaper. Watch the evening news on TV. Such behavior should obviously be condemned, but it wasn't the norm in Vietnam, just as it wasn't the norm in the Second World War.

So, why the enduring assault?

And why only with regard to the war in Southeast Asia and those who served there?

To be fair, however, *Platoon* did have the appropriate disclaimers at the end. Reading the credits, it did state that the story—the Oliver epic—was totally fictitious . . . Ollie made it up.

But then, why isn't it viewed as such?

Why do so many people relish that tasteless pile of male bovine excrement and find it palatable? Why such an appetite for shit-on-a-shingle . . . literally?

If people wanted to see a movie that more accurately portrays the real war (without ever showing the fighting and mayhem), a movie that more accurately portrays the real Uncle Ho (without ever showing the old boy himself), they should try *The Hanoi Hilton*. Then read the credits at the end. See who offered the insights into what went on in the North Vietnamese prison camps . . . the POWs.

But, not unexpectedly, the critics chewed up that big screen accounting of what it was like. American POWs could never have been treated as depicted in that film. The Saints from the North would never have been so cruel.

No way . . . it's not possible.

Jane was there—everything was perfectly fine for the POWs. She told us so.

Sure thing!

All hope is not lost though.

At least the subsequent war movie by the *Platoon* director didn't win as many awards as anticipated . . . someone rained on the jerk's Fourth of July parade. Perhaps the newspaper reports of blatant inaccuracies in that "true" story contributed to the unexpected shortfall at the Academy presentations.

Oh, too bad, Ollie . . . *you worthless sack o' shit.*

For me though, *Platoon* did accomplish one thing. It demonstrated that the book outline I was working on was, in fact, an important endeavor. Imperative is more like it.

Something had to be done to short-circuit the myths being propagated . . . to correct the malicious injustices about those who served.

The guys in Delta Company—those who made it back, those who didn't—the honorable vast majority deserved better . . . a ration of truth for a change.

Yes, I'd have to find time to write the book someday.

ANTI-AMERICA AMERICANS . . . LADY LIBERTY'S ACHILLES' HEEL

— Sanctimonious Amoral Moralists —

Enduring Truth: *Lies unchallenged become truth; truth dishonored begets more lies.*

Chapter 13

AMBUSHED BY FRIENDLY FIRE

Pinned down; hunkered in the academic bunker.

Platoon should have served as an omen of what was to come during the remainder of 1988.

God, what an odd-ball year that was . . . another emotional rollercoaster ride like the one after touching down in California in 1969, only this time the action was framed in slow, s . . . l . . . o . . . w motion. It spanned the better part of the year, not a few hours. The hills and valleys were once again measured in extreme highs and lows; it just took a hell of a long time to get from one to the next.

There was also one other difference from the earlier ride as well. The forces at work were clearly external this time around.

Well, most of them were at least.

Oliver's Odyssey may have contributed to one of the early stomach-in-the-throat plunges in 1988 (the first viewing having been on Saturday, February 6), but it turned out to be a minor dip in the road overall. The Cyclone Killer Coaster had bigger surprises in store.

And, regrettably, I thought I was out for a Sunday drive that year, coasting toward some unfamiliar R&R . . . way too long overdue.

Nonetheless, within days of watching *Platoon* that first time in early '88, a shot was fired—in the form of a simple, offhanded comment—that sent me plummeting into a Grand Canyon-size abyss . . . eventually.

The comment?

"Vietnam veterans don't count anywhere."

To put that pronouncement in context, it was the response I got when making an inquiry about a campus-wide affirmative action survey at *The* Ohio State University, my place of employment. Although I was unaware of any sort of legislation granting veterans affirmative action privileges with regard to employment, I had reason to believe such was the case—that Vietnam veterans should count somewhere.

During the previous year or so, I had applied for a few university positions in the west, since Marcy and I felt much more in tune with the western lifestyle and longed to return there . . . well, I did for sure. In each instance, the affirmative action forms I was asked to complete had a category for Vietnam-era veterans. I had no idea why, but there it was, listed along with sex, race/ethnicity, and disability status.

I was aware that women and minorities—categories one and two—were awarded affirmative action employment privileges under the federal Civil Rights Act, and it seemed as though individuals with disabilities were granted some sort of preferential status as well, although I wasn't certain of the statutory basis. However, since the only other box to check was for veterans of the Vietnam era, it seemed logical that they—we—must be covered by some legal means.

Why else would it be there?

Therefore, I asked Glenna, our department administrator, to look into it, suggesting there might be another individual the department could receive credit for on the questionnaire—me. But, after a thorough review of the survey materials and checking with the Provost's office, I got the official word: "Nope, Vietnam veterans don't count anywhere."

Nonetheless, that didn't put the matter to rest.

A week or two prior to that, I'd been named to chair a faculty search committee involving the departments of physiological chemistry and neurology. Fortuitously, a couple days after my discussion with Glenna, I received a booklet in campus mail outlining the affirmative action guidelines for faculty searches at the university.

And, guess what?

Veterans were covered by federal affirmative action legislation . . . the Vietnam Era Veterans Readjustment Assistance Act of 1974; the disabled by the Vocational Rehabilitation Act of 1973.

So, never knowing enough to keep my mouth shut, I sent an inquiry to the provost about it. Basically, I asked him why the university was including only women and minorities in its $7,000,000 affirmative action campaign for which the faculty-staff employment survey was being done.

What about veterans and the disabled? Shouldn't they be included . . . be part of the $7 million campaign?

If they're granted affirmative action employment rights similar to women and minorities (which is what the OSU booklet indicated), isn't the university discriminating against them by leaving them out?

Dumb move on my part. *Really DUMB!*

If one expects to tiptoe through the tulips of professional advancement, one should never pose a question about "Principles" when dealing with the "Peters" of the world. That's especially true when said paradigm of the "Peter Principle" is significantly up the administrative chain of command. An "up yours" can ricochet back at you all too quickly.

However, I'd shown a draft of the letter to the chairman of my department prior to sending it on March 3, asking if he thought any of the questions I raised were out of line. Gerry said the letter looked fine to him, "no problem," but eleven days later he called me with a question:

"Did you send that letter to the provost?"
"Yes. Why?"
"Well, that must be it."
"Must be *whaaat*?"
"The provost just pulled your promotion package."

From that point on, the specifics of the conversation get a little blurry, as I think my blood pressure must have jumped a couple hundred points or so. And, for certain, lots of four-letter expletives began spewing forth from my end of the line.

"The miserable, rotten prick, son-of-a-bitch, asshole, bastard!!!"

Then, when I found out what the provost wanted, I really started to curse. Gerry was to provide some lackey, go-between associate provost with the names of three outside scientists who could be contacted by telephone to comment on my qualifications for promotion.

Now, that may not sound too unreasonable, but there were—as required—multiple external letters of recommendation already among the materials forwarded in support of my promotion. The real kick in the balls in this instance was that the names Gerry was to provide were to be of people "who didn't know me."

"WHAT???"

That's right: *people who didn't know me!*

And they were planning to just telephone these total strangers without providing them with any information about who I was.

Now, perhaps I was being unduly paranoid, but isn't there something slightly bizarre about the approach of that "fact-finding" mission? Like, how in the hell is someone "who didn't know me" supposed to comment on my qualifications for promotion?

Gerry questioned the asinine concept with the doofus flunky asshole that called, but it was all to no avail.

As one might suspect, I went just a shade ballistic there for a spell.

When I finally calmed down enough to have a sit-down discussion with Gerry in his office, the strategy we devised was to provide names of prominent scientists who at least knew me; they just didn't know me very well. That way, they might have some knowledge of my research capabilities and, hopefully, they would be willing to respond to an otherwise dim-witted request.

There was also one other "peculiarity" that came to light during our discussion that day. It seems there were only five faculty members from the college of medicine recommended for advancement to full professor that year, and two of us were from the same department. As a result, the same departmental P&T—promotion and tenure—committee had assembled the promotion packages.

According to Gerry, the contents were, for all practical purposes, "indistinguishable" . . . something he knew for a fact having approved both. But I was the only one whose credentials were being challenged.

Curious, isn't it, that I would be singled out?

Two days later I returned to Gerry's office for a status check and found out he had even more cheery news from on high. It seems that the names and telephone numbers he had provided weren't going to do the job. They couldn't reach two of the people in a timely manner and the third said he needed to see a copy of my curriculum vitae before he could comment on my qualifications.

Gee, how strange.

The provost's office supposedly Fed-Exed the guy a copy of my CV, but they hadn't heard anything back yet. So, they now wanted the names *and addresses* of four or five additional references.

Having the intelligence of a band of untrained chimps, the great minds at OSU had come to the conclusion that scientists "who didn't know me" might have to be mailed copies of my CV before they could be asked to assess my credentials for advancement.

God, is it any wonder higher education is in the toilet?

Fortunately, Gerry was able to convince the associate puppet jerk-off that the department was capable of sending the CVs and requesting additional comments. Of course, the situation had now moved from something that could be resolved in days to something that would take weeks, perhaps months.

Terrific!

After fuming for a few more days, I finally dialed up our lawyer.

Basically, Sara suggested that I should "sit back, keep your mouth shut, and smile a lot." It was her recommendation that I wait to see if they backed off. If so, I could raise all sorts of hell once the promotion goes through. If not, legal action could be pursued later.

It was a tough assignment, but I *tried* to keep my mouth shut . . . at work, at least.

Sitting back? Smiling? Nope, those just weren't possible.

Then, gasping for air during the lull in that fiasco (and blowing blue smoke when not at work), the red flag of Vietnam was raised. Two of our best friends in Columbus, Owen and Sherry, were at our house for dinner at the end of March. At some point that evening, swilling brew while I was bitching about all the shit going on, Sherry asked me: "Why didn't the war screw you up like it did all the others?"

Holy crap! It wasn't the damn war! Not in *most* cases. It was the Goddamn, horseshit welcome home. And, besides, most Vietnam vets aren't that screwed up anyhow. Those are just the ones you hear about all the damn time.

Well, if someone we had known for years—one of our best friends—didn't understand, how could others?

It sure made me think, maybe my 1970 classmates in Speech were right; maybe I should have been speaking out. But this goes way beyond my "What War Is All About" speech. These issues would require hitting topics I left out of the speech purposely . . . whether the cause was worth fighting for, the pride felt by returning soldiers, and lots of other "screw the protesters" stuff. It would require taking things to a whole new level.

Wow!

There seemed but one good answer: Maybe the time had come to begin writing my book. Perhaps it was time to let people know what the realities *really* were—what it was like coming home to a slap in the face after serving with honor. What it was like to risk your life for an ungrateful nation—a life 58,000-plus forfeited. Facts were needed to counter all the fiction . . . all the bullshit . . . all the flat-out lies.

And once I got started, it seemed easy. Even after all those years of ignoring and forgetting, when the key to the lock was turned, the door to 1969–1970 burst open and I walked through as though it were yesterday. Everything was right there. After that, all that was left was to tell the story . . . put pen to paper. Or, in this case, fingers to the keyboard.

No sweat!

The briefcase was being left at work by then. Why should I use MY time for the bastards at work? Screw 'um. They got their pound of flesh—their decade. I'd brought a couple million dollars-plus of cancer research support into the university by then, and most of the grant writing had been done on family time, evenings and weekends. As far as I was concerned at that point, the place could get fucked. My grant writing days at Ohio State were over. My time was for me now . . . to take care of some long unfinished business.

Beginning spring break, the scant, Christmas-time outline for the book gained substance. With a crude blueprint to follow, text exploded onto the monitor in front of me. Emotion . . . emotion I didn't even know was trapped inside . . . burst forth. Hidden memoirs and sensibilities were sculpted into nouns, verbs, adverbs, and adjectives. Flesh was added to the skeleton before me. A form took shape.

Chapter 1. Chapter 2. Chapter 3. Chapter 4.

The words were all there. Reach for the keys, and the cursor seemed to march across the screen instinctively.

It really was going to be easy . . . another "walk in the park." Those first four chapters were roughed out in a matter of two days; *two long days*, granted, but two days nonetheless.

Of course, that rapid trek back in time surfaced at least one rather bizarre, totally irrational recollection from Vietnam that I didn't include in those chapters. Moreover, I still don't talk about it—the fact that I would have felt cheated if I hadn't been tagged WIA . . . wounded in action.

Yes, I know that's nuts—probably confirming Colonel Mess's original assessment: that I was at least *ti ti dien cau dau*, perhaps *beaucoup*—but it's the way I felt . . . nuts or not.

I answered the unknowns regarding combat: I performed under fire.

But what if I were wounded? Would I still pass the test?

Some didn't.

One example that really gnawed at me involved a lieutenant with a platoon we linked up with during a firefight. He had been shot in the arm just before we got there. The wound didn't look all that serious, and it sure as hell wasn't life threatening. But the guy was totally dysfunctional . . . gazing off into space, providing no leadership whatsoever.

That bothered me—*a lot.*

As the only officer, he was responsible for the lives of the men in his platoon, and he couldn't perform . . . *in a firefight*!

Jesus! At least he wasn't whimpering for his mommy.

I sure hoped the sight of a little blood—mine—and some pain wouldn't turn me into a useless, pathetic nothing.

Pain doesn't count in combat. It's not a justification to stop doing your job—*especially* someone in a leadership position. We were all in pain a lot of the time in Vietnam . . . everyone was, and you just sucked it up and kept going. You didn't complain about it. When you hit your limit, you just pushed past it.

I didn't want to let my guys down the way that lieutenant did. As it turned out, I don't think I did—the WIA question mark was erased.

Nonetheless, I figured that was one I'd better keep to myself. It would just confirm to some out there how crazy we were . . . or, I was, at least.

Besides, it was time to move on.

Chapter 5. Hmmm. What happened during those first three weeks back home? Why such a void there?

I spent the whole third day of my literary adventure plodding along on the fifth chapter, but got nowhere. It turned out to be a giant black hole.

Oh well, it could be bypassed for the time being.

The story wasn't about the good times coming back anyhow . . . the initial welcome. It was about the shit that happened immediately thereafter—chapters 6 through 10.

Except for the need to do a bit of library work in Wisconsin—to check the *Whitewater Register* and the *Royal Purple* for supplemental facts and figures—those chapters materialized from the vacuous depths even more precipitously. Each and every pertinent detail was still there, stitched into a decades-old wound. Scratch the still inflamed laceration and, quite astonishingly, blood gushed forth from 1969 and '70. It was as if a main artery had blown.

By the time those chapters were knocked out in first-draft form, spring break had slipped by the wayside, but so what?

I just continued to march. I'd go by the office Monday through Friday, but I had a computer there as well. If there wasn't something else I absolutely had to do, I kept on writing, editing, and rewriting.

Chapter 11: August 1970. According to the outline, the synopsis that had served me so well, the end of the story had been reached: graduation, getting married, and heading to Oregon . . . end of story.

A resolution had been found.

As I launched into it on the of April 17, 1988, however, the cursor didn't seem to think so. It struggled across the screen. Delete, delete.

Again. Nope. Delete, delete, delete.

Once more.

Okay?

Well . . . hmmm.

It was a battle, but eventually, a collection of words was compiled . . . a draft of chapter 11 was complete.

But was it?

Everything else seemed to fit. It flowed.

Why didn't chapter 11?

My problems had all been resolved in 1970. I was able to get on with my life, pursue that career in research.

So why wasn't that enough? Why didn't it serve as a fitting climax to the story?

The story was just about that one-year period . . . my welcome home in 1969 and '70.

Or was it?

It seemed there was only one thing to do at that point. It was time to flip the switch on the computer. Give it a rest, Bucko. You're getting nowhere fast, so you may as well give up the battle for now.

Besides, there was a rather consequential scientific research matter that was starting to press on my time. Months earlier I had committed to giving a talk at the national cancer meetings in New Orleans that year, and the date was starting to draw near.

Even if I was sufficiently fed-up to flick in my research career, I wasn't about to make a fool of myself in front of a national scientific audience. I had slides and a talk to prepare for the end of May.

Other than that (in the midst of all my writing), the only concern I didn't let go of at work was my almost daily status check with Gerry regarding the promotion.

Shortly after the middle of April he had received all the additional letters of recommendation requested and forwarded them to the provost's office. Soon thereafter, he got a call from the associate flunky, stating that they *probably* had sufficient material to complete their review. And, finally, two or three days prior to the cancer meetings, the word came down . . . it appeared that I was going to be promoted.

Hallelujah! At least I wouldn't have that noose hanging around my neck in New Orleans.

But, if there was ever so much as a microscopic, grain of sand-type doubt about what the shithead provost had been up to at Ohio State, that uncertainty was obliterated at the cancer meeting that year. I found a key witness to the sordid affair—a witness willing to talk.

Someone I trusted in the OSU administration (and, believe me, there were very few such animals) had found out the name of the scientist who had been queried by telephone at the very beginning. It was a guy from Purdue I had recommended to Gerry.

Since my OSU contact was convinced that something was "rotten in Denmark" with the whole process initiated by the provost, the name was passed on to me. And lo and behold, I ran into the Boilermaker scientist in question the day before my talk in New Orleans. We had an interesting conversation, to say the least.

I started out by employing my standard subtle approach . . . a frontal assault. After Bill and I exchanged greetings, I immediately thanked him for whatever it was he had done that was about to get me promoted.

Bill let out a noticeable sigh and began shaking his head back and forth. He responded by saying that he wasn't going to even mention the phone call he got if he saw me at the meetings. It was the strangest conversation he had ever had in all his years in academe.

It seems an associate provost from Ohio State had called him out of the blue and grilled him for thirty minutes or so. The strange thing about it was that nothing was ever asked about my scientific credentials, research track record, or qualifications.

Bill could never figure out what the guy actually wanted.

Finally, Bill informed the caller that while he knew who I was, he wasn't familiar with what I was up to at the time and would have to see a copy of my CV before he could offer an assessment. The associate provost was apparently less than pleased with Bill's request, but when he couldn't pump him for any detrimental info, he finally relented.

Bill said that his suspicions about the call were confirmed once the CV arrived. He stated: "Of course, you should have been promoted. That was obvious."

Unfortunately, Bill had to put up with another round of verbal parry and thrust when the guy called back, and from Bill's description, that conversation was even weirder than the first. Each time Bill tried to talk about the contents of my CV he was cut off. The associate provost wanted to hear nothing about my credentials or qualifications.

Bill concluded: "It was clear they were just looking for an excuse not to promote you."

At that point, I thanked him again and Bill apologized for the fact that he wouldn't be able to attend my presentation the next morning; he was scheduled to fly out before that. We then went our separate ways.

On my way back to the hotel room, I cussed under my breath a smidgen as I replayed the conversation over again, but all in all, I was too spent to blow my stack . . . not again. There just wasn't anything left to blow—nothing at all.

Besides, it didn't hit me back then.

I didn't recognize the magnitude of the problem I'd uncovered. I thought it was merely a case of being slapped down for questioning his eminence, the almighty provost.

Take that, you *lowlife bastard!*

I didn't know it was the question itself . . . doing something positive for veterans. As a result, I didn't see the punji pit—the sharpened, dipped-in-shit bamboo stakes—I was tumbling into . . . 1969 all over again.

I just knew I needed a break from the action.

Battle fatigue had taken its toll.

ANTI-AMERICA AMERICANS . . . LADY LIBERTY'S ACHILLES' HEEL

— Socialist-Loving "Intellectuals" —

Enduring Truth: *Antimilitary bigots lurk among the sham "intellectual elite" [sic/sick].*

98

Chapter 14

RETREAT

Hiding in the West and rediscovering pride on sacred ground.

....

Susan Ershler: *"Pain is temporary; pride is forever."*[1]

....

Cajun food—seafood gumbo, red beans and rice—must share some of the same healing elixir qualities with Mo's clam chowder. Sitting in the open air at Le Moyne's Landing on the River Walk, swilling beer and pigging out on the local cuisine, the trials and tribulations of weeks past began to just fade away. Even the most recent confirmation of what I had suspected all along—that the provost at Ohio State was a slimy, corrupt, scum-sucking dirt bag—seemed of no consequence.

Who cares?

Screw the bastard!

Marcy had made the trip to New Orleans with me—her first national meeting— and we were truly having a fun time. Of course, the fact that I wasn't bothering to attend any of the scientific sessions might have had something to do with it.

The meetings had been going on all week, but we dropped into town for the last couple days only. I stopped by the registration area to sign in on Friday (that's when I ran into the Purdue connection . . . my provost-gate informant), and I had to present my talk on Saturday morning, during the final hour of the weeklong event. Other than that, science was taking a holiday, thank you.

We hit Bourbon Street while there . . . so Marcy now knows what a urinal smells like . . . but mostly, we lollygagged around on the River Walk. We experienced zydeco music for the first time, and as a take-home remembrance, we grabbed a CD by Opelousas' own Clifton Chenier and his Red-Hot Louisiana Band.

Outstanding!

It was a great way to wind down; a great way to start a much-needed vacation.

My talk Saturday morning went off without a hitch. Well, more or less, without a hitch.

For some unearthly reason, I was exceedingly nervous during the presentation. That sure wasn't typical . . . not at all.

Hey, no one had an AK-47 leveled my way, so no sweat. I wasn't in anyone's sights. Only my "no sweat" recitation—my standard lock and load pep talk prior to joining the fray—didn't have the anticipated ice-water results that day.

But I survived.

With only sixteen people occupying the 200-plus chairs in the spacious hall that morning, what was there to be nervous about anyhow?

Most sane people had returned home to take advantage of the three-day Memorial Day weekend. The few remaining were of little concern . . . or should have been. There wasn't a shot fired by the lot of them worth ducking.

Next question?

It was weird. I hadn't had a case of nerves like that since my close encounters with the antiwar slugs in Whitewater two decades earlier, and I hadn't seen any of those freaks lurking around, cruising Bourbon Street.

A Mekong Delta flashback didn't seem to explain it either, although that was the last place I'd seen lots of aboveground gravesites like those around New Orleans. But that didn't make any sense as an explanation for the shakes. My only really vivid recollection about those Mekong topsider burial sites was one that caused me to chuckle every time I thought about it . . . not that it generated any laughs at the time.

It was the middle of the night and no one was sleeping particularly well due to recurring splashes in the flood zone surrounding us. We were in the midst of Charlie country and couldn't see shit, but we figured it must be rats jumping into the water to swim somewhere. The soggy 2nd Platoon was peppered around the area on six or eight gravesites, since those were the only dry spots we could find as nightfall closed in. Everything else in the area was either under water or water-logged.

And as if things weren't tense enough, about 0200 a blood-curdling scream echoed out of nowhere, damn near causing me to jump out of my skin. Talk about an attention getter! With guys scrambling for their weapons, there was an immediate consensus on our crypt that one of our compatriots must have just gotten stabbed or had his throat slashed.

But, who? Where?

And why were no shots fired?

Well, it turned out to be somewhat less traumatic. One of those vagabond rats looking for something to nibble on or a cozy nesting spot ran up the inside of the pant leg of one of our sound asleep troops.

Somehow, that got a little too "up close and personal" for our guy . . . a rude awakening as it were.

Everyone had fun with that one when we heard what happened.

So, no, it couldn't have been the gravesites making me nervous.

It didn't matter though. The talk was over. It was obviously a one-time aberration.

Thus, with my work for the trip completed, I headed back to the Double Tree, and about noon we checked out. We had a few hours to kill before plane-time though, so Marcy and I strolled back to Le Moyne's Landing to kill them in style. And it worked.

I was able to start the unwinding process all over again. Cajun cuisine, out of doors, by the Ol' Muddy . . . it certainly helped.

However, it was the next phase of the trip we were both looking forward to, our return to the Land of Enchantment . . . New Mexico. It had been seven years, seven long years, but we could remember the magic of the place as though it were yesterday. Le Moyne's Landing was a great spot to reminisce about our 1981 escapades.

Finally, a little after 1500, it was time to hail a cab.

Our 75-year-old cabby that day was a character and a half and he certainly put a real thrill into "sit back and relax folks" when we noticed that the speedometer reading was exceeding his age by more than 15 miles per hour. Nonetheless, he got us to the airport with plenty, and I mean *plenty*, of time to spare.

We could have savored another kettle of gumbo back at the Landing. Hell, we could have taken lessons from Justin Wilson—the ragin' Cajun chef extraordinaire—on how to prepare the stuff.

Our ahead-of-schedule luck didn't hold up though.

We ran into an absolutely monstrous, late afternoon thunderhead on the second leg of the flight out of Dallas. That flashy, 60,000-foot boomer cut in on our Ernest Tubb-inspired "Waltz across Texas," putting us into Albuquerque much later than scheduled.

Then, once inside the airport, it looked like a bomb had gone off; the place was in the midst of major construction that year. That slowed us down even more as we navigated untold numbers of obstacles and detours to the baggage claim area. What a mess. But, finally, well into Saturday night, we succeeded in collecting all our belongings and dragging our spent remains over to the Hertz counter to pick up our economy car.

Excuse me? We're late? You're out of economy cars?

But we had one reserved.

Oh, you're going to give us *what* for the same price?

A Lincoln Town Car?

Well, I suppose . . . if we must.

Things were definitely looking up. A burgundy Town Car was at our disposal, and within minutes we'd cruised to the nearby Radisson—a beauty—for our first night back home.

Yes, our first night back home. That's the way we both felt even though neither Marcy nor I had ever lived in New Mexico.

Perhaps it was because we'd been chased out of Ohio, but as we landed in Albuquerque, and even as we walked through the bombed-out airport, we both felt that way. We each admitted that fact as we sipped margaritas in the Radisson bar on into the night.

Then, the alarm blasted at dawn the next morning! Checkout time was soon thereafter, as we frantically loaded our limousine, the Burgundy Boat, and pointed it north. The real purpose of the trip laid to the north . . . 160 miles north . . . the Vietnam Veterans Memorial.

Marcy had been urging for years, every year since 1981, that we should spend the Memorial Day weekend at the chapel, but I was always too busy. The job just wouldn't let go. No matter how overpowering the effect of the chapel had been in '81. No matter that Chris had tapped me on the shoulder back then.

I couldn't tear myself away. The career took precedence over everything . . . absolutely *everything*.

But my friend the provost changed that. Thanks much, Myles, you worthless . . . miserable . . . rotten prick . . . *Mother*. . .

With the drive that morning, most of the sights—Albuquerque to Taos—were seen in the rearview mirror. The Lincoln's tires barely touched the asphalt. We had the agenda for the weekend activities at the memorial and we'd already missed day one. We were intent on getting involved in as much as possible from then on.

The pancake breakfast at the Legends Hotel was our first target event for the day, and we blew into Angel Fire well under the wire. Famished and a tad hung over, we put away a platoon-size order of grub. And considering there were only a couple other vets eating at the time, it appeared they needed our help.

Why let more or less edible food go to waste?

The next stop was at the memorial, and things had changed somewhat. It was now the DAV Vietnam Veterans National Memorial; the Disabled American Veterans having taken over the care and perpetuation from Victor Westphall and his family in 1982. Dr. Westphall was still the resident director, however.

A visitor's center had been added since our last visit and, fortunately, it had been done right. It complemented the chapel; it didn't detract. As a matter of fact, the visitor's center was almost totally underground, and from the parking lot at the top of the hill, you could hardly tell it was there.

We knew though. As a member of the DAV, I'd seen articles about the memorial every now and then in the DAV's monthly magazine, and we'd followed the progress, as the visitor's center was being built and then dedicated.

Marcy was especially fired up to make the trip out for the dedication on Memorial Day in 1986, but her ignoramus husband dowsed that fire with his usual wet blanket . . . naively sacrificing his soul to OSU.

God, what a dunce!

So, now that we'd made it, a couple years late, we wasted little time in heading over the hill to scope the place out, the visitor's center being a biggie on our agenda for the '88 trip.

The automatic sliding glass doors snapped smartly to attention as we approached, posting to either side so we could pass through. A military salute or a "well done" would have seemed in order, but we merely paused to log in, the sentinels of the entryway executing an abrupt about-face to our rear.

An imposing, backlit glass mural greeted us inside.

The mural was mounted in a large room divider, and it dominated the scene walking in. It was separated roughly into thirds, with a bright greenish-tinged map of Southeast Asia occupying the center portion, a few small pictures of the Vietnam countryside inset alongside in the South China Sea. The other two-thirds, one on either side of the map, had watery photos of the Delta at the top with historical and geographic descriptions of the region beneath.

Overall, I guess the mural was there to provide an inanimate "hello" to the visitor's center in Dr. Westphall's absence . . . sort of saying, "here's what the place is all about."

There was a veterans' room off to the right flank, a spot where guests could sit and relax at a table, browsing through literature about the memorial. A KIA roster of the war—the same green covered book used at The Wall—was there to peruse, as were a few hundred photographs of fallen comrades left by family members and friends.

And to the left flank of the glass mural was the real heart of the visitor's center, a museum-like display area, the exhibit room. Approaching the open double-size doorway, long banners were visible hanging from the ceiling almost to the floor. Unit insignia were outlined on each, two per side, one over the other, some in red, some green.

The 199th insignia was there; the Redcatchers' identifier silhouetted in red. Nice choice.

Rectangular green pillars were interspersed as well; a few with data informational in nature, KIAs by state and the like; others with long, narrow photographs, glimpses at those who had served. There were also benches here and there, where one could sit and absorb the whole scene.

But the real attention getters were the large pictures on the walls, all four . . . snaps of what life was about in Vietnam . . . and death. There were shots of the war: fiery tracks of projectiles arcing hither and yon. There were two guys in flak jackets and steel pots ducking and booking from a molten inferno; an exploding ammo dump, by the looks.

There was a picture of the fallen comrades' salute: the remainder of the company at attention, saluting rows of jungle boots lined up in the dirt. If that one didn't make a visitor stop and think, nothing would.

However, it was another shot, opposite the entryway, that got my attention. It made my skin crawl the moment I saw it: a door-gunner with M-60 at hand, a horrified look of helplessness on his face, a body slumped beside him. The expression said it all.

The gunners' mouth was wide open, but I'd be willing to bet no sound was coming out. I'm almost sure of it. The expression was one of searching desperately for divine intervention, wanting to shout for help and scream in agony, all at the same time, but with muted silence the likely result. There was no reparation at hand, divine or otherwise.

God, it had been a long time . . . a *looong* time since I'd seen that look. Almost 20 years, in fact, but the *look* stays with you . . . the frantic desperation, the helplessness of seeing a loved one, a blood brother, maimed or mortally wounded. It's a look of longing to change places; a pleading in the eyes, "take me instead."

The youthful face in the picture brought it all back. Kids, babes in the woods, their first time away from home, wishing their life had just ended. Wishing they had been blown apart instead of the buddy they'd risked their life for so many times before, the buddy having done the same for them, time and time again.

Yes, I'd seen that look before . . . somewhere in another life.

But there were other youthful faces on display in the exhibit room as well; youthful faces that made me remember why we were there . . . why the sacrifices were called for . . . why the sacrifices were made. The Vietnamese children!

My God, how could we have deserted them?

There was one absolutely beaming little girl, perhaps 8 to 10 years of age, looking up at a uniformed GI, M-14 slung over his shoulder. The girl's round, cone-shaped straw hat had slipped back, the string under her chin holding it in place behind her head. A much older man, the girl's grandfather I'd guess, was astride a water buffalo just behind her, the buffalo grazing contentedly.

I suspect the soldier had just given the girl a candy bar, as that's what it looked like she was about to bite into. Her happiness showed too. What a cute young lady. And what a typical scene.

Another of the large pictures was of a little Vietnamese boy, barefoot, in shorts and baggy striped shirt, getting a bucking ride on a Marine's combat boot. The little boy was standing on top of the guy's left foot, facing him, the two hand-in-hand, and he was being lifted into the air.

The American looked like a giant stork, arms raised, left knee cocked upward, maintaining his balance by keeping all his weight on his right leg. You could tell that the boy was having the time of his life, laughing ecstatically.

The kids, the Vietnamese children, that's why we were there.

Wouldn't it be nice if my three beloved coeds at Wisconsin State back in 1969–1970 would accidentally stop by someday?

Maybe they'd figure out "what war is all about" . . . at least, what the war in Vietnam was all about.

Damn!

But, the most compelling photo in the exhibit for me summed it all up—a picture worth a thousand words—a close-up of a Vietnamese girl sitting on a GI's lap. It wasn't a happy picture like the other two with the children, but then, war is not a happy time most often.

No, this picture actually depicted what the war in Vietnam was all about. It was about people . . . and the duo in the photograph clearly illustrated that fact.

The little girl had on an off-white, smock-like pullover, with three-quarter length sleeves and no collar. The garment was not clean by any means. She was wearing small hoop earrings, and had a no-nonsense, stern expression punctuated by her piercing, don't give me any crap, dark eyes.

It's possible, I suppose, that the photograph was staged and her less-than-enthusiastic look was in protest for having to sit on the lap of a total stranger. But I don't think so. The harsh glance past the camera was more likely in protest over the photographer's intrusion on a visit by a friend . . . the American serviceman she was with. The closeness of the two, just sitting there—vaguely surreal, yet totally mundane—argued that the latter was true.

The GI, a staff sergeant, had obviously just returned from the field, unshaven and dirty, large bags under his eyes. His was not a young face. It was an old-before-his-time, experienced face. Just looking at him, I could feel his dire state of exhaustion.

I'd been there.

Beyond the need for sleep, however, there was a haunting sadness in his eyes; a premonition, perhaps, of what was to come. Maybe somewhere deep in his soul he knew the little girl was doomed, like her country. Maybe he saw the tragic end we would leave her to after promising salvation . . . walking away . . . forgetting.

But the sergeant won't forget—'til death does he part . . . if then. How can he forget the children he fought to save being left to die?

* * *

There's no question, the exhibit hall was exceedingly well done. The photographs, the banners, the pillars, the inscriptions; whoever assembled the collection knew what they were doing.

It was a moving display. Not that it transmitted an aura of sanctity—the feeling of standing on sacred ground—comparable to what we'd experienced in the chapel in 1981, but nonetheless, it was powerful and inspiring in its own way.

Off the exhibit room was a small, theater-like area where we stopped to watch a twenty-minute video . . . also a grabber. It recapped the history of the memorial and was highlighted by numerous interviews and testimonials.

Also, nicely done; very touching.

It told how Dr. and Mrs. Westphall had lost their eldest son, David, in Vietnam in 1968, and how the chapel had been built in David's honor.

However, our last visit had made it clear that the site also serves as a memorial to *all* who perished in Southeast Asia . . . as well as to all who served, for that matter. Perhaps, most importantly, it's a place for meditation and reflection by the loved ones who didn't go, but who lost a part of themselves far, far away.

The changes over seven years hadn't changed any of that. Our visit to the chapel immediately after watching the video proved that to be true.

There was one small change enroute, however. Sidewalks to make the facility more handicapped accessible had replaced the circular, concrete steps leading to the chapel. That was certainly understandable, what with the DAV taking over.

Still, not having the names by the steps did take away from the impact prior to going into the chapel. The chills approaching the entryway were diminished, somewhat, from seven years before.

But the effect walking in . . . ???

Well . . . that was still a knock-your-socks-off experience.

Not that the first spiritual encounter could ever quite be equaled. But, close. Very close.

There was a woman inside strumming a guitar softly, and boy, did that set the mood. The chills up the spine and goose bumps head to toe reappeared instantaneously.

Wow! What an overpowering spot.

105

Marcy and I shared a few quiet moments together in the chapel—contemplating, reflecting—before whispering our goodbyes to the spirits in attendance and moving back outside. I felt physically drained by the encounter, yet spiritually rejuvenated.

A quick check of the weekend agenda indicated that a 21-mile bike tour was about to start, at 12:00 noon; a few minutes later, a 10-mile version was scheduled for the wimps in the crowd. Fortunately, we hadn't brought our bicycles with us, so we could wimp-out in good conscience.

What's the elevation here?

8,000 feet? 10,000 feet?

Whatever. Having just come from sea level, I think we'll pass.

We passed on the other sporting events for the afternoon as well . . . softball, horseshoes, etc. We were going to be staying in Red River, a rustic, old west-style town some 25 or 30 miles away, so we took off to check in at Riverside Lodge. We had a bit of time to kill, since the musical entertainment wasn't scheduled to start until 1600.

It turned out that Red River wasn't the most convenient place to stay—Angel Fire and Eagle Nest being much closer to the memorial—but it had been the most memorable nearby community during our 1981 excursion. As a result, that's where we made our reservations. The Town Car got quite a workout in the country, the high country, as we made the trek back and forth innumerable times over the next few days.

The first round-trip put us back at the memorial well in advance of the 1600 starting time for the Heart-to-Heart Concert. A whole bevy of local entertainers—professional-types—put on a great show for those of us who braved the intensely windy conditions that afternoon. The cold wind might have been rather biting, but the musicians really warmed the place up.

The low, wooden bandstand was against the back wall of the chapel, and those of us in the audience just sat on the ground. Since the chapel is situated just over the crest of a hill, we had a great view looking down at the stage.

Of course, the entertainment had hardly gotten started when there was a flurry of activity off to our left, down the hill. Moving to a better vantage point to check it out, we observed a haphazard, uniformed assemblage moving up the gravel road toward the memorial. With the American and New Mexico flags on a white Chevy pickup out front of the procession and a POW-MIA flag prominently displayed, it was clear where they were heading.

I walked over to the road to get some snaps of the group's arrival, and by chance, I was the first person they encountered at the top of the hill. The guy leading the procession surprised the hell out of me when he threw his arms around me and mumbled exhaustedly, "we made it!"

It wasn't until later we found out that Floyd somebody, the guy up front, had walked with five others from Truth or Consequences, some 350 miles away. More vets had fallen in at Espanola and the combined force was joined at the bottom of the hill by wives, kids, and other family members, so there was quite a troop on the last leg of the march. The Truth or Consequences and Espanola contingents were

106

raising money and awareness for "The Lady" . . . the statue of a nurse that was proposed back then to be added to the three soldiers at The Wall.

I guess Floyd's exhausted "we made it" was well deserved.

350 miles?

Whew!

Comparatively speaking, we had it damn easy the previous few days. Still, the long hours and overall chaos caused us to cancel out on the remainder of Sunday's activities . . . the after-dark KIA Candlelight Vigil at the chapel; a movie at the Legends Hotel; a dance at Zebadiah's Restaurant. After the Heart-to-Heart Concert, we just didn't have anything left. We headed for a quiet heart to heart of our own at Riverside Lodge.

Marcy and I might well have rated our 1988 trip as the perfect vacation had it not been for that Sunday night in Red River . . . a disaster-plus. Calamity Jane would have felt right at home in Red River that night.

We'd noticed a significant number of motorcycles around when we checked in at Riverside Lodge earlier in the day. Unfortunately, we didn't realize that every Harley west of the Mississippi was going to be in town that weekend, revving up repeatedly, day and night.

How were we to know that "drunk and disorderly" was a Memorial Day tradition for a few thousand bikers congregating in Red River?

Quiet, the night was not.

With no sleep at all prior to 0200 and a snad, at best, thereafter, it was tough getting up Monday morning. Nonetheless, there was no way we were going to miss the formal ceremonies at the chapel that day. So, a bit more bleary-eyed than usual, I jockeyed the Lincoln back over the 9,800-foot Bobcat Pass, and we rolled into the memorial parking lot about 0930, with a good 30-minutes to spare.

There was a nice crowd that morning—perhaps a thousand or two—and even though it was still rather brisk, they were an enthusiastic lot. There was a rousing cheer when three low-flying Hueys churned noisily overhead trailing green smoke.

The Hueys kicked it off . . . the ceremonies had begun.

And what an impressive Memorial Day service it was. From the welcoming remarks by Dennis Joyner, president of the memorial board, to the posting of the colors, pledge of allegiance, and invocation, it was all first-rate.

Gene Murphy, National Commander of the DAV that year, offered some preliminary remarks, as did Dr. Westphall. Commander Murphy convinced me of the importance of being a life-member in the DAV; political clout being gained by the organization based on the number of life memberships.

And Dr. Westphall is always inspiring . . . always!

He spoke of his family's personal loss in 1968 and of the memorial functioning as a shrine for all veterans who served, no matter the war, no matter the place. It's too bad every vet didn't have the opportunity to hear Victor speak. His commitment was unreal.

James E. Webb, Jr., Vietnam veteran, war novel author, and former secretary of the navy, followed Dr. Westphall. He gave the keynote address for the day. It was an impassioned speech, highlighting the importance of commitment by the nation when placing our servicemen and women in harm's way.

Gee, wouldn't that be nice?

And it would sure be a significant change from the situation in the '60s and early '70s, when most of us in attendance that day had served.

There were then a number of presentations on behalf of the Vietnam Veterans Women's Memorial before the grand finale, a twenty-one-gun salute and taps. And it was a finale you could only appreciate by being there. I've heard firing squads and taps before and since, but none with the impact of that day.

Man, what an eerie effect taps had up there in the environs of the chapel . . . on Memorial Day . . . echoing over centuries-old sacred ground for the Ute Indians. The ancient ones were close . . . *very* close.

It was a noble tribute that day to all those who have made the supreme sacrifice in service to the nation. And the selflessness of their sacrifice certainly deserves tribute . . . by everyone . . . always. It's likely, though, that only those who were there when they fell will ever truly comprehend the meaningfulness beyond the sheer loss.

That's why we all gather. We know the reverence and honor they deserve, each and every one.

"There but for the grace of God . . ."

* * *

For Marcy and me, the remainder of the day was spent mainly interacting with new-found friends, wandering in and out of the visitors' center and chapel, and basically, just kicking back, taking it all in. While most in attendance that day were from New Mexico and Colorado, we met vets from all over the country. One of them, Dennis, a Vietnam vet from Wichita, was decked out in his somewhat dated, but still fitting, dress uniform, complete with an old-fashioned, wide-brimmed horse cavalry hat to top it off.

"Nice hat, Dennis. Gosh, let me see if I can guess who you served with in Nam."

"Me?"

"I was with the 199th Light Infantry, between Saigon and the Cambodian border."

Dennis then laid one on me from out of the dark ages—a left hook that could have knocked me over—when he blurted out: "Well, welcome home."

"Damn! Twenty years, Dennis. It's been almost twenty years since the last time I heard those words."

Unbelievable, but somehow, the memorial has a way of inducing such spontaneous actions.

Dennis, like a number of other vets we talked to that day, discussed his belief— his firm belief—that the cause had been worth fighting for in Vietnam.

Yes, indeed.

He even mentioned his willingness to go back and fight again if it could be done right.

Unfortunately, not everything was so positive for him.

Dennis went on to describe his return from Southeast Asia when he was knocked down and spit on by a mob of protesters outside the airport in Los Angeles. His welcome home was so traumatic he wouldn't so much as mention his service in Vietnam for years. Somewhere along the line, however, he rediscovered his old pride in serving, so by 1988 he was giving talks about Vietnam in the Wichita schools.

"Well, welcome home to you too, guy."

You deserve it!

We wrapped up the day visiting with Dennis and his wife and two other couples before heading back across the pass to Red River. It was a nice visit and a nice welcome home, but Marcy and I were in dire need of some sleep. So, we excused ourselves and headed off to hit the sack . . . early . . . very early.

Fortunately, it was a much quieter night in Red River.

In fact, quiet is an apt description for the whole rest of the trip. We made an almost daily run to the memorial, but the crowds had all dissipated. It was like a ghost town, but that too was nice. We were able to study the pictures and such in the visitor's center in peace. And the quiet times in the chapel are always the best.

We went horseback riding in the upper canyon, above Red River . . . a half-day trail-ride over a 10,000-foot pass.

Beyond that, we cruised in the Burgundy Boat; we saw lots of sights; we rested; we ate.

For me, the peaceful mountains of northern New Mexico and, especially, the sanctuary of the memorial were just what the doctor ordered. With the bloody battles I'd just been through—blindfolded in front of an OSU firing squad—I needed a peaceful retreat. So, all in all, perhaps it was the perfect vacation.

The wounds I'd sustained back in Ohio had been sutured and dressed. And, yes, they appeared to be healing quite nicely, thank you.

Well, almost.

SURVIVAL'S BOTTOM LINE . . . "WE *NOT* ME" . . . FREEDOM'S BOTTOM LINE

Enduring Truth: *Memorials to selfless servants are best
built with citizens' hearts.*

Chapter 15

COUNTERATTACK

Launching a strike at OSU. Sinking in a bureaucratic quagmire.

There were lots of milestones along the high and low roads in 1988 and, surprisingly, St. Louis, on the flight back from New Mexico, signaled another formidable rut in the roadway. However, this one wasn't viewed with perfect hindsight like many of the others. I understood the significance instantly this time . . . Marcy too; St. Louis jumped up and slapped us both in the face simultaneously.

We'd just left Albuquerque and the bluest blue skies either of us had ever seen. You could see forever into the gemstone turquoise heavens that morning—clarity of vision to cleanse the soul one last time before departing.

Neither of us could stop looking skyward, and I know for a fact it was my last glance as we boarded the airplane.

Somehow, the flight to St. Louis then just evaporated into that pristine turquoise realm, as I barely more than blinked and the plane banked hard left on its final approach into the Gateway City to the west. As I peered out, down at the urban sprawl, a creeping nausea started to strangle my insides. The filth and grunge in the air was absolutely unbelievable, some of the worst pollution I'd ever seen.

It was like squinting through muddy skimmed milk. And at the same moment that visual shock wave was starting to hit home, a putrid, gag-inducing stench permeated the cabin.

Oh, God.

My stomach began doing rapid-fire cartwheels.

At once, Marcy and I knew what it foretold.

"Ohio," we blurted out almost in unison. We're going back to Ohio.

Oh, God!

It was a sick turn of events, but reality collided head on. It was time to face the facts of what lay ahead. My promotion may have gone through, but things would never be the same again.

I *knew* it; Marcy likely suspected it too. Nothing had to be said.

Believe me, I held Marcy's hand a lot tighter for the rest of the flight. Blue skies were a thing of the past . . . the vacation was over. It ended in the milky, sour-your-stomach putrefaction over St. Louis.

Yes, it was time to start looking ahead.

The R&R had ended, but it accomplished what it was intended to: I'd rested; I'd recuperated. It was time to jump back into the trenches, to go back into battle.

Oh, I suppose I could have continued following our lawyer's earlier advice, keeping my mouth shut and smiling a lot. I suppose I could have just forgotten about it, chalked it up as a lesson learned and gone on working around the clock as before.

I suppose I could have done that . . . maybe.

LIKE HELL I COULD HAVE!

There's no fuckin' way!

On the last leg of the flight from St. Louis to Columbus, the transformation—peacetime to wartime—was made. And it was made completely.

It's amazing what a little milk can do to fortify one's resolve. I was into formulating strategy. I was plotting tactics.

Air Force One is heading your way . . . *Mothers.*

Although it's probably not a trait to be proud of, over the years, I have been one of those people known to hold a grudge. And having committed totally, absolutely—100 percent—to my career for nearly two decades, I didn't take being screwed with all that well.

It was "get even" time.

If the big dogs at O-fucking-hio State needed some lessons on affirmative action, I'd show them affirmative action. A combat veteran understands that principle quite well, thank you . . . action of the affirmative, "pull the pin," variety . . . even if shit-for-brains university administrators at OSU don't.

Yep.

A white phosphorous grenade, a little Willie Peter, in the bastards' Fruit-of-the-Looms had a pleasing ring to it for starters.

So much for the highbrow, professorial approach.

* * *

Prior to the vacation, a friend back in the Washington, D.C. area had provided me with enough additional information about the '74 veterans' law to have me convinced that Vietnam-era veterans should be granted affirmative action rights and privileges comparable to women and minorities. However, I had been at OSU long enough—10 years at that point—to know that was not the case . . . not even close.

So, the day I signed my new contract, July 7, 1988, the U.S. Postal Service must have thought Christmas had arrived . . . six months early. Letters started flying all directions.

One nasty-gram was launched internally at the provost's assistant who had eventually answered my March query to her boss, but most of the correspondence was targeted to the seat of power in the east, the one along the Potomac.

Hello, Uncle Sam? Your faithful nephew, your humble servant of days gone by, needs some help at OSU—O' Shit U.

The published material I'd been sent stated that the '74 act "requires employers that have federal contracts of at least $50,000 and employ at least fifty workers to have a written affirmative action plan for veterans." That sure as hell included Ohio State; yet, the assistant provost had already told me that there was no program to increase the proportion of veterans at the institution.

Clearly, the university was in violation of the law. All I needed to do, I thought, was let the appropriate people in Washington know about it.

Unfortunately, the feds proved to be no more interested in enforcing the legislation than the university was in abiding by it. Dealing with Washington was an even bigger sham.

Want to be flimflammed?

Ask screw-the-public profiteers in the federal government for help. Public civil servants they "ain't" . . . nor particularly civil either.

Get this: I have a written statement from an assistant secretary of labor asserting that, "the (veterans') law was not intended to prosecute inadvertent violation."

Excuse me?

"The law was not intended to prosecute *inadvertent* violation?"

What the devil does that mean?

Is there a collection of federal laws we're allowed to violate . . . inadvertently or otherwise?

I don't think so!

Why would anyone bother to write them in the first place?

And isn't that a terrific philosophy for the guy in charge of the U.S. Department of Labor's *Veterans* Employment and Training Service at the time?

Jesus H. Christ!

Apparently, our custodians of federal policies aimed at the wellbeing of the citizenry enforce some laws, not others. Too bad veterans, yours is one they don't.

At least that worthless shitbird was replaced soon thereafter as the assistant secretary; he was no longer in a position to shaft the veteran segment of American society. I can only hope that my rather explicit written response, which was copied to the bozo's boss, the secretary of labor, may have had something to do with his abrupt career change.

Who knows? The timing was right.

Unfortunately, I found little consolation in that outcome, since nothing—nothing whatsoever—was accomplished by any of my subsequent forays into the Washington bureaucratic quagmire that year either. And it was not for lack of trying; the inch-thick paper trail for 1988 attests to that.

I sent letters to innumerable federal bureaucrats. I sent letters to elected officials, U.S. senators and representatives. I sent letters to 1600 Pennsylvania Avenue—the White House.

And what did filling postal bags with correspondence accomplish?

Zilch! Nada!

I may as well have pitched all the letters down a fourth-class depository in some backwoods, Park Service outhouse, forget about the big-time, Washington White House.

Weeks dragged on into months and nothing happened; violations of a federal law for veterans were a concern to no one. Oh, I'd still pen an occasional salvo at some new target of opportunity along the way, but my supply of ammo was definitely getting low.

I was about to flick it in, to raise the white flag and give up.

Chieu hoi . . . I surrender.

Then, two bits of correspondence arrived, one day apart, which changed the complexion of the war.

The university had never bothered to address my original concern about denying affirmative action to veterans and the disabled while providing it to women and minorities—the responses were always in some form of administrative double-speak. But, after months and more months of launching fusillades at the OSU hierarchy, they finally provided an explanation: "The concept of Affirmative Action does allow institutions to focus differentially on specific target groups for purposes of employment."

Oh, okay.

I didn't know that.

Huh!

It was almost a relief to be told I was wrong. At least, I'd finally been told something. That was a vast improvement over being attacked and coerced for merely asking a question.

And besides, I hadn't solicited an in-depth legal opinion regarding my concerns; I'd only read up on what I could find on the subject. So, "to focus differentially on specific target groups" sounded plausible for some obscure federal edict. I could live with that; I had a book to finish.

Besides, affirmative action wasn't going to do anything for me as a tenured full professor anyhow. I could do without the aggravation.

Incredibly, *utterly unbelievably*, the very next day a letter arrived from the Office of Federal Contract Compliance Programs, the OFCCP, an investigative arm of the U.S. Department of Labor in Washington, D.C. In response to one of my missives about federal affirmative action mandates for women, minorities, veterans, and the disabled, they responded: "We do not allow one program to take precedence over another."

Say what?!!

I went back and read it again: "*We do not allow one program to take precedence over another.*"

Damn! I was right all along.

Son of a bitch!

My blood pressure started its upward climb, as I recalled the crap OSU had tried to feed me a mere twenty-four hours earlier. But, I stopped, closed my eyes, took a deep breath . . . then, read on.

The letter from the acting director of the OFCCP concluded by suggesting that my rather pointed questions might be inferred to mean I was complaining about Ohio State's handling of affirmative action for veterans. Therefore, my concerns were being forwarded to their enforcement section "for appropriate action."

What?

Wow!

What a euphoric moment that was. I'd been bleeding for seven months on this issue—mid-March to mid-October—but at long last, a solution was in sight; a bandage had been applied to the open wound.

Kick ass and take names, Labor!

All I needed to do was sit back and let it happen. With a Department of Labor investigation forthcoming, I could finally let it go . . . the monster was off my back.

And the timing couldn't have been better. I had a few canned medical lectures I had to knock out beginning in early November, my annual biochemistry of amino acids spiel.

But with Labor taking over my battles with the university, I had a couple weeks to dust off my old lecture notes and handouts, so the task proved relatively unproblematic. In fact, the lectures were dispatched in short order, being finished off on Friday, November 18, and I'd have to say my mood at that point was better than it had been for months . . . since escaping to the west back in June.

Lounging around at home that weekend—relaxed with a brew—it was time to start looking ahead again, to move on to other, more important matters.

The Thanksgiving and Christmas holidays were fast approaching, and that period had proven to be remarkably productive for launching my new literary career a year before.

Why not finish off the effort twelve months later?

I'd spent most of 1988 at the computer anyhow. Now all I needed to do was put down the poison pen and pick up the literary quill.

That seemed easy enough.

I started out back at the beginning, reading chapter 1, editing and polishing as I went along. It was on to chapters 2 through 4—then peering into the void of chapter 5 where nothing of substance had changed—and cruising on into chapters 6 through 10. The time off had helped; the edited versions were much improved.

As I attacked chapter 11, I was confident that a fitting climax would be in the offing this time. But somehow, no inroads were made.

I hammered away, day and night, but nothing worked; every angle from which I launched a new attack proved futile. The stand I'd taken . . . the solution to the yearlong degradation I'd endured after Vietnam, just couldn't find its way to the printed page.

Well, that's not totally true. The "I dare you to say anything" attitude I'd developed in 1970—wearing my insignia-clad fatigue jacket everywhere I went—had served to get me through the year, and it sure helped to restore the pride that had slipped away hiding in the union and biology department.

Staff Sgt. Trewyn in a small fire support base in Vietnam in 1969. Trewyn, R.W., "Correcting the Record About Vietnam Veterans' Service," *ARMY Magazine*, 72 (11): 23–25, 2022.

Staff Sgt. Trewyn with a soon-to-be killer base camp mascot monkey. The monkey was tugging at his dog tags as well as hand grenades on his vest. A few days after the photo was taken, the monkey pulled the pin on a white phosphorous grenade in a resupply area, killing one Delta Company brother. Trewyn, R.W., "Combat Lessons Stick for Life," *ARMY Magazine*, 74 (02): 11-12, 2024.

Radioman Russell posing while Lt. Enyeart and Staff Sgt. Trewyn joust for the camera.

Staff Sgt. Trewyn flanked by two other patients at 3rd Field Hospital in Saigon. A booby trap had been tripped behind him that day, April 18, 1969. In addition to the two bandaged shrapnel wounds that are visible, a third metal fragment was in his left lung, about 2 inches from his heart at the time. It's still in there, but by the rib cage today. Trewyn, R.W., "Vietnam's Medevac 'Saints' Provided a Crucial Lifeline," *ARMY Magazine*, 73 (08): 49–51, 2023.

Vietnam Veterans Memorial Chapel on Memorial Day in 2001.

American flag enroute to the Vietnam Veterans Memorial.

Dr. Victor Westphall, welcoming attendees to the Memorial Day services.

Country Singer Lynn Anderson singing at the Memorial Day services. Lynn Anderson's Vietnam-era hit song, "I Never Promised You a Rose Garden," was adopted by the Marines in the Vietnam War as their unofficial theme song.

Westphall's granddaughter, Kimberly, speaking at the services.

Adrian Cronauer, keynote speaker on Memorial Day in 2001. He wrote the screenplay for the movie, Good Morning, Vietnam!

Adrian Cronauer signing autographs.

Victor Westphall and Lynn Anderson.

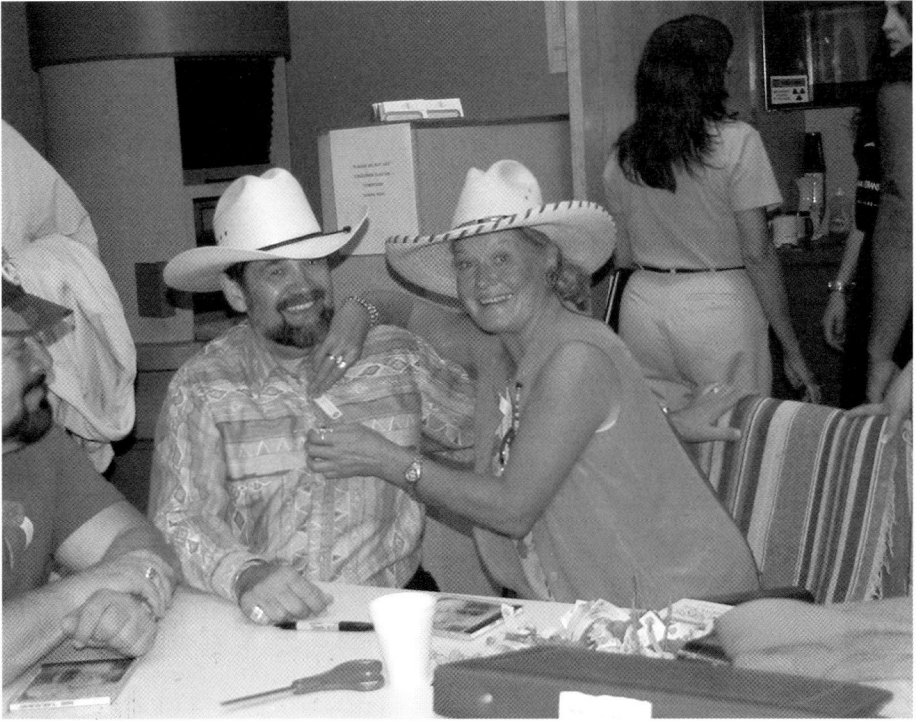

Author R.W. Trewyn and Lynn Anderson on Memorial Day in 2001. She's attaching a poppy honoring the casualties of war.

Vietnam Veterans Memorial Chapel on Memorial Day in 2001.

Author R.W. Trewyn when he was the vice president for research at Kansas State University.

That was easy enough to describe—the self-esteem and accompanying disdain infused by the staff sergeant stripes and Combat Infantry Badge (CIB). Nonetheless, a fatigue jacket attended by a major ration of "up yours" resolve no longer seemed to answer all the questions that had been raised . . . not from a vantage point nearly twenty years later.

But I knew there must have been more to my 1970 resolution than just delivering an olive drab "up yours" to the world. I was sure of it, since at the time, it totally answered all the questions burning inside. It allowed me to put the war and, more importantly, the antiwar creeps behind me, so all the answers had to be in there somewhere . . . they had to be.

As a result, I couldn't give up on old number eleven. I continued to do battle with it ever more frantically each day. I was certain the story had ended in 1970; I just wasn't saying it right.

One thing that was about to end though, no questions asked, was the Christmas break. Back to school was fast approaching, and distressingly, with every additional assault at the book's finale, an uneasiness from the past—a sporadic nervousness accompanied by a nagging knot in the pit of my stomach—began to increase in frequency and intensity.

It seems that chapter 11, the old version, had nudged yet another door ajar and damned if there weren't a few unexpected apparitions hiding back there . . . some ghoulish beasts that had to be dealt with before the story could end.

ANTI-AMERICA AMERICANS . . . LADY LIBERTY'S ACHILLES' HEEL

— Screw-the-Public Profiteers —

Enduring Truth: *Societal self-servants serve no one and, especially, NOT America.*

Chapter 16

DOWN FOR THE COUNT

PTSD? No way! Not a Ph.D., just reached the top, professor.

For a whole host of reasons, 1989 should have been a banner year for me . . . both personally and professionally.

It certainly didn't hurt that my yearlong running battle with the central administration might be coming to an end. Perhaps that could finally be put behind me.

Just prior to the first of the year I had to provide the Department of Labor with more details regarding my complaint against the university, but that was easy enough to accomplish; a scientist knows how to document and present evidence. And shortly after delivering my rather pointed exposé, an official notice arrived from the U.S. Department of Labor's regional office in Chicago:

"Trewyn *vs*. Ohio State University, Complaint No. E880445."

Yes!

I was formally on the books, and the wheels of the federal investigative bureaucracy were turning. And with what I'd been through in 1988, I was willing, for the most part, to leave the matter in the hands of the feds. I'd been back in the trenches long enough.

Of course, when the notice arrived in February of 1989, I had no idea how slowly the wheels of justice . . . or injustice . . . would actually turn.

After all, how could I have known back then that it would take a war in the Persian Gulf two years later, along with pressure from the news media and congress, to get the Labor investigation kicked into gear?

Apparently, my ESP wasn't working all that well.

Besides, there were a number of reasons to forget about the veterans' affirmative action diversion and turn my attention back to the job at hand, my career. First of all, 1989 was what one might describe as a "grand slam" on the professional front. It's hard to imagine an academic research scenario that could have topped the one I experienced that year.

As the year began, I was already serving as the program director on a large— almost a million-dollar—multi-year service grant with the National Cancer Institute. I had a sizable leukemia research grant from the American Cancer Society, as well as a small cancer therapeutics grant from the Burroughs Wellcome Company and a NATO travel grant with a research collaborator from Brussels, Belgium.

In February, I was named director of the Ohio State Biochemistry Program— the OSBP—the largest interdisciplinary graduate program at the university. The three major biochemistry units on campus were engaged in all-out blood-bath over the OSBP. Yet, somehow, the warring factions identified me as the one faculty member involved that might be able to save the disintegrating union. It's odd that my peers would have such faith in my abilities when the central administration looked upon me as some sort of pariah.

Regardless, by directing the OSBP, I had immediate access to the best incoming graduate students, a primary concern when one is trying to attain or maintain a top-flight research program. And, happily, my research endeavors were showing signs of achieving that status.

On the research front, I was the co-recipient of a substantial new grant to launch the commercial development of a cancer detection method another OSU researcher and I had co-invented. That arrived in February from a company in California.

Then, in March, I received a renewal of an Environmental Protection Agency grant that had expired a couple years earlier. It was a project to study the early, cryptic phases of cancer development induced by environmental chemical pollutants.

And finally, on July 1, my American Cancer Society grant on leukemia therapeutics was officially renewed for another two years.

These were all in addition to the National Cancer Institute, Burroughs Wellcome, and NATO grants that were still ongoing.

What a six months that was!

It was a run one might dream about in their scientific fantasies, but never truly believes will happen.

Professionally, how could things have been any better?

I had hundreds of thousands of dollars of research money at my disposal. I had access to outstanding students to push back the scientific frontiers. All those years of dedicated effort—losing sleep nightly and vacation-time annually—were finally paying off.

There's no question, I should have been reveling in the glory of it. As a bush league farm kid from Wisconsin—the first in the family to make it through college—I had beaten the odds . . . beaten the snot out of them.

Strangely, though, it no longer seemed to matter. I couldn't get myself psyched up about the grants or my career in any way, shape, or form. Something had changed inside; the fire had gone out.

Fortunately, I had two superb postdoctoral researchers—Bernie and Claudia—to hold things together, or the whole operation would have "gone to hell in a hand basket," as the old expression warned. Things didn't, but it was only because Bernie and Claud supervised the students and technicians and kept things running in the lab.

Throughout the spring of '89, I knew I was relying more and more on the two of them, but I rationalized that the OSBP activities—attempting to steer that would-be Titanic away from its fated rendezvous—was sapping all my concentration. However, I had invested too much of my life in a research career to just give it all up, so I continued to make a concerted effort to rekindle the scientific enthusiasm that had driven me for more than two decades. Nonetheless, I didn't seem to be gaining much ground, so I finally focused on one last-ditch attempt at a gathering of international scientists in June.

The biennial transfer ribonucleic acid (tRNA) meeting was being held in Vancouver, British Columbia that year, and the previous two meetings had proven to be highly stimulating and motivating events. The small cadre of scientists in the world working on the cellular molecule tRNA—the pivotal component in translating the genetic code into a multitude of proteins—would gather for concentrated sessions on topics of mutual interest. In my case, tRNA was central to all my cancer-related investigations.

The social interactions at this meeting tended to forge new research collaborations, the seeds being sown during thought-provoking debates in the formal presentations. The Brussels' alliance with my Belgian collaborator, Henri, and the subsequent six-year NATO travel grant arose in such a manner from my first tRNA meeting in Erlangen, Germany in 1985.

Then in 1987, Henri and I, along with a scientist from Montreal, drove from Brussels to the tRNA meeting in Umeå, Sweden . . . about a hundred miles from the Arctic Circle. That was one *long* haul from Brussels. The scientific discussions on that four-day, land and sea expedition were stimulating (as were the ten days in Umeå), but other aspects of the conversations were noteworthy as well.

I had been saying for years that I had no problem with those antiwar-types who left the country to dodge the draft, so long as the move was permanent. Of course, that was easy to say, since I didn't know anyone like that.

Now I did.

Bob, the Montreal scientist with us, had split for Canada (from Minnesota, I think he said) to avoid the war. But, unlike so many who left for cowardly reasons and then raced back with a Jimmy Carter pardon as soon as possible—"the war's over; we didn't really mean all those anti-American things we said"—Bob stayed in Canada. Eventually he became a citizen there and a faculty member at the University of Montreal.

Good man.

Although I never got to know Bob extremely well (he died of cancer not too much later), we spent enough time together on that trip to become friends . . . not exchange cards at Christmas-type friends, but university faculty members who respected one another scientifically and personally. Bob considered it a lifetime decision when he moved to Canada, and he stuck by his principles, giving up his U.S. citizenship.

I could respect that . . . and did.

Yes, the tRNA meetings tended to be thought provoking . . . scientifically and otherwise at times as well. They functioned in the way I thought universities were supposed to when I entered the profession—places for open dialogue with all viewpoints respected.

It seemed reasonable, therefore, to head off to the Pacific Northwest in 1989 to try to resuscitate my scientific curiosity from its cataleptic state. I hadn't forgotten about that part of the country contributing its own special magic way back in graduate school either. I was hopeful that, together, the lively tRNA clan and the exhilarating Northwest would come through for me once again. They had already done remarkable things to help push my research career up the ivory tower staircase.

Of course, it didn't hurt that a two-week vacation was going to be tacked onto the end of the meeting. That added a little something extra to look forward to . . . especially, since Marcy was going along for the second year in a row. We had created lots of enduring memories in that part of the world.

When June 6 rolled around, it was with great hope and anticipation that we boarded USAir for the flight to Seattle. Then it was on to B.C. in a rental car.

And it turned out that seeing old friends and scientific colleagues at the meeting was nice, but it was the social activities—Pacific salmon feeds and the like—that held my interest much more than the research-side of the agenda. The science—thought provoking discussions or not—just didn't cut it.

The presentations seemed totally blasé. They did nothing for me whatsoever. Zip!

In fact, two days of technical talks was all I could stomach.

Marcy and I caught the ferry for Vancouver Island before the meeting officially ended, and from there, we headed for the Olympic Peninsula in Washington a couple days later. Once we made our escape, it was a relaxing, enjoyable time as we meandered down the Pacific coast, eventually winding up in Newport, Oregon, dining on good old Mo's clam chowder.

The trip may have been stimulating in various ways, but try as I might, I just couldn't get the flame of scientific intrigue to ignite. Even Mo's tried-and-true elixir failed to emote a spark.

Of course, it probably didn't help that there was an issue gnawing at me during the whole trip that I just couldn't shake . . . or resolve. It's something I'd think about when there was a lull in the conversation while driving through the Olympic forests or while sitting quietly in a rustic motel room after Marcy had gone to bed.

It was a totally monstrous—Number 10—case of the nerves that was starting to follow me everywhere I went. The first symptom, I suppose, was that uncharacteristic nervousness I'd experienced the year before at the cancer meeting.

Unfortunately, it was becoming a much more frequent, highly unwelcome visitor in 1989. That had a lot to do with why I went to Vancouver as a spectator rather than as a presenter. I had purposely avoided getting my name on the tRNA meeting presentation list. I left that chore to my Belgian collaborator and friend, Henri.

The problem was, I couldn't put my finger on why the "Nervous Norvis" condition was continuing to escalate. In New Orleans, I had presumed it to be a one-time aberration, and it hadn't really recurred that much during the summer or fall of 1988. Oh, perhaps, now and then when the letter writing tirades would build in intensity, but not so much in the public speaking domain.

I could recall a couple sneak attacks at the start of the medical lectures . . . a tightening in the chest, a trembling break in the first few words to the half-awake class. But, all in all, those were relatively tame.

It was after the first of the year when the situation truly began to get out of hand. I'd start to go into a panic mode if I had to open my mouth in a gathering of more than two people.

It made no sense. In departmental faculty meetings, among a dozen familiar faces, I'd feel a lump building in my throat if it looked as though I might be forced to say something.

It would all start innocently enough. Topics would ebb and flow—departmental fiscal matters, who was up next in the medical lectures, results of a recent exam— when someone would comment on a student or seminar in the OSBP.

Incoming!

The internal alarms would go off as various faculty members' eyes would glance my way. I could feel myself starting to hyperventilate while trying to hide and hold my breath. It was as if someone was sitting on my chest . . . a noose was tightening around my throat.

Would I be able to breathe at all?

Would the intense pounding in my chest cause the straining pump to explode?

The strangle hold that would constrict on my Adam's apple—FOR NO REASON—was worse than when I was about to head over the rim of that damn gully back in Vietnam. I was becoming a basket case; afraid to go anywhere I might have to say something. And at the time, I had no idea why . . . none, whatsoever.

Naturally, I never told anyone about it. But I'd begin to get clammy, almost breaking out in a cold sweat wondering: Do they sense the anxiety, the panic? Can they hear the quaking changes in octave level in my voice? What about the herky-jerky speech impediments?

What a rat's ass situation. Like some old Star Trek episode, the shields on the Enterprise were wearing down. And I was going down with them.

During those quiet, reflective times on the trip, I poured over every aspect of the previous few months hunting for clues. I couldn't help thinking that as a new full professor, I had it made. I was at the top of my game in the grant-getting business, the yardstick by which one measures success in the research arena.

The battles with the provost didn't seem to explain my shaky mental state either. After all, as a tenured professor, there was nothing the Peter-principled provost or his even less capable associates could do to me. That's what having tenure is all about. So, why wasn't I enjoying my newfound status at the top of the academic ladder?

Strangely, sitting in Moolack Shores—a great little motel in Newport, Oregon we'd stayed at with my folks more than 15 years earlier—my thoughts started drifting back to Vietnam. But, not to the war per se. It was more with regard to what the Vietnam experience had done for me over the years.

Vietnam: Whenever I needed a vantage point from which to put some seemingly bad situation into focus, I could always rely on Vietnam to bring forth a ray of sunshine through even the murkiest, threatening fog.

Take butterflies in the stomach, for example, the ones that would congregate there just prior to speaking in front of some large gathering of scientists and academics. Those winged beauties would instantly scatter when a momentary flashback to Vietnam was conjured up from the past . . . Russian and Chinese green and white tracers kicking up dirt all around, grenades exploding, wounded comrades crying out in agony. No, somehow this audience doesn't appear to be much of a threat, thank you.

Those instant replays worked so well early on, in graduate school and beyond, that they proved mostly unnecessary as my career progressed. The self-confidence that developed along the way—embellished with a touch of that 1970 "up yours" resolve—was enough to carry me through without needing to look back. There'd been sufficient repetitions to convince even the stubbornest old Monarchs that their services were no longer needed, or welcome, for that matter.

So, what was happening to me in 1989?

The problem went way beyond a simple case of butterflies.

And why weren't those images from the past able to chase away the demons anymore?

Why had the post-Vietnam shakes—those induced by the antiwar freaks in Wisconsin—returned once again?

I was having a devil of a time figuring it out, and nothing of substance came out of those hours of reflection in the inspirational Northwest. The trip came and went with nary a bit of comprehension.

Upon returning to Columbus though, one thing was clear: My research career was over. There was no getting around it anymore.

However, beyond that realization, I didn't have a clue what it meant. There didn't seem to be anything at the university that still interested me, but I had no idea what to do instead. I'd spent twenty-two-and-a-half years of my life going to school preparing myself for what I was doing at the time. I hadn't considered any other alternatives for decades.

Now what?

Shit!

A good question, but not exactly the sort that soothes one's already deteriorated nerves, much less a case of self-confidence that was heading straight into the toilet.

* * *

Back at work, I stuck to my OSBP duties pretty conscientiously—I owed it to the students—but beyond that, I let most other things slide.

I was into a "hide from the world" mentality at that point, trying anything and everything as a diversion.

There was silversmithing at the Cultural Arts Center one night a week. That was a terrific change of pace, and at least for a few hours, hammering away at a defenseless piece of metal, it offered a "no worries" refuge from the skittering jumpies.

Then, somewhere from deep within the gray depths, my alter ego appeared that summer: Thurl E. Fedup, Ph.D. Yes, that was me alright.

Few could have been more bummed out—fed up—with life in general at that point, but Thurl knew how to vent by getting it all down on paper. Set him down at a computer, and he would become one prolific, word-generating machine.

Short stories, a couple thousand words in length, just flowed from some pent-up well. It was amazing the speed with which the stories gushed forth. The first was entitled, "Affirmative Inaction: Someone Turned Out the Lights in the Bureaucratic Attic." It recapped my fun times with the university hierarchy and federal "public servants" the year before.

Then it was on to "Peter, Your Principle No Longer Cuts It . . . Cranial Rectitis Rules," followed by "Acanemia: Dandelions Grow in Your Own Back Yard," and "Acronymatic Rectacranial Spasmatology Syndrome (ARSS): Pull Your Head Out Uncle."

None of these latter literary gems garnered what might be called "rave reviews" from the magazine editors I forwarded them to, but Thurl's first undertaking, "Affirmative Inaction," was eventually snatched up for publication by *The World and I*, a Washington-based magazine. What's more, they actually paid $600 for Dr. Fedup's allegorical masterpiece.

Regrettably, even that magnum opus never made it into print. *The World and I* shuffled editors shortly after the deal was signed, and the new guy hated Thurl and Thurl's writing style from day one.

I guess it just wasn't meant to be, since the editor who had purchased the rights to begin with, Madeline something or other Italian, had been very supportive and encouraging. She even suggested during a telephone conversation that there was a likely niche for one Thurl E. Fedup, Ph.D., and a fed-up audience that would surely be receptive to his offbeat message.

Oh, well. I can always tell myself it was their loss, not mine, and I did derive certain "benies" from the overall exercise.

Probably the only times I ever really felt good in 1989 were those occasions when I assumed the Thurl E. Fedup character in front of the computer screen. The nervousness and chronic frustration would quickly dissipate as Thurl's fingers slashed away at the keyboard. I could feel my blood pressure drop, as if some safety valve had been released.

I even had business cards printed up for Thurl, a professor at The Olentangy Scioto University, specializing in "investigative acanemic curmudgeontary and bozocratic commentary." Those unfamiliar with The Ohio State University and Columbus, Ohio, probably wouldn't know that the Olentangy and Scioto Rivers converge there, but Thurl's writing was intended more for those who did know.

I'd lost all respect for the shithole place where I was employed, and I guess I wanted those folks who bled scarlet and gray to know there was a dissenting point of view.

Later on, I came up with an even better, more accurate name for the place Thurl worked—*The* Orwellian Stalinist University—but the shortage of writing revenue couldn't justify an outlay for additional new cards. Not that I didn't use the name around OSU at times though.

It may have been pessimistic, cynical old Thurl who finally sensed the basis for why I was falling apart. He'd done his homework.

If Thurl was going to be successful in the short-story game—selling his wares to magazine publishers—researching the industry was key. That meant spending significant time and effort reading all sorts of magazines and newspapers, looking for trends, content, and ideas.

Of course, reading anything other than scientific articles was totally new to me—I normally didn't even bother to read the local newspaper—but I quickly adapted to the new order. And, damn, there was an entire literary world out there I didn't know existed. One could actually be informed and even entertained by what was available.

How odd!

Something else that surprised me when I started reading newspapers and magazines was the number of stories about posttraumatic stress disorder (PTSD). At the time, I wouldn't have thought it to be a particularly big problem . . . or particularly newsworthy, for that matter. But there they were, a bevy of vignettes about Vietnam veterans suffering from their exposure to combat in decades past.

I probably would have paid little attention to the stories except that the symptoms described in the first one I perused had a familiar ring to them; they struck rather close to home. Even though the correlation made no sense since I wasn't having any problems with flashbacks to the war, every article I looked at subsequently had some twinge of commonality to what I'd been experiencing. There was enough of a correlation with the psychological turmoil described I began to think that I too was in need of an emotional overhaul.

Did I need to visit a shrink?

On the verge of seeking professional help, I also began to make a connection between my "newly" developed psychosis and the book I had been forced to walk away from. Perhaps more accurately, it was a correlation to fragmentary lessons learned from that literary undertaking. After all, if the story didn't end in 1970, there must have been something wrong with my rationale for believing it did.

Right?

Even though it made perfect sense to me in August 1970 that I had "gotten my shit together" concerning the protests and all, it now appeared that I really hadn't. And that's nearly two decades later.

What a bitch!

Apparently, my recaptured self-esteem, and the accompanying self-confidence back then, were based on little more than building an impenetrable shell. Putting on a flak jacket and blinders hadn't resolved the real problem at all. It merely allowed me to get on with life.

Not only that, my public speaking capabilities must have been developed on the same "I dare you to say anything" approach. As a result, once the shell started to disintegrate, everything else attached to it started to fall apart as well.

While looking in the rearview mirror, it also appeared that my decision in 1970 to pursue a career in science must have set as a subconscious goal the attainment of the rank of full professor. That's the top of the academic ladder.

Otherwise, why would all the aforementioned complications have arisen when they did?

Yep, that aspiration must have been hidden in there somewhere.

Then, when you couple the reaching of my career goal with the nearly synonymous discovery of the affirmative action problem for veterans on campus—a problem likely caused by the old '60's creeps—it's no wonder a few old ghosts bounded out from the shadows.

Vietnam veterans don't count anywhere?

Damn!

Ain't that the truth?

The discoveries—like the burning of Old Main almost twenty years earlier—certainly didn't solve the psychological warfare going on inside my head. But, at least the spark of understanding kept me from sinking any further into the quicksand.

There was also a crutch I discovered that could get me through the worst of times: the high blood pressure drug, Inderal. One of my MD colleagues at OSU had mentioned that a couple of his physician buddies would take an Inderal prior to any major public speaking engagement. Apparently, it would keep them from coming totally unglued on stage—the scared shitless anxiety would fade away.

Tucking that bit of information away for later recall proved useful.

I had a small stash of Inderal left over from a ten-week cluster headache I had a few years back. That localized skull-splitter was finally diminishing when Marcy and I left on our Four Corners camping extravaganza in 1981. It quit completely after we crossed the Continental Divide. Since I had enough pills to last through the trip, there were a few left, and for some reason they never got tossed out.

So, eight years later, I tried part of an old Inderal before a required lecture, and it eased my trip to panic city . . . a lot. For scheduled presentations, a half or even a quarter pretty much did the trick. Unfortunately, that didn't help much in those unexpected, extemporaneous situations that arose quite frequently on campus, but my supply wasn't big enough to take them any more than sporadically.

Besides, I was becoming an academic hermit anyhow. I didn't go out of my office any more than absolutely necessary.

Why should I?

Nothing on campus interested me—nothing at all.

* * *

Once I understood that my book didn't end in 1970 and had avoided what seemed like an imminent crash and burn, I was also able to put Thurl back on the shelf occasionally and get back into the book-writing mode . . . as me. I wasn't sure how the book was going to end at that point, but I knew it was going to be in the present day, not decades earlier when I finished my undergraduate work.

Obviously, the non-welcome home festivities had lasted more than that one year. I just didn't know it at the time.

As a result, I knocked out a new chapter 11; one that transitioned from 1970 to 1988. That was easy enough . . . finally, after a hundred and one dead-end attempts.

And drafts of the next three or four chapters rolled right off my fingertips and into the computer as well.

Now we're getting somewhere!

I also had the chance to fill in some passed-over details in the earlier chapters, after doing some research in Washington, D.C.

We spent lots of long weekends—drinking—in Gaithersburg, Maryland with our longtime friends, John and Mary Lou. That friendship had started at Oregon State, and it was renewed for a time in Denver when we all landed there.

John was in his last year as a Micro Met when I started graduate school, and he had the best damn arm I've ever seen. Being on the receiving end of the missiles he launched from left field was the downside of playing third base—being smacked in the kisser by a bad hop really *was* "no sweat" by comparison.

And Mary Lou was the friend who had bailed me out on the veterans' affirmative action front at O–Screw-over-veterans–U, providing me with the federal regulatory info early on . . . something she had access to in her beltway job. It was a God-send.

Anyhow, on a break during one of those recurring drink-a-thons, I took the bus from downtown D.C. to the military records section of the National Archives to dig out the daily battalion action reports corresponding to my stint in Nam. Even though I was confident about my recollections across the big pond, I wanted to be certain that the specifics were in order . . . time and place-wise.

Those reports allowed me to pin down—to the minute—the timeframe for the dustoff pickup when I got hit. It also clarified some things about the Groundhog Day fiasco . . . sort of.

The only day for which two different action reports existed for the 2nd Battalion was February 2, 1969. One meshed very well with my memory of the events. The other one didn't: the order that things reportedly happened was shuffled . . . a lot.

Strange!

Although I never have been able to figure out the relevance of the changes, I'd be willing to bet our battalion commander who fucked everything up that day tried to falsify the timelines for some reason.

Why else would two different versions exist?

Maybe the two-star duo from the 25th Division that came around investigating the events a couple weeks later figured it out. Perhaps that contributed to the shitbird battalion C.O. getting relieved of command.

We didn't miss the asshole.

And it was sure a world of difference when Colonel Mess took over. He was terrific . . . in the know about what was happening on the ground, concerned about his men.

Definitely "Number 1" as far as I was concerned.

Yes, the battalion action reports provided lots of interesting facts and contradictions to think about. Plus, the time and place details were helpful as well.

Of course, that's when I stepped on another "ignorance is bliss" landmine . . . a big-ass, Bouncing Betty, blow-you-away-type landmine.

In rereading some of the early book chapters to plug in specifics and to ensure that everything tied together, a thought flashed through my mind that utterly scared the crap out of me. It jarred all the core values I thought I understood and made me question whether my whole life—the last twenty years, at least—was based on a lie . . . a lie I'd told myself.

Could it be possible? Might I have convinced myself that the war in Vietnam—the cause—was worth dying for in 1969 only because that was a likely outcome?

Was it nothing more than a survival tool . . . a rationalization one concocts just to fool themselves when death appears imminent?

Oh, shit!

Could I have been that stupid? Might the antiwar protesters have been right all along?

Oh, my God, maybe so.

HOLY FUCK!

What a horrifying thought.

I sure had to figure that one out. *I had to figure it out fast!*

ANTI-AMERICA AMERICANS . . . LADY LIBERTY'S ACHILLES' HEEL

— Antimilitary/Antiauthority Zealots —

Enduring Truth: *Antiwar carnage can be worse than horrors of war . . . MUCH worse.*

Chapter 17

JOHNSON'S WAR? NIXON'S WAR?

What the hell happened? Victim or killer . . . or just plain stupid?

George Patton: *"If everyone is thinking alike, then somebody isn't thinking."*[1]

Was it a big con job?

Did I convince myself the cause was worth dying for merely out of necessity, since that likely prospect was being encountered day in and day out?

Was it nothing more than a grand illusion . . . some sort of reality-induced rationalization?

Was I that gullible? That naive? That *DUMB*?

Then? Now?

No, I don't think so, do I?

No . . . I sure hope not.

Well, you bet your life on it, dummy. You'd damn well better figure it out.

Was the cause not worth fighting for, worth dying for?

Boy, there's a $58,000 question that needs answering.

After a couple decades of going around with my head in the sand . . . or some other even less enlightening locale, I had a ravenous need to know: What was the Vietnam War all about?

I was there, but I had no real clue about how we actually got there.

What were the real issues?

Damn!

That's not reassuring. I was ready to die for a cause, and twenty years later I figure out that I didn't even know what the cause really was.

Crap!

Maybe the protesters knew what they were talking about all along.

Did my first-hand experience count for nothing? Did being up to my ass in it actually taint my opinion?

Okay, I knew about domino theories and the like. Uncle Sugar indoctrinated the troops on that front . . . and we heard the company line from the politicians on TV as well.

But, was Vietnam a domino worth 58,000-plus American lives?

Was it worth Chris' life?

The way it turned out, the obvious answer is "no," or in the jargon of the time, "HELL, NO!"

However, what about twenty years ago . . . twenty-five?

If I thought my thirst for scientific understanding in years past was a real driver pushing me up the academic ladder, it paled by comparison to my need to know on this topic. I had a voracious appetite to read anything out there regarding Vietnam and the Vietnam War. I absolutely flew through everything I could get my hands on.

Forget about scientific literature. It no longer mattered.

I also started sitting in on a Vietnam War history course taught by a retired Air Force officer, Joe Guilmartin, who did two tours in Southeast Asia. He was there in 1965 and 1975, flying Jolly Green Giant rescue missions. Between '65 and '75, he earned his Ph.D. in military history from Princeton, and the 1975 tour got him involved in creating military history in a big way . . . participating in the evacuation of Saigon.

I read books from Joe's reading list. I created my own much longer list. I read articles and books on Vietnam that tilted to the left. I read those skewed to the right. I read material where I had nary a clue as to the political leanings of the author.

I didn't care. I was on a fact-finding mission. A scientist needs data on which to base decisions.

Hmmm. That's not reassuring either.

How could I have gone along for decades on nothing more than gut feelings?

I would have chewed up and spit out any students—would-be scientists—if they tried to bluff their way through on something totally intangible.

You're basing *what* on a gut feeling?

Where's the evidence, the data, to support your conclusion?

Maybe there was a valid reason my safe little world was falling apart.

I was ready to die . . . *for what?*

Okay, let's go at this again, systematically this time. So, from what I recall, Johnson got us into Vietnam. That's probably the place to start.

But, no, that doesn't appear to be true, not once I started looking back at the historical record. There were already a hundred or so American casualties in Vietnam by the time Kennedy was assassinated on November 22, 1963.

Wow, I remember when that happened. I was in the car with my high school buddy Piep and his clan on the way up north to go deer hunting.

It started way back then? Kennedy got us into Vietnam?

Well, sort of, but digging deeper suggested that he and his whiz kids—those brainy easterners Johnson inherited and hated—just implemented a counterinsurgency plan in Vietnam developed while Ike was the man with a plan on Pennsylvania Avenue.

Say, what? Eisenhower was the architect who got us into the whole mess?

Well, no, that's not right either. If you keep going further back, Eisenhower started out just endorsing the policies Truman had initiated to help the French in Vietnam.

Truman, concerned with the spread of communism, began officially providing aid to the French all the way back in 1950; he sent thirty-five advisers to Vietnam that year as well. Unofficial U.S. financial aid might go back as far as 1946.

Eisenhower then continued providing financial assistance. Not only was aid provided, "in fiscal year 1954 [it] reached $1.063 billion"[2] which accounted for one-third of the total U.S. foreign aid budget.

One-third! In the rest of the world, the remaining countries receiving assistance got to divvy up a paltry two-thirds of the budget?

Even so, after initially considering the possibility of U.S. air strikes at Dien Bien Phu in North Vietnam to help the French, Eisenhower stopped short of crossing the line to military intervention. Nevertheless, when the French were run out of the area in 1954, the counterinsurgency plan was developed . . . just in case. Ike, the military strategist, didn't want to see the communists in control of that whole region either.

My, my, that certainly puts a little different spin on the whole affair. Since at least 1950, the Truman, Eisenhower, Kennedy, and Johnson administrations were all convinced that Vietnam was a critical place to make a stand against communism in Southeast Asia.

Huh!

Who would have guessed it?

Of course, that doesn't mean the rationale was sound, but it sure represents a significant data point. Both sides of the political aisle had bought in.

Although there were some other interesting nuances associated with these early historical digs, the big-time changes in U.S. philosophy and strategy in the region appear to fall squarely in Johnson's lap. That was in spite of the fact he had promised the voters in 1964 that he would keep "American boys" out of Vietnam.

However, the move from Americans as advisers to war fighters occurred on his watch, and I had known that pretty much all along. Still, there were numerous aspects that my reading marathon and Joe's course did help clarify.

Take, for instance, the feeling many of us had in Vietnam that Commander-in-Chief Johnson wasn't concerned with winning the war. In analyzing the issue, it appears President Johnson considered Vietnam to be more of a nuisance than a major agenda item.

It detracted from his first love—"The Great Society"—that he fantasized to be his presidential legacy. Beyond his grand domestic agenda, little else seemed to matter, especially in the early years when Vietnam was little more than a pesky gnat on an elephant's rear . . . or, more appropriately, a donkey's ass in this case.

Johnson's dream for "The Great Society" was so vast and self-consuming it's not clear that he actually had any genuine agenda items two, three, or four. A war of attrition was fine so long as it didn't interfere with agenda item number one—an easy assessment, I guess, for someone with only daughters' ineligible for the draft.

Unfortunately, Commander-in-Chief Johnson had to order, reorder, and then order yet again escalations in troop strength to keep from being blamed for an embarrassing U.S. defeat on the battlefield. So much for his adamant promise while campaigning not to send American boys to Vietnam. However, the order was never given to go win the war.

The rational appeared to be, what's the minimum we can get by with to keep from losing?

And, of course, more Americans were being "attrited" every day with no mandate to win; just don't lose.

In thinking back to that time, I can't recall Commander-in-Chief Johnson ever launching into a "fire and brimstone" speech to rally public support for U.S. efforts in Vietnam. I could find no evidence in my reading that it ever happened either. Evidently, all the fire and all the brimstone were saved for President Johnson's Great Society.

Johnson's decision not to mobilize units of the National Guard or the Reserves to address growing troop strength needs was consistent with his low-profile approach to warfare as well.

Of course, there was probably nothing more despicable during his presidency than the way Johnson and his defense guru, Robert S. McNamara (or, more correctly and appropriately, as Joe always referred to him in his course, Robert *Strange* McNamara), got around this problem . . . by launching "Project 100,000 . . . to help disadvantaged youth."[3] That little gem lowered I.Q. standards for military service . . . *substantially.*

And once they started down this path, why should they bother stopping at 100,000? It seems that well over 350,000 were ultimately placed on active duty under this program.

Although I had never heard of Project 100,000 or knew of the change in standards in 1968, I can recall seeing the consequences of it first-hand while pushing troops through AIT at Fort Ord. One of the guys in 4th Platoon with 12 years of education, in fact, had 12 years of special ed. He could barely read or write. More importantly, he couldn't clearly comprehend what the instructors were talking about in the classroom or in the field. It was totally nuts to consider putting him in an infantry unit.

How could this young man follow orders . . . *instantly* . . . when his life depended on it? How would the guys in his unit know that he'd make the right decision . . . *instantly* . . . when their lives depended on it?

Jesus! Not a good situation.

Before I headed out on leave, then on to Vietnam, I did manage to get paperwork into the system to have this kid's qualifications for military service reviewed, but I honestly don't know what happened. Nonetheless, I do know what should have happened to the lowlifes that designed this little experiment.

Fragging would have been too good for the worthless bastards.

Little did I realize back when I was on active duty how demented the politicos in charge really were. Someone would have to be pretty sick to lower the I.Q. standards for military service for the not-so-subtle purpose of producing "cannon fodder" with those unable to defend themselves.

However, it allowed Johnson and McNamara to keep from calling up the National Guard and Reserves. That could have created some community-based backlash in support of local citizen-soldiers, not a good thing when one is trying to maintain a low profile.

Even more importantly, implementing Project 100,000 meant that college student deferments wouldn't have to be messed with substantially. Hey, there were enough problems with the *intelligencia* on campus already. But the university elite wouldn't care if a little societal culling of low I.Q. guys was undertaken. These weren't the frat boys competing for those life-saving S-2 deferments.

Who gives a shit?

How Darwinian. Natural selection at work, except, in this case it was Johnsonian-McNamarian "unnatural selection" on the battlefield.

What a pair of unprincipled, scum-sucking dirt bags!

* * *

Something I hadn't realized back when I was "up to my ass in it" was that my hitch in the service corresponded almost exactly to the most active stage of the war, the period with the greatest number of U.S. casualties. The month I was hit—April of 1969—was the peak for American troop strength in Vietnam.

Gee, perhaps I started the downsizing—launching Nixon's Vietnamization program when he moved into the White House—by getting wounded and shipped out of country.

Apparently, I had been in the thick of the action while I was there as well. One reference noted: "Enemy contact during the first weeks of 1969 remained light, however, for most units. Among the exceptions was the 199th Infantry Brigade (Light) patrolling the approaches to Saigon. The 199th encountered numerous groups of Communist troops attempting to filter back toward the Capital."[4]

Yes, indeed, we certainly encountered a few near Cu Chi.

Then there was a Lieutenant who complained that his "hopes of joining an airborne unit or the 1st Air Calvary (in 1969) were ended by the large numbers of killed and wounded suffered by the 199th LIB in the past weeks."[5] Welcome to the Redcatchers' Old Guard.

Lieutenant Lanning arrived in Vietnam three days after I got hit. He wound up in Charlie Company, but he knew about my old unit . . . and why some of the troops were "reupping" to escape into a non-infantry MOS: "a six-year extension sounded better than the finality of death which seemed the Infantryman's fate in Delta Company."[6]

Undeniably, Delta was in the thick of it in 1969. I guess that explains why I wasn't watching the nightly news much back then.

Investigating what went on during the time I was out of the information loop (on active duty) one realization outweighed all others: very little was as it seemed. What was going on in Vietnam had almost no bearing on what was being reported back home.

And you know what?

This was beginning to explain what happened to my civilian world—the one I knew and loved—while I was away between January 16, 1968 and August 18, 1969. It wasn't nearly the same when I got back.

Oh, sure, I was different. The two uncles—Sam and Ho—had mediated their subtle influences . . . and their head-on collision-type influences as well. But that didn't seem to be it; at least, not all of it.

The world—the people back home—had changed more. They had changed much, much more.

It made no sense at the time, but that's the way it appeared to me. They hadn't gone anywhere, hadn't been in combat, but they seemed to be the ones who were different.

Now, examining what went on back then, it was beginning to make sense.

Sure, the United States suffered heavy casualties during 1968 and the first half of 1969 as reported, but they paled by comparison to those inflicted on the enemy. Somehow, that information was less than factually transmitted by the media. Or when it was, the propaganda indicated that numbers meant nothing to the enemy. After all, the "yellow hordes" have unlimited bodies to throw into the fray.

Hundreds? Thousands? Millions?

What's the difference?

In checking the historical record, it appears that even before I got drafted, something was terribly wrong with the reporting of events related to Vietnam. On May 13, 1967 "in New York City, 70,000 march[ed] in support of the war, led by a New York City fire captain."[7] Captain "Gimmler's branding for the event was simple: either you supported the troops, or you supported the flag-burning communists."[8]

That was in the liberal Big Apple . . . *70,000 marchers in support of the war and the troops!* Old photos suggest there may have been three to four times that number lining Fifth Avenue cheering them on.

Yet, the march had zero national coverage on TV or in print. Nada!

Why not?

Every time ten protesters congregated on a street corner was covered. Protests were national news. Apparently, the converse wasn't.

It is also clear in looking back that the Tet Offensive in '68 was *the* turning point of the war. And since I was being pummeled into shape in basic training at the time, I totally missed it. Newspapers and TV were not provided to the trainees at Fort Campbell.

Somehow though, based on what I had heard over the years, I had the impression we did poorly on the battlefield during Tet. Yet, examining it from a historical perspective, the U.S. and South Vietnamese troops kicked ass . . . big time.

General Weyand noted this in a detailed analysis in 1976: "the real losers of Tet-68 were the South Vietnamese Communists (the Vietcong or PRG) who surfaced, led the attacks, and were destroyed in the process"[9] *Destroyed* in the process.

The Vietcong were never a significant factor in the war after Tet. They got absolutely creamed . . . a fact that had long-standing consequences as also noted by General Weyand.

By moving to a conventional warfare mode, "the North Vietnamese eliminated their southern competitors with Tet-68. They thereby insured that the eventual outcome of the war would be a South Vietnam dominated and controlled, not by *South* Vietnamese Communists, but by the *North* Vietnamese."[10] Uncle Ho might not have had this in mind at the time, but it was one of two beneficial outcomes for the North.

The other even bigger advantage was described by General Davidson: "The irony of the Tet offensive is that the enemy failed miserably to attain the effect he planned for, but accomplished his purpose by an effect he did not foresee and did not intend (the destruction of internal American support of the war)."[11]

Ho could thank the American media for the latter outcome. They misreported almost everything related to Tet.

On January 31, 1968, VC sappers attacked the U.S. embassy in Saigon. They got inside the compound, but not into the embassy.

It was reported otherwise on TV back in the States.

Why?

With the siege at Khe Sanh, innumerable analogies were drawn to Dien Bien Phu where the French got stomped in 1954. It was suggested on TV that the same general was there—on site—calling the shots.

Again, why?

There was no such evidence.

It must have made the "story" sound more interesting. Since General Giap had been able to out-soldier the French in 1954, why not the trapped Americans in 1968?

That idea undoubtedly gave the people back home something to chew on.

What's the difference whether it was true or not?

By the end of the siege, 199 U.S. soldiers had been killed at Khe Sanh. *Ten thousand* or more enemy soldiers had been.

There was an especially notable statement made by one of the CBS correspondents during the encirclement that stated, "the North Vietnamese decide who lives and who dies at Khe Sanh."[12]

Now how do you suppose that came about and then got broadcast over the airwaves back in the States?

Jesus! The NVA must have been awfully damn suicidal if that were the case.

They decided that fifty times as many of their soldiers would die?

Of course, the biggest crime (in many different ways) took place at Hué in 1968. During the three weeks that the "liberators" from the North and their VC chums controlled that ancient city, over 5,000 of its citizens were taken from their homes for "reeducation" purposes.

They must have been slow learners. Those good people never made it back to their loved ones . . . NONE of them. And it wasn't just hooch girls at American bases, either. Students, religious leaders, the educated . . . all were gone.

Then, sometime after Hué was actually liberated, mass graves were found outside the city. Three thousand or so bodies were ultimately discovered. The extent of the coverage on TV network news back home was apparently one throwaway line on NBC: "Hundreds of government workers were killed and thrown into temporary graves."[13]

Hundreds?

That was it, period. None of the usual gory pictures were shown. The Hué massacre was barely mentioned in the print media either.

Why not?

Where was the journalistic outrage that became so commonplace back then?

3,000 bodies don't constitute news?

Catholic priests apparently buried alive . . . not news?

What about finding the bodies of children in the graves?

Were there no American correspondents in Vietnam old enough to remember the holocaust?

Another war crime discovered about the same time, the much smaller one on our side, certainly got vivid coverage.

Yes, My Lai was tragic, a criminal act that never should have occurred. Yes, it deserved to be exposed and the perpetrators punished.

But, the discovery of *thousands* of civilians being slaughtered isn't newsworthy?

How could our watchdogs of freedom and human rights in the media view those infamous events so differently?

It makes no sense.

Lack of concern for reporting the truth was perhaps the biggest travesty perpetuated by the media during the Vietnam War.

One of the most blatant cases I ran across in my 1990 readings dealt with NBC news. When a reporter suggested to a news chief there in mid-1968 that an effort should be made to correct the misinformation reported during Tet, the response was that Tet had already been accepted "in the public's mind as a defeat, and therefore it was an American defeat"[14]—a correction would not be aired.

The facts be damned. It was no longer relevant that Tet was a crushing loss for the Vietcong.

Isn't that peachy?

And to keep from getting nauseous, I won't even start on Walter Cronkite . . . arguably the most loved and respected TV newscaster back then. In fact, he was probably the most biased reporter of all when it came to Vietnam. The grandfatherly one didn't want his adoring public to have to worry about interpreting the news from there; he took care of that for them. After all, he knew all about "that pathetic country."[15]

At least I was able to find reference to one principled TV reporter back then.

William Hammond's analysis noted, "News commentator Howard K. Smith provided one of the few counterpoints to the mood of defeat. With the charge that the American press was contributing to the 'confusion and frustration now damaging the American spirit,' he resigned his position at ABC News because he no longer felt he was participating in 'a great age of journalism.'"[16]

Smith went on to state that "news coverage of the Vietnam War was replete with examples of bias."[16] Apparently, Mr. Smith had a son who served in Vietnam, so he didn't have to rely totally on biased accounts by his media colleagues.

It's amazing what some real, first-hand information can do.

And amazing doesn't even begin to describe the slanted historical cluster—record—I was uncovering with my research effort. The military half-a-word "cluster" is more accurate though.

Clearly, the annals being written by anals about the Vietnam War had little semblance to what actually went on there.

What a crock!

God, there's no way this bullshit could get any deeper.

Could it?

ANTI-AMERICA AMERICANS . . . LADY LIBERTY'S ACHILLES' HEEL

— Mass Media Manipulators —

Enduring Truth: *Transforming fiction into fact, lies into truth—*
"reporting" it isn't.

Chapter 18

BROKERS OF COUNTERFEIT TRUTH

Sham reporters, smug intellectuals, antiwar moralists, and other frauds.

Aldous Huxley: *"Facts do not cease to exist because they are ignored."*[1]

Well, maybe the bullshit could get deeper . . . history changing-wise.

The problems with biased reporting about Vietnam clearly didn't end with the war. I could recall a PBS special on the Vietnam War that ran in the mid to late 1980s. I started watching parts of the series on three or four different occasions, but became frustrated and flipped it off (literally and figuratively) after just a few minutes each time.

It had absolutely no correlation to what I experienced in Vietnam a decade-and-a-half or two before, none whatsoever.

From what I could discern, Uncle Ho and his merry men were being depicted as the good guys . . . stealing from the rich to give to the poor. Oh, wait, perhaps I'm mixing up that latter part with some other fantasy, but regardless, the NVA and Vietcong were certainly depicted as the good guys in the PBS special. There was no question about that.

And while I couldn't stomach the TV version of "Vietnam Reinvented," I was able to slog through "the bestselling companion to the PBS series"—*eventually*—Stanley Karnow's book, *Vietnam: A History*. It was purported to be "the first complete account of Vietnam at war."

Fittingly, it didn't claim to be a "truthful" account of the war.

Karnow was a journalist in Southeast Asia with *Time*, *Life*, and the *Washington Post*, so he should have been in tune with the issues and the outcomes—NOT SO! I'll grant that the book may not have been as bad as what I remembered of the brief PBS segments I watched on TV, but it was the most blatantly propagandized account of the Vietnam War among the many, many works I read.

Karnow didn't bother hiding his partiality either, stating "South Vietnam's leadership *and population* (emphasis added) were apathetic, corrupt, and undisciplined."[2] The book couldn't have been more sympathetic to Ho Chi Minh and the communists of North Vietnam if a communist had written it.

But, then, who knows?

Maybe one did.

At the very least, Karnow must have gone to the same South Vietnam appreciation school as Walter Cronkite. Both certainly detested the South Vietnamese people for some unfathomable reason.

Even though *The New York Times* praised Karnow's work as being "free of ideological bias" and "profound in its understanding," blatant contradictions and authorship prejudices were peppered throughout the book. Beyond his assertion that the *population* (poor peasants for the most part), not just the leadership, of South Vietnam was "apathetic, corrupt, and undisciplined," there were lots of other illustrations.

After harping about the corruption of South Vietnamese officials, Karnow comments that at the end of the war, "senior South Vietnamese were either too honest or too incompetent to enrich themselves."[3] He gives as examples former Prime Minister Nguyen Cao Ky, General Tran Van Don, and Washington Ambassador Bui Diem. None of them had used their positions for personal monetary gain; they arrived in America essentially broke.

Boy, I can see why Karnow would have so much contempt for these folks. And, obviously, he didn't think they were "too honest."

With regard to the thousands of civilians the communists executed in Hué during Tet, Karnow states, "paradoxically, the American public barely noticed these atrocities."[4]

"PARADOXICALLY," you say? Are you fucking kidding me?

It would have been a hell of a lot easier for the American public to notice those atrocities had journalists—*like Karnow*—actually reported on them during the war.

That would have been a novel approach: reporting facts, the truth.

Of course, the benevolent Karnow tries to let himself and other members of his profession off the hook for biased reporting by alleging that, "the press, with all its shortcomings, tended to follow rather than lead the U.S. public."[5]

But, again, that doesn't square with Saint Karnow's own assertions later on.

While reluctantly noting that a majority of the American public supported the Nixon-ordered incursions into Cambodia, he points out that, "once again, however the opinion leaders set the pace. Press commentators lashed out at Nixon."[6] Moreover, after complaining that "the public response in the United States was relatively muted" to the Christmas bombings in 1972, he then proudly declares, "by contrast, news commentators reacted with outrage."[7]

Somehow these examples sound like they were intended to *create* public opinion, not just report or "follow." But reading Karnow's book did help me understand a lot about what went wrong back then . . . history fabricators in the media were out of control—*totally* out of control.

Thankfully, not all of the historical accounts I read bought into the load of bull being sold by North Vietnam.

Guenter Lewy's assessment was that "contrary to communist propaganda, the southern insurgency was never a spontaneous uprising but from the beginning was a deliberate campaign, directed and supported from Hanoi."[8] This was from a political scientist who actually studied it.

The Vietnam War was not about nationalism. It was not a civil war. It was about a separate country, North Vietnam, conquering South Vietnam. But, most members of the media in the '60s and '70s bought the full, unabridged load of crap being sold by their trusted Uncle Ho.

The notion of a civil war probably resonated in America because of our own civil war a century earlier. We understood the concept.

However, it wasn't a matter of some transparent, easy-to-traverse state line separating North and South Vietnam. It wasn't an arbitrary 38th Parallel like that dividing North and South Korea or an Iron Curtain–Berlin Wall between East and West Germany.

There were nearly impassable mountains separating North and South Vietnam. The North and South Vietnamese people didn't wander back and forth and intermix; except for old French-built route 1 on the coast, there were no roads connecting the two countries.

There's a reason the Ho Chi Minh Trail went through Laos and Cambodia. You couldn't get there easily going straight north and south in the mountains.

No, the Vietnam War was not about reuniting a split-apart country. That was sheer, unadulterated bullshit.

The myth propagated by the media that Uncle Ho was really a nationalist rather than a communist was bunk as well. He was a communist. He lived in France for two decades (returning to Vietnam in 1941) and was a founding member of the French Communist Party.

Somehow, though, the American media seemed to believe everything their beloved Uncle Ho told them. He wouldn't lie. Besides, his Vietnamese name translates to "he who enlightens."[9] Surely, the Enlightened One always tells the truth.

The fact that he gave himself that name probably wouldn't have raised any suspicions either, would it?

Give me a break!

* * *

By 1972, Nixon's Vietnamization of the war was almost complete; few American combat troops remained in South Vietnam. The few Vietcong troops still alive after the annihilation in 1968 were on the defensive and the South Vietnamese were performing admirably.

As a result, North Vietnam decided a change of strategy was needed. What they came up with was an all-out invasion of the South—the 1972 Easter Offensive.

Conventional warfare replaced guerrilla warfare.

I was locked away in graduate school at the time, and I barely recall anything about what went on during that time war-wise. Reading about it almost two decades later proved to be very interesting and informative.

North Vietnam committed "14 divisions and 26 independent regiments, practically all of their armed might, but the invasion failed to accomplish its goal."[10] Moreover, North Vietnamese losses were "close to 100,000 killed." The ARVN bent—significantly—but they didn't break, thanks in large part to the resumption of full-scale bombing support and the mining of Haiphong harbor ordered by Nixon.

Then, in December of '72, Linebacker II—the "Christmas bombing" of North Vietnam—was launched . . . a subtle push to get the North back to the bargaining table. As assessed by General Davidson, the chief military intelligence officer in Vietnam for two years: "From an American viewpoint, the results were spectacular. North Vietnam's military potential, its industry, and its economy lay in ruins. . . . For the first time, it seized the strategic initiative from the enemy."[11]

Wait one: What does that mean?

Did our side have the war essentially won in 1972?

No, that can't be true.

However, Joe Guilmartin mentioned a similar assessment in his Vietnam War course at one point. John Hasek, a Canadian who was in South Vietnam as an observer in 1973, told Joe that he had driven around extensively in provinces north of Saigon: It was perfectly safe. A province chief took him out *at night* shining for deer.

No sweat!

There was no danger.

The war was over.

But, true or not, things changed dramatically soon thereafter. Peter Kissinger, Nixon's renowned policy strategist, gave away whatever military advantage there might have been at the time.

The 1973 Paris Peace Accords were a disaster in the making for South Vietnam. It allowed any NVA forces in the South to remain there, and there was no effective way to ensure that North Vietnam would not violate the conditions of the agreement . . . something they started to do almost immediately.

Our Australian allies knew it was a sham as well—"a shameless bug-out"[12] as one of their commanders referred to it—but President Thieu of South Vietnam was forced into accepting it.

Thieu fought like hell about it, but finally gave in when he received personal assurances from President Nixon that he would "take swift and severe retaliatory action"[13] if North Vietnam violated the terms. Of course, that was a promise Nixon couldn't keep when the Watergate damn burst and spewed sewage of his own making all over him.

The enemy knew the handwriting was on the wall also, as noted by Truong Nhu Tang, the former Vietcong Minister of Justice. In a book he wrote after the war, he states: "In fact, the Paris Accords created vast new opportunities to bring the Thieu government to an end through political means. However Nixon and Kissinger might have regarded what had happened in Paris, it was clear to us that the concessions were largely in our favor."[14, 15, i]

So even before Watergate, the probable outcome was established.

It took the North Vietnamese a while to recover from the Easter and Christmas shellackings they took in 1972, but with the help of their Russian and Chinese allies, they were ready for another major invasion of the South in 1975. By that time, the economy in South Vietnam was in a shambles, and reductions in U.S. military aid were sufficiently severe it was unlikely the ARVN could mount a credible defense.

The resupply situation was so bad, in fact, that ammunition was being rationed. ARVN soldiers were receiving a paltry "85 rifle bullets per man per month."[15, 16, ii]

Hell, that's not even a good "one-minute quickie" with an M-16 when shit hits the fan. If you set that sucker on "spray," you can pop a lot of magazines in and out awfully damn fast. Eighty-five rounds a minute out the business end wouldn't be all that tough.

So, we expected the South Vietnamese to defend themselves . . . HOW?

Jesus H. Christ!

We sold them down the river . . . men, women, and children.

Worst of all, though, was the Case-Church Amendment that the Democrat-controlled congress imposed with assistance by Senator Clifford Case (R-NJ). After making commitments to the South Vietnamese concerning our withdrawal from the conflict, the Case-Church Amendment put the final nail in the coffin. The legal mandate: There would be no American combat activity in or *over* Southeast Asia.

Forget air support. Case-Church killed that option.

And the enemy knew what it meant.

Again, Truong Nhu Tang wrote: "With the Nixon administration in obvious disarray, the U.S. House and Senate were busy with legislation that would put a definitive end to further sustenance for the Saigon regime. Then, on June 4 the Case-Church amendment passed, blocking funds for Indochina military involvement after August 15."[17] The obituary was written and enacted.

Why should the North Vietnamese honor the Paris Peace Accords?

We weren't even going to be able to offer air support or any other kind of support to our long-time ally if the treaty was violated.

What a crock!

Fill the coffins with soldiers, old men, women, and kids in the South. Their fate is sealed . . . a Case-Church gift that would keep on giving.

Things went downhill mighty fast in 1975 when the North once again launched an all-out invasion. North Vietnam's allies—China and the Soviet Union, intent on an American defeat—provided assistance, materiel, and motivation for a final victory.

South Vietnam's supposed ally—America—did not.

Although it provided no real gratification, it was interesting to discover that the last major battle of the Vietnam War was fought where my involvement in the war had started, at Xuan Loc. The events are described by James Banerian: "At Xuan Loc, the 18th Division, considered to be one of the worst units in the South Vietnamese army, held off and also counterattacked the much bigger and better equipped North Vietnamese soldiers of Gen. Van Tien Dung. While the battle was eventually lost, it stands as a tribute to the determination of Gen. Le Minh Dao and his men who defended their capital."[18]

So, these folks who we didn't resupply didn't just throw in the towel. They put up a pretty good fight at times in spite of being abandoned by America.

Boy, I don't get it. These were our longtime allies.

And, wait a second!

Those of us who fought there are being blamed for losing?

How?

None of us had been there for at least a couple years. And things appear to have been in pretty good shape when we left.

We didn't lose shit. Our politicians gave it away—with lots of help from the media and antiwar sacks-of-shit.

Look in the mirror, assholes, if you want to see who lost the war.

And you know what?

The war could have been won. The books I read pretty well confirmed that. Moreover, I had it right all along: the cause *and* the people were worth the effort and commitment.

And I wasn't alone in feeling that way either.

Bob Greene—not believing it could have been true—posed a question in his syndicated column: "If you are a Vietnam veteran, were you ever spat upon when you returned to the United States?"[19] In reading the compilation of letters he ultimately published in *Homecoming*, a follow-on book, it's clear that lots of other Vietnam combat vets shared my opinion about the war: that it was a worthy cause. It's also clear that lots of them were spat upon . . . both literally and figuratively.

I can certainly identify with the latter.

Mr. Greene was surprised that one of the respondents "actually felt happy"[20] when he got back to Vietnam after a month in the States. However, Bob notes that it became a recurring theme in many of the letters, and he surmised that the "ugly Stateside experiences" the soldiers had to deal with must have made Vietnam feel "strangely like home."[21]

Now, there's a welcome home none of us would have expected.

But, twenty-plus years after the fact, I had to concur with Bob's assessment. In late '69, early '70, Vietnam did feel more like home to me than Whitewater. I was ready to go back, but for a "Towering Inferno."

Thankfully, there were also lots of letters in Bob's book that talked about things like honor, pride, and compassion.

Many veterans—whether spat upon or not—spoke with reverence about their comrades in Vietnam. They spoke with fondness and concern about the Vietnamese people too. Being proud of having served America was in there as well, as was the willingness to serve again . . . in spite of the horseshit welcome back in the real world.

Of course, it would be easy to consider the letters Bob Greene received as anomalies, not representing the majority of veterans who served in the war. However, a study for the Veterans Administration in 1980—a full decade after America's peak effort in Vietnam—indicated that a majority of those who served in Vietnam did, in fact, feel proud of their efforts there . . . just as I did.

Moreover, of the fifty-plus troops that rotated through 2nd and 3rd Platoons during my time as Platoon Sergeant or Platoon Leader with Delta, I knew only one that didn't earn the right to be proud. All my other brothers—98 percent—served with honor and pride.

Even with more than a decade of bombardment by the media and antiwar protesters over the futility and horror of American efforts in Vietnam—and the war having been lost—71 percent of the veterans in the V.A. survey indicated they were "glad" to have served in the war. 66 percent would have been willing to serve again.

Pretty amazing, but why am I not surprised?

I would have voted with the majority on almost all the questions.

And I'll bet the percentages would have been even higher if the survey would have been conducted prior to all the years of antiwar brainwashing.

Not surprisingly, good old Stanley Karnow found the V.A. results "astonishing," although he managed to rationalize his way through it. Pay attention: Since 82 percent of Vietnam vets thought America's political leaders lost the war, it meant that the soldiers' "zeal was eroded by frustration, and they sought to attribute blame for their disappointment."[22]

Excuse me?

How, exactly, does this explain their willingness to serve again?

And where in the questionnaire was the "zeal eroded by frustration" question?

Brother, what a worthless piece of crap.

As 1990 was winding down, with America—and perhaps our daughter Lorna—facing the bona fide possibility of going to war in South*west* Asia, my reading marathon led me to ask one last question for the year:

What could be worse than war?

The obvious answer: Nothing, right?

But that didn't jibe with the way I felt back home in 1969 and '70 or with the results of the V.A. survey, for that matter.

Moreover, if it was really true, where were the "boat people" in 1968 and 1969 . . . at the height of the war?

Think about it. The South Vietnamese regime—along with its military and police—was supposed to be corrupt and brutal. The media told us so.

The U.S. troops in Vietnam were supposedly warmongers, committing war crimes daily. People heard it daily back then; everyone knows it now.

The ravages of war . . . any war . . . are ghastly and grotesque. The carnage was at its peak in 1968 to 1969.

So where were the "boat people?"

Escaping the horrors of war should have been first and foremost on everyone's mind in Vietnam, shouldn't it?

And, as Marcy asked after watching *Platoon*, why did so many Vietnamese want to come to America . . . home of the alleged "baby killers?"

Odd, huh?

Maybe it's because the allegations were bullshit!

Somehow, the horrors occurring in Vietnam must have gotten worse—*substantially worse*—after the country was "unified" by the North, by the folks her holiness Jane assured us were the good guys. It appears they weren't quite the humanitarians that America's opinion makers and antiwar protesters thought they were.

In fact, the South Vietnamese people knew it all along.

Even before the fall of Saigon in 1975, huge numbers of Vietnamese—tens upon tens of thousands—were fleeing from the advancing NVA forces.

They knew what North Vietnam had in mind . . . and it wasn't liberation.

Even the Vietcong Minister of Justice, Truong Nhu Tang,[23, iii] figured it out eventually and became a boat person himself to escape the horrors.

Since he was one of the lucky ones who survived the voyage, he was able to tell what happened after the war: "In the first year after liberation, some three hundred thousand people were arrested—a figure based solely on the number of officers, state officials, and party leaders who were summoned for thirty days of reeducation. To my knowledge, none of these had returned after a month or even after a year. Up until the time I retired from government in the summer of 1976, not a single one had been freed. This figure of course does not include people who were arrested in the sweeps by governmental organs and military authorities that terrorized both Saigon and the provinces during that period. It is simply impossible to estimate the number of such people. This all happened during my tenure as minister of justice."[23]

Some justice!

So, various true believers inside Vietnam figured it out and, remarkably, even a few outside did as well. For at least one antiwar protester, his eyes were finally opened by one of the maiden voyages of the Vietnamese "boat people" as their country was about to be conquered.

Professor Peter Berger—fervent in his opposition to American involvement in Vietnam—saw a ship full of refugees on TV. "Piles of corpses were on the beach, mostly of children who had died of hunger and thirst. A woman was carrying her dead child in her arms. The question was inescapable: is *this* what those of us who opposed the war helped bring about."[24, 25, iv]

Clearly, the answer was, *YES!* And that was based on but a minuscule sampling in 1975 of the horrors yet to come.

Assessing the ongoing exodus through the intervening years, Berger concluded in his 1980 article: "as far as the peoples of Indochina are concerned, the consequences of Hanoi's victory have been a human catastrophe of monumental dimensions."[24]

True, so true. But if it was a human catastrophe in 1980, what does that make it a decade later?

The exodus continued at least that long, with estimates that more than a million Vietnamese fled their homeland. Not a few thousand, but likely HUNDREDS of THOUSANDS lost their lives at sea trying to escape.

Unbelievable!

Something that makes it even more extraordinary is the ancestral allegiance I saw in the hamlets and villages in Vietnam . . . the devotion linking them to a specific locale. No matter how bad things got, the villagers wouldn't abandon their roots, their family, and their heritage.

How much worse must it have gotten? Tens, then hundreds of thousands, and no one did anything about it. Well, Hong Kong did.

The compassionate souls there initiated the forced repatriation of the "boat people" at the end of 1989. Since the 56,000 Vietnamese in Hong Kong were being "held in squalid camps,"[26] it was probably easier for people to turn their heads and ignore the screams for help.

I certainly had to commend Professor Berger though for recognizing that "one must not walk away in silence from positions stated at the top of one's voice in the past."[24] It says a lot about the man.

It's too bad so few of his campus contemporaries have seen the light . . . or have his morals and integrity. But for most of them, once a chicken shit bastard, always a chicken shit bastard, I guess.

"One must not walk away in silence from positions stated at the top of one's voice in the past."[24] Joan Baez—one of Jane's early compatriots—figured it out.

Why have so few others? Where are those high-minded "humanitarians" [sic] . . . the antiwar moralists . . . out preaching human rights and salvation for the poor and downtrodden?

Where's the journalistic outrage?

Two-faced slugs!

By the end of 1990, I knew where I stood on the issue of the Vietnam War . . . essentially where I was before it all started, only with some actual hard data in hand now. I had it right from the beginning. The reading and analyses weren't finished, but there was enough information in hand for the moment.

Johnson's screwed-up approach to war could be relegated to a second-tier activity. My critical life and death query had been answered.

Besides, America was preparing to go to war for the first time since Vietnam. So was I . . . at *The* Orwellian Stalinist University. There were just too many injustices and atrocities to ignore.

Fortunately, I knew a bit about going to war. A war of attrition didn't cut it; the Johnson method wouldn't do. There was a better way . . . a much better way.

Dau tranh: The Vietnamese expression for warfare on all fronts—the approach utilized by Uncle Ho. That made more sense.

It was Mao's guerrilla warfare model as modified by the Vietminh in their battles against the French in the 1940s, then perfected by the Vietcong in the 1950s and '60s.

And while I knew how it worked—Uncle Ho taught me that—I first learned about the term *dau tranh* in Joe's course. The few other Vietnamese expressions in my vocabulary, I remembered from Nam.

But I saw *dau tranh* in action in Vietnam: military warfare, political warfare, psychological warfare, social warfare . . . "you don't know where or how you're going to get hit next" guerrilla warfare.

Yep, that's what I was preparing for at Ohio State.

There were wars to be fought . . . and won this time.

ANTI-AMERICA AMERICANS . . . LADY LIBERTY'S ACHILLES' HEEL

— Mass Media Manipulators —

Enduring Truth: *Hypocrites loath integrity; it exposes the treachery in their hearts.*

Chapter 19

REPENT AND YE *MIGHT* BE EMPLOYED

Or go hide in a closet. That works just as well . . . probably better.

Eleanor Roosevelt: *"No one can make you feel inferior without your consent."*[1]

Veterans' activities were eating up more and more of my time in 1990, Ohio State-related duties less and less.

Gradually over the ten years since joining the VFW, my involvement with various functions at Post 4931 had increased. Somehow, the need to deal with real people rather than narcissistic "intellectuals" and their self-righteous crap had become increasingly important . . . especially the past couple years.

During 1990, activities for the post included lots of time helping to raise funds for a $30,000 veterans' memorial in Hilliard. Fund-raising was formally launched on Memorial Day; the 8-foot-high, black granite monument was dedicated on Veterans Day.

Our VFW crew, in partnership with the local American Legion post and the city of Hilliard, kicked butt.

You couldn't have raised the funds any faster. And the finished product is absolutely awesome.

What a great feeling that was . . . a real high point for the year.

Along the way, I had also joined the American Legion and the DAV—sometime later, the Military Order of the Purple Heart . . . the MOPH. That added a few more hours of veterans' activities to my recurring agenda; there were monthly meetings to attend.

Furthermore, those off-hour activities started occupying even more of my time once things began heating up in the Persian Gulf at the end of 1990. With the specter of a new group of war veterans on the horizon, the treatment of veterans of previous wars became newsworthy. At least the general concept tweaked the interest of a couple local reporters.

Then, when the Gulf exploded into war in January of '91, that interest turned into actual newsprint in *The Columbus Dispatch.*

The first story broke on January 25. The title read: "Professor says OSU ignoring vets job law," and it had a large picture of the rabble-rousing professor—ME—sitting in front of an old "I want you for U.S. Army" recruiting poster with

Uncle Sam on it[2] . . . a poster that lived on the wall of my office at Ohio State just to piss-off the big dogs there.

If there was ever any doubt about switching from a "hide in the weeds," guerilla warfare mode to a conventional warfare, "all-fronts" offensive at Ohio State, the *Dispatch* article took care of that. War had been declared, and I was back on the battlefield assaulting a fortified institutional bunker—ready or not.

But the response that story created was absolutely unbelievable.

In the next month, six different black Vietnam veterans stopped me on campus . . . one slamming on the brakes of his OSU delivery truck and letting it sit in the street so he could catch me before I walked in the back door of the hospital. All six had seen the story in the *Dispatch*, and they all conveyed essentially the same message: *When Ohio State discovered they were Vietnam veterans, they LOST their affirmative action rights as African Americans.*

Say, WHAT?

Can you prove it?

Probably not, but all six of them came to essentially the same conclusion . . . independently, I presume, since these were all separate, one-on-one discussions. And until the article came out in the newspaper, not one of them had a clue that being a Vietnam-era veteran was actually supposed to *add* affirmative action rights for them, not subtract. Of course, they were accustomed to rights being subtracted; that just seemed like business as usual.

Holy crap! If I thought I had things figured out, those guys certainly added a new twist I hadn't ever considered.

Being a Vietnam veteran must really be perceived by lots of people as being something pretty awful . . . much worse than I had imagined. However, none of the six vets who stopped me seemed to think it was so terrible. They were all proud of their Vietnam service, and each of them encouraged me, in one way or another, to "have at it" with the university.

They wanted me to know that they were on my side. That helped—*a lot.*

Something that didn't help—something I couldn't ignore—was a complaint by a *Dayton Daily News* "reporter" published in the Columbus paper soon after the OSU story came out.[3] This hack was distraught because he felt the Vietnam War protesters of the '60s and '70s were being improperly maligned in media coverage about the Gulf War. He claimed that the concept of Vietnam protesters being anti-troops was "a rewrite of history." In his delusional recollections, "the anti-Vietnam demonstrations were fundamentally expressions of concern for the troops and potential troops."

Say what?

Are you kidding me?

Just because they were carrying North Vietnamese flags and spitting on guys in uniform, why would anyone think they were anti-troops for Christ's sake?

I couldn't let that B.S. go, and fired off a letter to the editor.[4]

God, what a fucking bonehead! But he probably would have fit right in with the old Vietnam War protesters—now faculty and senior-level administrators—at Ohio State.

146

In one of those "déjà vu all over again" encounters, it was mind-boggling to watch these "sleazoids" come out of the woodwork. When things were cranking along hot and heavy in the Persian Gulf, over-the-hill hippies and other "People's Army" remnants in the Department of English were displaying pictures of the Commander-in-Chief, George H.W. Bush, in a dress along with a bevy of pro-Iraqi posters.

It was just like back in Whitewater, with the English department supporting the enemy . . . supporting the killing of Americans.

Where do they find these worthless slime balls?

Regrettably, I think I managed to figure it out: They found them by checking old SDS membership rosters. But, since they were no longer students, these creeps now created organizations like Teachers for a Democratic Culture (TDC) and Union of Democratic Intellectuals (UDI).

And just like the old days with Students for a Democratic Society and the Democratic Republic of Vietnam (DRV, i.e., North Vietnam), the "D" for democratic really wasn't. They're all just fronts for card-carrying and would-be socialists and communists trying to disguise that fact by calling themselves the exact opposite of what they are.

Obviously, I wasn't looking forward to dealing with those assholes again. Whitewater in 1969 and '70 had been enough . . . more than enough and then some.

Damn!

Luckily, I wasn't out on the escalating battlefield by myself this time around. Reinforcements charged into the breach as soon as the first shot was fired.

Dave Aldstadt, the governor's adviser on veterans' affairs, jumped in instantly, providing comments and assessments critical of Ohio State in the very first newspaper article. Dave Bradley with the Ohio chapter of the Vietnam Veterans of America (VVA) was in there as well, noting that the university had "blatantly disregarded" the federal law for Vietnam-era veterans.[2]

Joe Andry, executive director for the Ohio DAV in 1991, then fired a few rounds across the university's bow soon thereafter by asking the DAV's national headquarters to look into the employment complaints at OSU.[5] Joe had served as the national commander for the DAV, so he was well connected back in Washington. He knew where the buttons needed to be pushed. And he didn't let the loss of a leg and an eye in Vietnam slow him down either.

The timing for Joe's request couldn't have been better either, since Marcy and I were about to head to the D.C. area. As chance would have it, we were going to Gaithersburg in early February for another of those extended weekends with our friends, John and Mary Lou.

While we were back there, I was able to visit the DAV command center. It was a start. And although little of substance was accomplished with the national DAV folks, it established a beachhead for some extensive efforts at the federal level later on.

Of more significance on that trip was a meeting with a University of Cincinnati professor of political science, Jim Stever, who was doing a sabbatical at the general accounting office. Jim was also an "in-country" Vietnam veteran, and he was tangling with his institution over veterans' rights as well. His expertise in public policy, along with the investigative skills he honed at the GAO, proved to be invaluable to the battles over veterans' employment rights over the next few years.

A number of off-campus veterans in key leadership positions in Columbus also joined the crusade right from the get-go in 1991. These included George Ondick with the Ohio AMVETS, Don Lanthorn with the American Legion, and Wes Leggett and Carl Price with the U.S. Department of Labor's Veterans Employment and Training Service.

Plus, there was Gene Watts, a state senator from Columbus who happened to be an on-leave OSU history professor *and* a Vietnam veteran. He wasn't one to shy away from a fight with the university.

The Vietnam vets at Ohio State would have been toast without all the logistical support and covering fire these external coalition forces provided. The coalition forces in the Gulf had nothing on the collection assembled for the war against OSU.

Senator Watts and the leaders of the veteran service organizations were able to roust the Ohio Senate into action in just a couple weeks. Hearings were called to examine the hiring practices for veterans at the state's public universities. The political warfare phase of *dau tranh* was launched. Senator Schafrath—the former Cleveland Browns lineman and chair of the Senate's state and local government and veterans' affairs committee—called the hearings, which occurred over a two-week period.

What a spectacle those inquiries turned out to be.

The first session focused on sorting through the rhetoric from both sides . . . from the universities and from the veterans.

An OSU staff member and I made the case for campus veterans. John, who worked in the residence and dining hall area, chaired a Vietnam Veterans Issues Committee on campus, and he had been fighting for veterans' causes long before I realized there were such causes out there. Between the two of us, we made the case that veterans were being denied their legally mandated rights at Ohio State.

University officials countered, testifying that without question they were in compliance with all federal employment provisions for veterans. They "talked the talk" really well. Of course, the two weeks of hearings proved they couldn't "walk the walk." The director of human relations at Ohio State, especially, stepped in it—BIG TIME—while trying.

Her trouble started in week one when one of the senators asked if OSU had "consulted with veterans' groups" when the hiring policies were developed. Her immediate response was, "yes, *too* much."

Not an astute response, but Sue probably couldn't help herself.

I had seen the loathing flash in her eyes when she was first confronted with the Vietnam veteran's issue on campus.[6, i] It was that same burning hatred I'd seen in the eyes of that young coed in Whitewater when she found out I had been in the infantry in Vietnam. Apparently, Vietnam veterans are the devil incarnate to some. Thus, for Sue and her friends, even thinking about us is probably "too much."

George Ondick jumped all over her off-the-wall comment. He testified that in his capacity as executive director for the AMVETS in Ohio, he had never been contacted by OSU (or any other university in the state) about such matters, not once.

A week later, Dave Aldstadt had a stack of documentation almost a foot-high refuting, point-by-point, essentially every assertion made by Sue and her colleagues.

Hmmm.

Isn't there some name for it when one is less than truthful—when one lies— during a legislative hearing?

Ah, yes, "perjury" isn't it?

When ol' Sue—still spouting the institutional party-line—tried to get Ohio State's chief legal counsel to come forward to bail her out in week two, the guy just sat in the back of the room waiving his hands back and forth and shaking his head . . . *no way!* He recognized that the first week's congressional lasso had been retied into a hangman's noose, and he wasn't about to trade places up on that horse.

Guess what, Sue?

It's your neck in there, not his, so you're on your own.

What a great bunch.

The major outcome of the hearings was a requirement that a detailed report be submitted by each of the thirteen public universities in Ohio documenting their efforts to hire disabled and Vietnam-era veterans. The reports were due no later than April 15.

Remarkably, Ohio State, Cleveland State, and Youngstown State missed the deadline. Yes, they all managed to get the reports in sometime later, but only after being threatened by the governor's office.

Two things happened soon thereafter that served to launch the veterans' activities at OSU into the national spotlight. First, the *Akron Beacon Journal* broke a story indicating: "Only one of 889 new employees hired at Ohio State University (in 1990) was a Vietnam veteran."[7] At a time when Vietnam-era veterans accounted for over 6 percent of the civilian labor force, an employment rate of 0.1 percent didn't cut it.

That put OSU's credibility regarding affirmative action for veterans' employment right where it belonged . . . in the toilet.

Then, a couple articles came out in the local suburban newspapers that highlighted Ohio State's "unofficial" three-tiered classification system for military veterans[8, 9]:

- "A career military person, who included his long service on his resume."
- "A 'closet veteran,' who didn't mention it on the resume unless it related to the OSU job."
- "An 'unrepentant veteran,' who included his service for no apparent reason."

A high-level university official—the senior legislative assistant to the Ohio State president—attempting to mend fences with the governor's office made note of them. Apparently, he had too many drinks at the bar and got a little too honest.

Way to go, Herb!

He indicated to Dave Aldstadt and a few members of the veterans' service organizations that the university had no significant problems with the first two categories, but they really worried about the last group, those *unrepentant* veterans.

Why would anyone include military service on their resume if they didn't have to?

EXCUSE ME?

Without question, Herb's comments about unrepentant veterans did more than anything else to rally our comrades-in-arms around the cause. A lot of vets in the undecided camp came aboard.

What did we have to repent for, SHITHEAD?

From that time forward, the fax machine I'd put in my faculty office at OSU used the header, "Unrepentant Vets 'R' Us."

Thank you, Bricker Hall. We probably couldn't have launched the psychosocial warfare component of *dau tranh* without you.

Attempting to provide some damage control along the way, President Gee named a task force at Ohio State to assess what the university was, or should be, doing for veterans. He made a huge tactical mistake, though. He asked ten people to serve—faculty, staff, and students—who actually cared about the topic. It wasn't your typical "talk about it, but don't do anything about it" university committee.

Joe Guilmartin, the Vietnam War course historian, chaired the group. With a hundred-plus combat missions and two Silver Stars to his credit, Joe wasn't one to take a lot of crap and, man, could he spread it on with the written word when he got on a roll. And, believe me, that's something he managed with ease while launching armed torpedoes disguised as harmless, nonlethal footnotes.

I've never known anyone who could weaponize footnotes like Joe.

Between Joe and Phoebe (our English department envoy on the task force who had been in the Air Force and helped with the Vietnam baby lift), the university didn't stand a chance challenging the written findings.

The final report nailed the university on all fronts. "The university has no approved program for veterans delineating the necessary pro-active measures. The overall result is that federally mandated civil rights are being denied 'protected' veterans at The Ohio State University."[10]

Guilty as charged!

Amazingly, exactly one day after the task force story appeared in the *Dispatch*, it was reported that the Department of Labor—the Office of Federal Contractor Compliance Programs, the OFCCP—was finally going to investigate my 1988 complaint about discrimination against veterans.[11]

It was about damn time . . . but not too damn bad timing-wise.

Considering that an OFCCP finding of noncompliance by the university could lead to the termination or suspension of $100 million in federal contracts, the task force report had OSU's backside exposed BIG time . . . hanging in the wind. Obviously, the Pres had a problem if he accepted the findings of the task force he created; they had already concluded that OSU was violating the 1974 law.

He couldn't agree with that . . . not with $100 million at stake.

So, when the high road wasn't available, President Gee took the more familiar low road instead—one he and OSU traveled frequently it seemed. Yes, President Gee blasted his own task force.[12]

The timetable chosen to do so was really cute too.

Joe had submitted the task force report on July 29, 1991. No response was forthcoming from the president in August or September. Joe left Columbus on October 1 for a research fellowship in Spain.

President Gee dispatched his scathing response to Joe on the 2nd.

Incredible!

My money would have been on Joe in any public battle of wits regarding the findings. Apparently, the university's money was as well.

And, naturally, the English department luminaries at OSU couldn't let things rest either. They couldn't let their sworn enemy of years gone by—Vietnam veterans—off the hook.

Their departmental colleague, Phoebe, had put up a poster outside her office supporting the Vietnam women's memorial. The poster had a woman's dog tags on it and it read, "Not all women wore love beads in the '60s." In early October, someone penned across the bottom, "Yeah some were murderers."[12]

Jesus Christ, are you slime balls nuts?

For one thing, the few thousand women who served in Vietnam were there almost exclusively in life-saving roles . . . nurses and the like. But I suppose it may not have actually been a faculty member in the English department who did it though. Someone on the faculty in English *might* have known to put a comma after "Yeah."

Regardless, President Gee didn't think that comment was indicative of anything problematic. Oh, he did indicate to Phoebe privately that it wasn't nice, perhaps even a tad objectionable, but that never came across in any of his public comments. Publicly, there was no basis for *any* of the veterans' concerns.

Somehow, we disagreed.

Of course, there's nothing like a public pissing contest to display an institution in the best possible light to a group of outside compliance investigators. Although the accusations and counter-accusations moved off the pages of the *Dispatch* for a time, the OSU student newspaper along with the faculty-staff tabloid featured plenty of contentious, back and forth arguments. And, with perfect timing, many of those were published in October, right when the OFCCP investigators were on campus gathering data.

Not that we were complaining. If anything, OSU's administration was helping to make our case. Thus, this was a major exception to my mother's old advice of staying out of pissing contests with skunks.[13ii]

To be perfectly fair though, even President Gee was willing to acknowledge to the press that a veterans' affairs office was needed.[14, 15] I'm sure the fact that state and federal hammers were about to come crashing down on his head had nothing to do with his enlightenment. Senator Watts, as chair of the Ohio Senate committee responsible for the university's budget, had already inserted preliminary stipulations regarding veterans' rights, and the OFCCP was hot on the university's tail.

The public battles and notoriety sure didn't hurt our recruiting efforts for a new AMVETS post on campus either. Since we had managed to be a major thorn in the side of the university administration as a disorganized mob, the Ohio AMVETS executive director, George Ondick, suggested that an organized mob might be even more effective.

So, we decided to give it a try.

During that late fall and early winter, we added quite a number of faculty, staff, and students to the roster of the Colonel David H. Zook, Jr., Memorial AMVETS Post 1974. Colonel Zook was an Ohio State graduate and a decorated Air Force officer who was killed in Vietnam. He had been listed for quite some time as missing in action—as MIA—one of way too many in Southeast Asia.

Naturally, an AMVETS membership then had to be added to my growing list of veterans' associations. And this one resulted in substantially more work on my part, since I ended up being elected the first post commander. That imposed daily responsibilities—interactions with members of the post regularly and with George at the state level and his counterpart at the national level periodically—not just once-a-month meetings.

Hey, what could I do?

Duty called.

My AMVETS activities weren't limited to just those duties with the new post either. The AMVETS slot on the Franklin County Veterans Service Commission came open, so George and his colleagues put my name in for the judicially appointed position.

The county service commissions in Ohio provide emergency relief to veterans in need, and in Franklin County that amounted to over a million dollars annually. So, once I got the university to sign off that this was an acceptable use of my one-day-per-week consulting time, that ate up most of my Wednesdays.

Veterans' activities were definitely becoming a huge part of my daily routine. But that was okay. I wasn't being motivated or challenged by anything else I was doing (or supposed to be doing) at the time . . . things like teaching, research, and service at the university.

Besides, the daily networking was proving to be invaluable for our escalating *dau tranh* campaign.

In some ways, it was like being back in the Army, all the veterans' stuff. I was once again surrounded by people I could trust . . . just like Enyeart, Russell, Perry, and Petite; Cunningham, Hardison, and Rodriquez; Rogers, Martin, and Holmes, plus many, many more.

Only the names and places had changed from 1969 to 1991. Now it was Jim, John, Joe, and Phoebe; Arnie, Gene, Rick, and Stuart; Tom, Bob, Paul, and many, many more.

And there was still a clearly defined enemy out there as well, no question about that. Of course, this one didn't seem to be quite as bright or capable as Uncle Ho and Charlie.

As in Nam, I was also managing to survive some things I probably shouldn't have. Let's hear it for academic freedom and the safety net of tenure at the university! The untenured staff and students probably couldn't have gotten away with all the frontal assaults I lived through.

Not that there weren't some consequences though. The herky-jerky voice inflections may have gotten somewhat better, but my blood pressure seemed to be on a continual upward spiral. Those readings of 180 or so over 90, 95, 100 were not a good sign. Neither was a resting pulse rate in the mid to upper 80s. That had been in the low 60s.

Something had to be done.

One approach I tried was switching from a twelve-month appointment at OSU to nine. That at least gave me the summers to go hide out in the mountains of northern New Mexico with Marcy.

We sure took advantage of it too . . . taking off with our tent camper and dogs to Cimarron Canyon, almost 1,600 miles away. Spending time conversing with the Native American's Standing People—ponderosa pines, pinions, and spruce—near Ute Park was a great escape . . . and the dialogue was certainly more substantive than most exchanges with the politically correct assholes at Ohio State.

I'd take Kodi, our Siberian husky, for walks along the Cimarron River two, three, four times a day. We'd stop and sit in the Standing People's cathedral, listening to the river . . . or listening to absolutely nothing, enjoying the peace and quiet.

Marcy and I made lots of terrific friends among the retired Texas regulars there in the state campground. Talk about nice, caring folks. More of our Christmas cards each year went to the panhandle of Texas than anywhere else in the country. More came from there as well.

Of course, you couldn't find better people anywhere than Norma and John, the owners of Pine Ridge—a gas station, grocery store, motel, and everyday gathering place—a mile-and-a-half down the road from the campground. Lots of hours were whiled away on the porch at Pine Ridge, and not once did I encounter a "Go Bucks" cheerleader among the old-timers hanging out there.

It was great.

You could also count on John and Norma for anything and everything you needed—ice, milk, gas; a fishing license . . . a shower.

Car trouble?

No sweat!

Leave it for John to work on. Take Norma's Lincoln for a couple days until the parts come in.

Norma and John wouldn't have fit in back in Ohio. They are way too nice.

There were also ample opportunities for me to head to the memorial to sit alone in the chapel . . . visiting quietly with Chris and comrades. We would reminisce about valued friends and friendships, recalling the commitments so many made, one to the other.

Other times, I would just wander the memorial grounds, photographing the undulating, wind-blown sea of wildflowers and sage—purples, yellows, and oranges on a sage-green canvas. The finest artists in the world couldn't create anything more striking . . . the centerpiece, undeniably, being the Moreno Valley's signature wildflower, the Indian paintbrush . . . diminutive, yet conspicuous, dipped in autumn orange.

Those peaceful, aesthetic times were sure nice too.

And for additional inspiration, lots of hours were spent visiting with Dr. Westphall, an absolute saint who dedicated his life to the memorial and Vietnam veterans. There could never have been a more inspirational soul anywhere for veterans to encounter than Victor Westphall.

Old wounds troubling you?

Victor's soothing words provided powerful medicine.

Marcy and I spent lots of quality time together as well . . . most by choice, some clearly not. It can turn rainy for days on end up in the Sangre de Cristo Mountains in the summertime. Yet, we managed to spend week after week together in a tiny tent camper—cooped-up for hours and hours during sometimes-daily downpours. Somehow, we survived it though . . . and the dogs did too.

However, rain or shine, we didn't watch TV, listen to the radio, or buy a newspaper the whole time we were out there in God's country.

When we escaped, we escaped.

And, you know what?

It was great!

We didn't miss a damn thing.

Unfortunately, at some point we always had to head back to Ohio. Then, rolling east down I-70, an invisible band would start to constrict across my chest . . . tighter and tighter, the closer we got to Columbus. When the skyline came into view, it was almost impossible to breathe.

God, I sure wanted to do an about-face and head back west.

And that crushing tightness in my chest didn't go away when we got home either. It would reappear, big time, whenever I started to back out of the driveway to head for work.

Clearly, a nine-month appointment wasn't the answer. I needed to find some other solution . . . something that might actually work.

ANTI-AMERICA AMERICANS . . . LADY LIBERTY'S ACHILLES' HEEL

— Socialist-Loving "Intellectuals" —

Enduring Truth: *Unrepentant vets gave us freedom; the "elite" gave their worth: SHIT!*

Chapter 20

NOT SO HALLOWED HALLS

The feds' assessment: "harassment, intimidation and coercion."

....

Henry Kissinger: *"University politics are vicious
precisely because the stakes are so small."*[1]
[Except maybe for vets]

....

Heading into 1992, OSU veterans seemed to have gained the upper hand.

We were well organized and had lots of allies on our side. Moreover, with the Labor compliance review hanging over their heads and lots of surly state legislators threatening to take even more action, the big dogs at OSU weren't marking quite so high on the tree anymore.

The campus vets wanted to keep it that way. We'd served as their "pissonya" tree long enough.

Although the regular newspaper stories about veterans on Ohio campuses slowed to a trickle in early '92, one dandy recap came out in the university's own alumni publication—the *Ohio State Quest*. The story entitled "A Peacetime War" captured the essence of the ongoing battles with the administration at OSU[2] and, remarkably, it portrayed the veterans' side quite accurately.

My Purple Heart and Combat Infantry Badge (CIB) were prominent among the artwork for the story.

The editor of *Quest*, Earle Holland, wrote the account, and he absolutely nailed it. Even after years of brainwashing at OSU, Earle still retained his antiquated, "honesty is the best policy" values, and he always contended that a university is not well served by cover-ups.

Nonetheless, "A Peacetime War" landed him in the camp of the enemy in the eyes of the administration at Ohio State; not the best career advancement move Earle ever made. Owning up to sleazy institutional behavior doesn't gain many points with inherently dishonest lowlifes.

Although it was quiet on most other fronts, one campus event did garner some local press coverage that spring, a formal ceremony in Bricker Hall on March 5 for the establishment of the Ohio State AMVETS Post 1974[3] . . . the number being selected in honor of the 1974 Vietnam Era Veterans Readjustment Assistance Act.

Somehow that had a poetic ring to it.

And if there was ever a reason to form a veterans' post at a university, we certainly had one.

There were a number of state and local politicos in attendance at the ceremony, and even President Gee was there to accept the "Reflections in the Wall" framed print from our AMVETS members. To Gee's credit, he did hang the print in the entry to his office . . . for a little while, at least.

The post dedication marked a short break in the action—a forced R&R—for me though. That morning I had a needle biopsy on a tumor below my right ear, and the surgery that followed shortly thereafter knocked me off the line for a few weeks.

The tumor turned out to be a benign parotid variety (a tumor in the gland where one gets the mumps), but the scheduled hour-and-a-half procedure turned into more than four hours due to the damn thing having grown around the major facial nerve. Fortunately, my Cancer Center colleague Bill Farrar, the cutter, took his sweet time and got it right; the nerve wasn't severed. As a result, there was no permanent, stroke-like paralysis on that side of my face, a relatively common occurrence in those types of surgeries . . . about 5 percent of the time back then.

Thank you, Bill!!!

It paid off questioning my friend Mike Grever (the best of the best MDs in my book) and multiple in-the-know nurses (always providers of truthful insights regarding MDs . . . the good, the bad, and the ugly). All those testimonials I heard about the quality of Bill's work must have been true: "a surgeon who'll think his way through difficult situations, where most others will cut their way through it." I guess the New York head and neck training many years before stuck with him, so picking a breast cancer guy to do the slicing and dicing worked out.

Marcy had some real questions about that to begin with though.

From her vantage point, the mug she was looking at had changed rather appreciably in those few hours. About a six-inch incision had been carved down around my right ear, then down my neck. Apparently, the ear had to be pulled up out of the way during the surgery, so when everything was stitched back together, the ear was left sticking straight out for a time.

When Marcy first saw me, it gave me that suave, Dumbo-the-flying-elephant look.

Then, the next day, I wound up with a patch over my right eye when it was determined that the blink response on that side had stopped working. Between the black eye patch and all the stitches along the ugly red gash on my neck, I looked like I'd come out on the losing end of a sword fight in some old pirate movie. When asked about it, I just told people Marcy had come after me with a butcher knife.

Things eventually returned to normal though . . . more or less.

Not that things were normal on campus, however. There were a few flashbacks to the turbulent, down-with-America 1960s that spring. The Rodney King court case was occupying lots of attention on the news, and the verdict caused an eruption on campus. On May 1, a few hundred students marched on the administration building, and at the end of their rally, a '60's-type faction tore down the American flag and burned it.[4]

Yes, indeed, just like on campus in Whitewater in 1969 and '70.

Wow, here we go again.

Fortunately, there were some cooler heads among the students. Jordana Shakor, an African American student from Mississippi, organized a peace rally the following Monday and donated a new flag.[5] Jordana's father was career military, and his flag-draped coffin served to instill some additional respect for the red, white, and blue standard he served.[6]

That spring and early summer, when I was back up and about, I spent lots of time working with Jim Stever and his buddy Abe Miller in Cincinnati to establish a not-for-profit institute to study veterans' issues. It was clear we weren't going to be able to conduct such studies at either of our universities, or any other in Ohio the way it looked. So, the Center for the Study of Veterans in Society (CSVS) came into existence in 1992, with the three of us as founding directors.

We all suspected that a glut of PhDs in the '60s had contributed to the antipatriotism predilections on our campuses decades later, and a scholarly publication in early 1992 provided corollary evidence. With Vietnam as the apparent motivator, there was an "extraordinary upsurge in undergraduate enrollments" in the 1960s, and that was accompanied by an unprecedented three-fold jump in "the absolute number of doctorates awarded to U.S. residents" during the decade.[7]

The anomalous proliferation followed decades of minuscule growth. The increase was gender specific—males—and the numbers dropped like a rock once graduate school deferments were eliminated in 1968.

Now there's a surprise.

And where did the draft dodging glut end up?

Our guess was right back where it started . . . on college campuses.

So, to put more troops on the line for the campus wars, Jim Stever spearheaded the establishment of an AMVETS post at the University of Cincinnati to complement the one we had at OSU. With CSVS collecting data and a growing number of pissed off troops at our two posts, we had multiple means for raising hell from that point forward.

We managed to raise just a bit along the way too by continuing to employ Uncle Ho's principles of *dau tranh* . . . warfare on all fronts.

We wrote articles for veterans' magazines and any other publications willing to print the stories.[8-11] We interfaced with veterans' service groups and other organizations at the local, state, and national levels. We sponsored resolutions and presented at their meetings.[12-14] We submitted congressional testimony[15] and lobbied elected officials to take action.

We harassed intransigent bureaucrats and antivet university administrators at all levels—CONTINUALLY. We told anyone and everyone who would listen about employment discrimination against veterans on college campuses.

Basically, we were a major pain-in-the-ass on the topic of veterans' rights. It was time to put an end to all the wrongs.

We really thought we were winning too. The results of the Labor investigation seemed to be taking forever, but veterans in Ohio appeared to be victorious on every other front. There was no reason to believe we wouldn't be there as well.

Not that there weren't some more storm clouds on the horizon though. Fiscal problems in the state were taking a toll at Ohio State and the other public universities in Ohio as well. A few employees had already been laid off and as we were heading into the summer months, it looked like more cuts might be forthcoming.

President Gee started taking public shots at the governor about the budget shortfalls (not the most intelligent approach ever), but he was unconcerned about veterans or the disabled being terminated in any potential cutbacks. His priority concern: "it is vital that *women and minorities* not be disproportionately affected by reductions in force."[16]

Unbelievable!

With everything that had been done up to that point—state legislative hearings, a federal investigation, a university task force, tons of correspondence from veterans and veterans' groups—the university administration still didn't believe it. They wouldn't accept that veterans and the disabled were protected on par with women and minorities.

What was it going to take?

The OFCCP compliance review at Ohio State finally gave us the answer—at least, we thought so. After months of hassling to get an update on the status of the review—sending innumerable letters to government officials and filing multiple Freedom of Information Act requests, all to no avail—a conciliation agreement was issued on September 16, 1992 . . . eleven months after the on-site investigation.

FINALLY!

OSU was cited for seven major violations of the U.S. Code of Federal Regulations (41 CFR 60.250 and 41 CFR 60.741) that implement the relevant federal statutes. These included two biggies: (1) *not having affirmative action programs for veterans and the disabled as required by law,* and (2) *failing to maintain "a working environment free of harassment, intimidation, and coercion" for veterans.*[17]

Bingo!

Just what we'd been saying all along. And the law for veterans had been on the books for *eighteen—EIGHTEEN—God-damn years*!

It was about damn time.

Then, just as the furor was calming down from that kick in the old Bucks' groin, all the hell we'd been raising with various federal legislators delivered another nut buster: The feds from the GAO were on their way. Ohio State had been selected as a "target of a nationwide investigation into the hiring of disabled and Vietnam-era veterans."[18]

YES! All those letters to Washington had finally paid off.

Our train is coming in, guys. Maybe the GAO will finally come down on the sorry-ass OFCCP for failing to enforce the '74 veterans' law. Better yet, maybe congress will actually put some teeth into the law once they find out how worthless the damn thing has been.

So, finally feeling somewhat more confident about where things were heading on the veterans' employment front, I began spending additional time on other diversions. For one thing, I was getting more involved in the Agent Orange health issue.

Although I had never worked on dioxin or any of the other nasty chemicals found in the herbicides sprayed in Vietnam, a significant part of my cancer research program focused on chemical carcinogenesis; the principals involved are the same regardless of the specific cancer-causing agent. As a result, I agreed to participate on a campus panel discussing Agent Orange, and my involvement grew from there.

Herbicide exposure in Vietnam was a major focus of most of the veterans' service organizations—especially in the early '90s—and I became good friends with the person honchoing that effort nationally for the American Legion, Dick Christian. He was able to provide assistance in Washington on our veterans' employment issues, and I supplied scientific expertise for the Legion's Agent Orange efforts. It was a very workable, mutually beneficial partnership.

Dick was a close friend of retired Admiral Elmo Zumwalt—the former commander of Naval operations in Vietnam—so I got acquainted with the admiral as well. What a nice guy.

As most Vietnam veterans know, Admiral Zumwalt's son died of cancer—non-Hodgkin's lymphoma—a type suspected to be caused by Agent Orange. Since the admiral had ordered the spraying of Agent Orange while his son was serving in the Delta, he became a real advocate for addressing the health problems suffered by other veterans who had served over there.

Of course, the admiral may have gotten to spend additional years with his son just *because* he ordered that herbicides be used. The casualty rate for the brown water Navy in Vietnam—the Mekong Delta Riverine Forces—was absolutely through the roof prior to the spraying; it was much more likely than not that a brown water sailor would be killed or wounded during a full hitch there. The casualty rate dropped appreciably once the riverside ambush sites were diminished.

As a result, the younger Zumwalt's life being shortened by cancer wasn't the only issue to consider. He may not have lived long enough to get cancer . . . caused by Agent Orange or not . . . had his father not ordered the spraying.

I'm sure it was Admiral Zumwalt who gets credit for one of the most unusual situations I got into back in February of 1993. I was invited by the National Academy of Sciences to make a presentation to their congressionally mandated committee reviewing health outcomes associated with Agent Orange exposure.[19]

In and of itself, that might not have been so strange, since I was conducting research on the causes of cancer at the time. However, that isn't what they wanted. They asked me to present the U.S. Army infantry perspective in Vietnam.

You want me to do what? Give an overview of what it was like in the infantry in the Vietnam War?

Unreal!

One Vietnam veteran from each branch of the military was asked by the National Academy to provide an overview of that branch's activities in Vietnam. As a draftee, shake 'n' bake NCO who spent less than four months in Vietnam, it seemed rather strange that I would be asked.

With about a million-and-a-half Army personnel having served in Vietnam, why would I be singled out to give the U.S. Army perspective?

Really?

Normally a retired general or someone like that would have been tabbed. Clearly, it had to have been my interactions with Admiral Zumwalt—my cancer research background adding a bit of relevance, perhaps—that got me pegged for the job.

I was up to the task though.

By the time the hearings were held in early 1993, I had a large collection of color photos from the National Archives illustrating issues of importance to the committee. I had copies to leave with them and slides for my presentation.

The photos portrayed what life was like for the troops slogging around in the paddies and humping in the highlands.

There were pictures of soldiers sitting in muddy river water bathing and one with a guy washing his hair in a water-filled bomb crater. Some depicted riverbanks and areas around base camps denuded by Agent Orange. Others documented the spaying of herbicides from fixed wing aircraft, helicopters, half-tracks, and boats. Those where personnel were visible, none were wearing respirators or any other protective gear.

A picture of three guys spraying Agent Blue (an arsenic-based herbicide) from a boat tweaked a few recollections for me as well. In the background, a Chinook was landing, bringing in supplies for the building of fire support base Elvira on the canal. I had spent time at Elvira in 1969.

While I was there, Delta Company was rocketed one night from the edge of the village nearby. The guy or gal launching those suckers must have been an RPG novice though. The first two flew way over the base, missing us by miles. The last one blew a monstrous crater in the rice paddy between the base and the first hooch, about 25 yards from where it was fired.

The next morning, we found an RPG instruction sheet on the ground nearby. Either the person couldn't read or was one hell of a bad shot.

On another occasion, late one afternoon, I was just heading out with a squad to set up an ambush on the other side of the village . . . villagers didn't go out socializing at night, Charlie did. I was about halfway to the hooches, walking point, when all sorts of shit broke loose somewhere beyond the village. Our two other ambush patrols that night were being dropped off by an Army landing craft down the canal a short distance. They got clobbered just as the front ramp was being lowered.

Luckily, I decided to go back to Elvira in case we needed to head out to help. We were almost back inside when Charlie opened up on us from the village and a tree line nearby. No question about it, they had planned to nail us on our way out that evening as well.

None of my guys got hit, but there was sure enough crap flying back and forth for a bit. Our 50-caliber machine gun on that side of the base took the fight out them though.

All we found the next morning were a couple dead water buffalo.

Yes, I was definitely able to make my presentation to the National Academy committee somewhat personal in nature.

Of course, we had tried to make it personal for our replacements at Elvira a week or so after those ambushes as well. But they had just come from the enemy-controlled "Pineapple." They were tough, so they didn't need to rush to set up their defensive positions . . . in the middle of the day, for God's sake . . . at a cushy-duty fire support base.

We were no more than a couple miles down the canal in the landing craft when Charlie brought the max. I don't remember which unit it was that replaced us (probably just as well), but they had multiple casualties just because they were "tough."

Dumb!

Yes, Committee, I can tell you about my old girlfriend, Elvira.

As the various photos were being shown on the screen, I talked to the committee about chemicals that initiate cancer and those that promote it, and I covered the concept of synergistic effects among chemicals in cancer development. I talked about the importance of different routes of exposure, and hammered away at the fact that no one had yet done an appropriate study to prove or disprove whether Vietnam veterans were suffering from adverse health effects . . . caused by Agent Orange or anything else. Such controlled studies needed to be done.

By the time I finished, I was convinced that a retired general probably wouldn't have hit all the pertinent issues the committee needed to know about. Maybe Admiral Zumwalt had the right idea all along.

All the other presentations that February 8, 1993 in Irvine, California were highly informative, but some side conversations with the L.A. lawyer who spoke about the Navy brown water guys in Vietnam were especially intriguing. And, they weren't about his activities in the OJ trial.

Nope, they had to do with Hanoi Jane's like-minded—socialist-at-heart—twin in the 1970s, John Kerry. The consensus among most Vietnam vets I talked to back then was that Kerry's antiwar crap was likely just for self-serving political purposes; antiwar was the direction the political winds were blowing. However, hearing about Navy guys who served with him made it sound like he had absolutely nothing—*zero*—to be proud of from his time in Nam.

What? Two of his three Purple Hearts most likely weren't real?

Apparently, three Purple Hearts could get you out of the field in Vietnam—something I'd never heard of—and Kerry knew it. The attorney indicated Kerry's crewmates questioned whether his "wounds" were really caused by enemy shrapnel. Knowing him, their assumption was they were either caused by him diving for cover or were self-inflicted. Plus, most didn't think the minor wounds—two of three times for sure—were worthy of a Purple Heart, regardless.

But Kerry demanded them, then got pulled out of the combat zone.

Hmmm!

A pattern was developing regarding the small percentage of Vietnam vets who returned home protesting against the war. If they tasted combat and failed to perform while their comrades fought and died, that would explain a lot.

161

Cowards need something to blame . . . other than themselves.

So, our pot smoker in 2nd Platoon, Oliver Stone (probably), and John Kerry (almost certainly): They could pontificate about warmongers in Vietnam and an amoral war as a way to hide their spinelessness back home.

Wow! That actually makes a lot of sense.

I wonder if that allows them to look in the mirror and not see a gutless slime ball peering back. Maybe that's where banding together and making up stories about their units' atrocities day-to-day blurs the image.

My response to the worthless cowards: *BULLSHIT!*

* * *

In early 1993, while I was messing with the Agent Orange issue on the side, the campus AMVETS posts, CSVS, and the whole veterans' coalition continued to press forward. They kept the pressure on at both the state and federal levels regarding veterans' employment issues.

Initially at the state level, Governor Voinovich issued an executive order regarding the employment of veterans on college campuses in Ohio, and that was followed up by state congressional action. However, both measures relied mainly on voluntary compliance.

It became clear that wasn't enough.

Data collected by CSVS indicated that Vietnam-era veterans made up 6.4 percent of the civilian labor force in Ohio in 1991, but only 2.8 percent of the new hires by federal contractors in Ohio that year had been Vietnam-era veterans. At the University of Cincinnati and Ohio State, the levels were an appalling 0.7 percent (9 of 1,215 new hires) and 0.2 percent (5 of 2,097), respectively. That was for employees at all levels—custodial workers, grounds keepers, food service personnel, etc.—not just faculty.

Obviously, a bigger stick was required. Neither the state's actions to date nor OFCCP's conciliation agreement had made a damn dent—none whatsoever. The state continued to try though.

Additional legislative action was undertaken—Concurrent Resolution #51—which created a joint select committee to study affirmative action for veterans at all public universities and state agencies in Ohio. Affirmative action employment programs for veterans were to be judged on the basis of technical adequacy, implementation, and parity with programs for women and minorities . . . all based on recommendations by CSVS (Jim Stever, really) via the veterans' service organizations. CSVS then helped draft questionnaires to assess these parameters, and Jim's background with the GAO really helped in that regard.

Site visits by the select committee were scheduled on all campuses, and deadlines for preliminary reports and final reports were set at the end of June and December of 1993, respectively. However, those dates were eventually pushed back six months when the committee discovered that many of the state universities had no clue what was required. Even after all the news stories, they were oblivious to the federal and state laws regarding veterans' employment rights.

Not a good sign.

Moreover, the reports turned out to be absolute abominations when they finally did come out. At Ohio State, President Gee was successful in his goal to not have women and minorities adversely affected by the budget-mandated reductions in force . . . but that accomplishment came at the expense of veterans.

Ten more Vietnam-era veterans were terminated in one year (51) than had been hired the previous four (41 of 4,484 total new hires), and 135 other military veterans were sacked as well.[20] One of the Vietnam veterans was within 16 months of being eligible to retire when he was given the boot.

Nice caring folks at *THE* Orwellian Stalinist University.

There was no question that military veterans were being terminated disproportionately, that is, at a higher ratio than they were employed at the university. That selective targeting should have given us all the ammunition we needed to bring down the max, or the ax, or something. However, when Representative Malone—the outspoken chair of the joint committee—didn't get reelected, the other members of the committee ducked for cover.

In the end, the whole effort at the state level amounted to little more than a resounding splash in the latrine.

Moreover, once the conciliation agreement was signed, the U.S. Department of Labor wanted nothing more to do with the matter either.

Hey, they didn't want to investigate my original complaint, so why would they want to come back and look at this issue?

If an individual veteran couldn't prove it was his or her veteran status *explicitly* that caused the termination—an essentially impossible task—it was irrelevant. Screw the data.

Screw "harassment, intimidation, and coercion."

Each case was required to stand along. Where's the unequivocal—you've been fired because you're a veteran—proof?

The only success we had (which Labor had nothing to do with) was a single case involving a gay Vietnam-era veteran with AIDS. Bob had been unable to get assistance from the administration or any of the gay rights, politically correct sectors on campus after getting his walking papers. He was disenfranchised by everyone . . . *almost*.

To his surprise, our AMVETS post took up his cause. Veterans understand how the freedoms in this country—*all the freedoms*—were gained, even if the PC crowd doesn't. And although Bob wasn't an in-country Vietnam vet, he had served America in the Air Force for four years during that era.

Therefore, AMVETS 1974 stepped into the fray.

We were able to enlist the aid of U.S. Congresswoman Debra Pryce (thanks to Marcy McCreary in her Columbus office), and she put enough pressure on President Gee's office to keep Bob employed. At least he was able to keep his university medical insurance coverage until he succumbed to the disease a couple years later.

That was our only bona fide win (if you can call it that)—186 veterans canned, 1 saved. And at least the one saved could die later as an Ohio State employee.

Clearly, our victories were measured in small increments.

And while I probably shouldn't have been surprised based on how things were going, the GAO report didn't turn out as we had hoped either. In fact, it was absolutely worthless . . . Number 10 and then some.

The title said it all: "Federal Contractor Hiring—Effect of Veteran Hiring Legislation Is Unknown."[21]

Basically, it was determined that federal contractors didn't use veteran status as a consideration for hiring (even though it is mandated by law), and the Department of Labor didn't use the veterans' employment data collected since 1988 for anything. It was just collected, then ignored. As a result, the GAO couldn't tell whether the 1974 legislation was working or not.

Apparently, they didn't care either.

Talk about letting the air out. Damn!

Almost two decades had elapsed, and still nothing was being done. It was just so matter-of-fact. Nope, we looked, but we can't tell whether the law has done any good.

The GAO didn't nail federal contractors for not complying with the law. They didn't rip the OFCCP for failing to enforce the law.

They didn't even suggest that congress fix it . . . or do anything about it. They just did a "Gooberesque" "gee, golly, gosh, we can't tell."

And this is the congressional investigative arm?

What a worthless damn waste!

Plus, it was beginning to have the feel of 1969 to 1970 all over again.

Fortunately, for my sanity if nothing else, we discovered some additional allies in Washington at about the same time all this cheery news was coming down. It seems that the old '60s antiwar factions on college campuses that had been reawakened by the war in the Persian Gulf were taking new shots at the military, and at least a couple members of congress were rather pissed off about it.

We were able to convince some of their staffers that there was an obvious relationship to the antiveteran issues we were dealing with in Ohio—these are the same campus assholes mentality-wise. They hate anything military or military veteran-related.

In New York, Representative Gerald Solomon was irate, and then some, when he discovered that universities in his home state were not allowing military recruiters on campus to meet with students. As a result, he sponsored an amendment to the DOD appropriations bill to prohibit colleges with such practices from receiving DOD funding[22] . . . an attention-getter for money-hungry university administrators.

Similarly, Congressman Pompeo from California decided something needed to be done when university loonies in his state tried to have ROTC thrown off campus at Sacramento State. He joined forces with Solomon and eventually they were able to get legislative prohibitions imposed on almost all federal funding if the antimilitary fanatics interfered with either military recruiting or ROTC on college campuses.

The ivory tower rationale, of course, was that the military discriminates against gays. Therefore, military recruiters and ROTC shouldn't be allowed in the intellectual elites' hallowed halls.

So where were these hypocrites when our gay Vietnam-era veteran at Ohio State needed help?

They sure as hell weren't interested in Bob's rights being violated. But that was probably just another instance where an individual's military veteran standing canceled any other protected group status.

You're a gay veteran? You're a black veteran?

Sorry, there are no affirmative action rights for you on campus; those are canceled if you've been in the military.

What a bunch of two-faced frauds . . . PC *assholes!*

* * *

Not surprisingly, the word was starting to get around nationally about our veterans' activities and the campus wars in Ohio. That notoriety was even getting me out on the rubber chicken circuit a bit, starting with the Veterans' Day festivities in 1993.

First, I was invited by the Vietnam Veterans Institute (VVI) to write an article for publication in their journal[23] and to give the keynote address on discrimination against veterans at their Council of Scholars Colloquium on November 12.[24] The event took place at the Army Navy Club in Washington, D.C., and it was a first-class affair.

Peter Rollins, an Oklahoma State English professor—of all things—organized the colloquium, along with Jerry Yates, the VVI president, and Adrian Cronauer, the vice president. And, yes, it was the real "Goooooooood Morning, Vietnam" Adrian Cronauer played by Robin Williams in the movie.

Among the experts on the Vietnam War attending was Michael Lee Lanning, the officer with Charlie Company, 2nd of the 3rd with the 199th who wrote the book where I found out what happened to my old unit after I got wounded and shipped out. He's the author that described "the Infantryman's fate in Delta Company" . . . "the finality of death."[25]

Even recalling "the finality of death," it was sure great to get totally away from the politically correct campus crowd for a while. It was even better to interact with a group of highly informed individuals who really understood what the Vietnam War was all about.

Of course, Michael Lee and I didn't see eye-to-eye with regard to the war-fighting leadership of Colonel Mess. Michael Lee—a Texas A&M Aggie—much preferred the "cowboy" approach of the guy who replaced Colonel Mess as battalion commander when his tour was up.

I strongly favored the "kick butt, while keeping your guys alive" tactics employed by Colonel Mess. I saw too much of the "body count regardless of cost" attitude of his high-flying predecessor to endorse cowboy as the way to go.

Regardless, the Council of Scholars discussions were certainly interesting and informative. And they were one hell of an improvement over the conventional dialogue in the OSU intellectual wasteland.

That evening was interesting as well . . . terrifying, but interesting.

An Evening of Blues, Poetry, and Prose—a black-tie affair—was scheduled for the Arts Club of Washington, in James Madison's former home. Adrian was the MC, and I was the prose part of the event . . . reading from my draft of *VIETNAM'S WAR OF HATE* as it stood at the time.[26]

Scary!

It was about like crawling over the rim of that damn gully back in Vietnam.

Laying your guts out there for everyone to see isn't all that easy.

And the gaggle of elderly women—members and officers of the Arts Club—didn't help the matter either. Reciting some of the more colorful language in the early chapters to guys who had served in Nam was one thing; I wasn't sure how understanding a refined group of 70- and 80-year-old socialites might be.

To play it safe, I started out by apologizing for all the four-letter words they were about to hear in that tranquil setting surrounded by beautiful works of art. I didn't want my finale for the evening to shock any of them into some sort of coronary episode.

It didn't go too badly though.

In fact, I got a standing ovation at one point and did an encore reading from a section I hadn't planned to recite. Afterwards, the very prim and proper president of the club . . . one of those advanced-age, elegant ladies I was worried about . . . gave me a big hug and whispered in my ear: "I've really heard all those words before."

What a terrific feeling . . . laying it all out there and not getting laughed off stage.

* * *

All in all, there were probably a lot more lows than highs those last couple years I was at Ohio State, but I survived. My mental health wasn't what it should be—and neither was my out-of-control blood pressure. However, the nine-month appointment gave us lots of time in New Mexico in the summers.

Looking for another way to make a living became a major pastime while there. Marcy and I considered the possibility of purchasing a gift shop, looking at one rather generally in Red River and one quite seriously in Eagle Nest.

I looked into real estate sales as a possibility—gathering information on the Norris School of Real Estate in Albuquerque. That got serious enough to line up a verbal commitment for a job from a broker in Red River if we made the move.

I considered teaching opportunities at community colleges in New Mexico as an option. Anything, anywhere looked better than staying at Ohio State.

Finally, though, it came down to some consulting I was doing related to my Ohio State responsibilities that gave me a way out. I had run the Comprehensive Cancer Center's Tumor Procurement Service for more than a decade, and the

National Cancer Institute routinely rated it as one of the top services in the country during their regular reviews.

My old business training paid some dividends in that regard.

Based on the reputation we established for running an unbelievably cost-effective operation, I started to be asked to consult for other cancer centers on efficiency management for various centralized services they were providing. For some reason, those were really enjoyable diversions.

Most importantly, though, I was good at working out what needed to be done to improve the effectiveness of these shared services.

So, all that was left to do was to figure out how to make a living at it—*anywhere else*—before Ohio State pushed me over the edge.

I was teetering *waaay* too close.

ANTI-AMERICA AMERICANS . . . LADY LIBERTY'S ACHILLES' HEEL

— Socialist-Loving "Intellectuals" —

Enduring Truth: *Elitist third-rate intellects vilify first-class patriots as second-class citizens.*

Chapter 21

GOODBYE COLUMBUS

Good riddance is more like it.

Mahatma Gandhi: *"Truth is by nature self-evident.
As soon as you remove the cobwebs of ignorance
that surround it, it shines clear."*[1]

With the benefit, yet again, of perfect hindsight, it's clear that the beginning of the end of my multi-decade-long journey in search of that elusive welcome home occurred in 1994. It began with our move to Manhattan, Kansas for my new job at Kansas State University.

Reaching the end of that meandering trail took another seven years. Elusive it was.

Moving to Kansas had never been on my list of lifelong goals . . . the opposite is more like it. Kansas was a far-too-wide state to drive through while heading to New Mexico for a vacation in God's country or heading back home to Ohio. Stopping never seemed like a good idea except perhaps when a kidney call or gas was needed.

Of course, there was one curious exception in 1993.

While blowing down I-70, heading home and thinking we were never going to make it through this damn state, Fort Riley emerged on our left. Not that that was anything new. We'd been down this road before.

However, this time as I glanced at the Big Red One up on the water tower and the row upon row of military vehicles parked near the highway, a yearning for the comradeship of the military swept over me.

Fort Riley looked welcoming and safe.

It had been years since I thought about that aspect of Army life . . . the close-knit family. I'd been away from that family far too long.

Just for an instant it felt like Fort Riley was calling me home.

But, in another moment, the fort and the yearning for that past-life comradeship disappeared in the rearview mirror behind us.

Keep the hammer down. Home—the place where we live—is another 800 long miles ahead.

Kansas wasn't totally out of the picture for the year nonetheless.

Because of all my veteran's activities in recent years, I was one of about a hundred Vietnam vets invited by the VVI to a Christmas party in Washington. The Kansas senior senator, Bob Dole, was the host.

Marcy convinced me that it was a once-in-a-lifetime opportunity, so denting our savings to cover the trip would probably be worth it.

It was.

Senator Dole spent almost the full four hours with us and his wife Elizabeth joined him about halfway through the party in his huge office in the capitol. She had been at some White House function and immediately informed the senator, "Bill sends his regards."

The senator—rolling his eyes—shot back: "Oh, yeah, I'm sure!"

That certainly brought a chuckle from the vets within earshot.

And there were lots of bigger laughs exchanged with our veteran host that December 17 evening. What a droll wit the man had.

It's too bad the news media never bothered showing the humorous side of Senator Dole back then.

Never in my wildest, most off-the-wall prognostications did I consider the possibility that we'd be living in the senator's home state within a few months. No way!

The Cancer Center at the University of New Mexico—where I had been consulting for a couple years—was in the process of creating a job for me. So, I presumed it was just a matter of time until we would make the move to my favorite place, the Land of Enchantment. Since I helped write the job description, I wasn't too worried about being competitive in the mandatory university search process.

Creating a university position takes time though, and this one seemed to be dragging on forever. So, when I saw an ad in *The Chronicle of Higher Education* for a job at Kansas State with university-wide responsibilities almost exactly like those I'd drafted for the Cancer Center at UNM, I shipped off a letter of application.

Associate vice provost for research, huh?

What the heck, it couldn't hurt anything to toss my hat in the ring.

Little did I know that the search at K-State would move along at light speed . . . but it did.

By the time the search process at New Mexico was getting to the point of selecting finalists to invite for interviews, I had an offer in hand from K-State that I had to accept or turn down. And while I knew I'd get the offer from the Cancer Center if I stayed in the race, there were lots of conflicting issues to consider.

New Mexico felt more like home than anywhere I had ever been. At the time, it was my top choice; Marcy still liked Columbus though.

One rock-solid vote for New Mex; one . . . oh, maybe, vote.

Of course, the job that was created at the Cancer Center was not a tenure-track position. I'd have to give up the security of a tenured—you can't be fired—faculty position at UNM. The tenure safety net could probably be maintained at K-State, and heaven knows that had been of critical importance at Ohio State in recent years.

The big dogs at OSU would have sent me packing in a heartbeat if they could have. Sorry, but I've got tenure.

Then there was the fact that the job in New Mexico would have required taking a 15 percent pay cut, while the one at K-State would provide a 40 percent increase. Although that should have made the matter a "no brainer," it still turned out to be a difficult, agonizing decision.

New Mexico was a powerful, powerful draw.

Eventually, though, there were just too many intangibles that tilted things in favor of K-State. Most importantly, the people I interacted with in Manhattan during the interview process all seemed great. They were real.

The phony PC crap floating knee-deep everywhere around OSU didn't seem to exist at K-State . . . or was minimal at most. And then there was Fort Riley right next door to Manhattan. Somehow that was a real plus as well. It just felt right . . . that welcoming call while speeding by.

I also knew that Vietnam vets at New Mexico were getting dumped on just like at Ohio State. Without tenure or the ability to keep my mouth shut, that could be a case of jumping from the frying pan into the fire.

The final "vote"—not that there really was one—was probably one for Kansas and one abstention, but the move was made in early August of 1994. My lab operation at OSU was closed down the end of June, we spent July getting ready to go and hit the road in August.

Goodbye, Columbus! It's time to *didi mau* out of here.

Except for our daughter, Lorna, and grandson, Zeke, being left behind, the image of Columbus disappearing in the rearview mirror was a marvelous sight. I was definitely in need of a permanent change of scenery. However, leaving Lorna and Zeke behind was really tough, particularly on Marcy, but on me too.

I was going to miss seeing them every week, but I had to get out of Ohio. To me, it was essentially life or death . . . literally, no choice.

Beyond the simple fact that I was enjoying my new job from day one, there were a few other things that confirmed the correctness of the choice that was made, Kansas over New Mexico, at least. First, the director of the Cancer Center at UNM who created the position for me was forced out a few months later . . . not a good sign. Then, the position I would have held and the person who filled it were eliminated soon thereafter.

That's fairly convincing—it could have been me out on the street. That lack of tenure would have been a biggie.

However, there were some positive indicators as well.

Not long after we moved to Kansas, an official-looking letter arrived from Washington. It was from Senator Dole congratulating me on my new job at K-State. He touched upon the Vietnam veterans' Christmas party in his office the previous year, and then commented that he was "delighted that a fellow veteran will be making a difference in Manhattan."

That was certainly a plus.

The real clincher, though, was provided by our family doctor in Manhattan, Scott Coonrod.

Having spent twenty years of my life in medical schools, I tend to stay away from MDs as much as possible (I know how few of them actually go into medicine for the right reasons—helping people *versus* making money). Nonetheless, I had to go see Scott (one of the really good ones) soon after we moved to Manhattan in 1994, but then it was two, two-and-a-half years before I went back to see him again.

When Dr. Coonrod came into the room that second time, glancing over the vitals the nurse had written on the chart, he looked puzzled. He asked me to roll up my sleeve so he could take my blood pressure again, which he did.

Then, mumbling under his breath, "that can't be right," he asked me to roll up the other sleeve. After checking both arms, he finally said:

"How do you explain the fact that your blood pressure is 40 to 50 points lower now than it was the first time you came in here?"

Huh!

How, indeed?

Even being in a university administration position that by its nature should have been stress-inducing (my signature went on all grants and contracts assuming legal liability for compliance with the terms), I suspected I knew the answer. Escaping the corrupt antiveteran bigots at *THE* Orwellian Stalinist University may have had something to do with it.

K-State proved to be a remarkably military-friendly, veteran-friendly campus . . . unbelievably so. Although my veterans' activities diminished appreciably when we moved, those that were undertaken were all done openly for everyone to see.

Nobody at K-State seemed to think that was a problem.

I had already made a commitment to attend the November 1994 VVI Veterans' Day events prior to taking the job at K-State, so I had only been on the job a couple months when my first veterans' function came up. The Hoffberger Center for Professional Ethics at the University of Baltimore was hosting *The History and Legacy of Those Who Served in Vietnam*. Jim Stever and I, plus an attorney, did a presentation entitled, "Employment Disparities and the Vietnam Veteran," and my boss at Kansas State thought that was perfectly acceptable.

General Westmoreland was the honoree at the event, so the tux had to be dragged out again for an exceptional reception the evening before the program. Then, I shared a booth with the general the next morning at breakfast . . . another oddity for a draftee shake 'n' bake NCO.

The folks at K-State had a number of opportunities to find out the specifics about my veterans' activities as well.

In April 1995, my picture showed up in the *Washington Post*[2] and I was quoted in two articles regarding discrimination against veterans on college campuses—"No Glory, No Parades, No Jobs?"[2] and "Missing in Action: Vietnam Vets in the White House."[3] A friend back east, Jack Wheeler, did the companion White House study.

Jack had determined that within the Vietnam generation age group at the time (ages 39 to 59), 30 percent of the men had served in the armed forces.[3] Only

5 percent of male members of the Clinton White House staff of that age had done so, compared to 34 percent in the Bush White House. So, when I pointed out that "many college campuses remain inhospitable to vets largely because so many antiwar students in the 1960s are professors today,"[3] the same rationale could apply to other non-university situations as well.

On Memorial Day in 1995, Bob Edwards on the Morning Edition of National Public Radio interviewed me—along with Jack in Washington—about the same topics. The feedback I got from numerous K-State faculty members and administrators who heard the NPR interview or saw the stories in the *Post* were uniformly complimentary. They congratulated me on my role in uncovering and publicizing these outrageous injustices.

That was certainly a refreshing change from what I encountered at Ohio State.

Jim Stever and I also wrote a rather pointed article for the VVI's journal that year entitled, "Academe: Not So Hallowed Halls for Veterans."[4] It summarized much of the data we had collected concerning veterans' discrimination at universities across the country and it outlined some of the probable causes and effects.

That article followed up on the one I did the year before nailing the U.S. Department of Labor for failing to enforce the law for veterans.[5] Again, the folks at K-State who saw the articles were appalled by the findings. Clearly, such things wouldn't be tolerated if women or minorities were the group being targeted.

It's funny how obvious that can be to people with some common sense and an understanding that diversity is supposed to be inclusive, not exclusive. Unfortunately, that doesn't appear to be the case at most universities.

Jim and I were surprised to discover that the data we'd collected from some universities was even worse than at Ohio State . . . as hard as that was to imagine. At American University in D.C. and San Diego State University, the official reports they filed with the federal government documented that 0.7 and 0.05 percent of their employees, respectively, were Vietnam-era veterans.[4]

APPALLING!

Evidently, the problems we discovered span the country, coast to coast. Considering that the reports cover everything from custodial workers to faculty and administrative positions and these were at a time when Vietnam-era veterans comprised 6 percent of the American work force nationally, the numbers were abysmal at best.

At the New School for Social Research in New York City where Adrian got his master's degree, they were employing forty-eight Vietnam-era veterans in 1988 when they filed their first federally mandated veterans' employment (VETS-100) report. It took only three years to purge the system—*zero* were employed in 1991.[4]

A clean sweep: Now you see them, now you don't.

"VETERAN CLEANSING," as we referred to it in our VVI article,[4] was not uncommon at universities once they discovered that they had Vietnam-era veterans on the payroll. Most just weren't quite so blatant about it as the New School.

The basis for this phenomenon came about in 1987 and 1988 when the U.S. Department of Labor began requiring all federal contractors to report annually on the new hires and the total number of employees that were Vietnam-era veterans.

Prior to that time, most universities didn't know they were even employing these folks. But, a large number of universities—advocates for affirmative action that they are—took corrective action, cleansing their rosters of these undesirables when they found out.

My colleagues at Kansas State who became aware of the issue seemed to find that reprehensible.

Odd for a university campus, isn't it?

They considered the financial penalties for Vietnam veterans to be reprehensible as well. A study we reported on from Harvard documented a negative impact of 15 percent on the annual earnings of Vietnam vets compared to non-veterans a decade and a half after their service.[4, 6]

Myra MacPherson had it right when she said, "Vietnam was a war that asked everything of a few and nothing of most in America."[7]

Sadly, the few—and their families—are still paying the price.

And far too many universities are responsible for this injustice.

Regrettably, the injustices aren't limited just to employment issues either. Neil, a graduate teaching assistant at Ohio State in Joe Guilmartin's Vietnam War course, discovered firsthand that educational opportunities can be impacted as well . . . impacted significantly.

Neil was older than most of the GTAs (graduate teaching assistants) at Ohio State. He had recently retired from the Marines as a lieutenant colonel, having made the corps a career after serving in Vietnam a couple decades earlier. But when Neil decided to retire and go to graduate school, he looked at some of the most prestigious history programs in the country, believing he had the credentials to go anywhere he might choose.

Wrong! Yale University rejected his application.

So, employing standard Marine "assault the beachhead" tactics, Neil called the History department's graduate program director to find out why he hadn't been admitted. The guy informed Neil that he didn't have the records in front of him, but the history Ph.D. program at Yale turns down LOTS of good applicants (*they admit only the best*) . . . it was probably his undergraduate grade point average.

So, Neil told him what his GPA was, to which the guy replied, "Oh, that couldn't have been it. It must have been the scores on your graduate record exam."

When Neil relayed his rather outstanding GRE scores, the increasingly addled prof began stammering away, "Oh, ah, gee . . . ah, that couldn't have been it either. Gosh, I don't know."

After hemming and hawing a bit longer, the light bulb finally went on though. The crystal-clear explanation from this elite Ivy Leaguer went something like: "Wait a minute! Are you the *Marine*?"

Bingo!

How's that for the basis to be denied admission to a university?

As incredible as it may seem, it's probably not that uncommon. And, unfortunately, it's also not something that affects only over-the-hill Vietnam vets or university admissions decisions either.

Jim Stever knew of a young student at the University of Cincinnati who was a proud member of the school's Army ROTC unit during the Persian Gulf crisis in 1991. The first time this fresh-out-of-high-school teenager wore his military uniform to English, the professor asked him in front of the class: "Why do you want to be a murderer?"[4]

How could anyone—*theoretically* an educator in this case—justify asking such an outrageous, despicable question?

Clearly, the young man was not going to be judged fairly by this antimilitary bigot.

How much did the student's English grade suffer as a result? And how many of his other teachers felt the same way, but were more clandestine in conveying their hatred?

There are lots of ways to dole out punishment.

These hypocrites—extolling the virtues of academic freedom and diversity day in and day out—only adhere to those principles when everything is excluded they don't believe in. The social engineering carried out by the university "thought police" is still in the mold of Hitler and Stalin . . . it's just less obvious in the campus ivy-clad stalag/gulag.

The diametrically opposed difference in the administration's attitude at K-State regarding veterans' issues compared to those back in Ohio became crystal-clear when I was asked to sit in for my boss at a president's staff meeting. Congressman Ryun was going to be in attendance, and I was asked to give an overview of the research efforts at the university.

When my turn came, President Wefald (knowing the congressman's pro-defense stance) introduced me by launching into a ten-minute oration about all the great things I was doing for military veterans. Not once did he express any misgivings about hiring "unrepentant veterans"—like me—at K-State.

Thanks, Jon! It's *reeeally* appreciated.

And, as expected, the president's comments resonated with the congressman, a supporter of all things military-related—*big time.*

But if I thought the hawkish Jim Ryun could beat the military service drum, a visit to Pat Roberts' senate office in D.C. introduced me to the leader of the percussion section. I've known since my active-duty days that there's no such thing as a former Marine . . . once a Marine, always a Marine . . . but Senator Roberts shows the world that he remains "one of the few, the proud, the Marines." His office was chock-full of corps paraphernalia.

He's proud all right, as well as the ultimate class act and a hoot to boot.

I'd go into battle with him any time, any place.

God, it's great to be around people you can count on.

And at the time, I didn't think anything could surprise me regarding the level of contempt for military veterans back in Ohio. Nonetheless, I was blown away to discover that the universities back there wouldn't even take money—research dollars—if the research results might be helpful to veterans.

Yes, the contempt must run awfully, awfully deep.

Soon after I arrived at K-State, the state legislature in Ohio appropriated $100,000 for a study of Ohio Gulf War veterans, focusing on health and other outcomes of their service. None of the public universities in Ohio applied for the funds. Even a follow-up request by the governor's office asking each university president to have their researchers submit proposals was unable to get any to comply.

That deeply felt hatred must be commonly felt as well. Not one of the thirteen state-supported schools—*zero*—could dredge up a single social scientist willing to do the project.

The study was done though.

CSVS, the Ohio not-for-profit corporation with Jim Stever at the helm (and now with Adrian Cronauer on board as a director), applied for and was awarded the funds . . . with a major subcontract to Kansas State. It turns out that we had lots of faculty expertise of relevance out in Manhattan to do such studies. Moreover, Ohio got a superb analysis and report for their money even though they had to cross a few state lines to find a military-friendly, veteran-friendly campus to help out.

But the K-State president thought these are good things to do . . . things I should help cultivate. Most other folks here seemed to as well.

Strange the difference 800 miles can make.

Concerns over Gulf War Syndrome and other adverse outcomes of serving in the Persian Gulf caused legislators in Kansas to want similar studies done in Kansas. I testified before committees of the Kansas House and Senate regarding the work K-State had done for Ohio, and the legislature followed up with the necessary funding.

Lastly on the list of veterans' activities early in my tenure at K-State, I was named by the U.S. Secretary of Health and Human Services to an oversight committee for a massive Agent Orange health study. The Air Force was in the midst of 25-year, $145 million assessment of the health impacts of those involved in Operation Ranch Hand in Vietnam, the spraying of Agent Orange and related herbicides. The prospective study had already been ongoing for many years and the oversight committee was in place to assess progress and, supposedly, make recommendations.[i]

Once again, Admiral Zumwalt and Dick Christian with the American Legion were involved in getting me named to the committee, just like 1993 when they got me to testify before the National Academy committee. In this case, my role was to review cancer-related aspects of the study.[8, 9, ii]

And as opposed to what had happened to me in Ohio, all these veterans-related activities didn't hurt my credibility in Kansas—overtly or covertly. I was made president of the KSU Research Foundation in 1995, overseeing the patenting and commercialization of university inventions . . . finally able to use my old business training in a relevant way. Facilitating company start-ups in Manhattan based on university technologies was great fun.

I was promoted from associate vice provost to vice provost for research and dean of the graduate school on an interim basis in 1998 when my boss retired.

Those appointments were made permanent in 1999 following a national search and interview process.

Fostering university-wide research and scholarly activities at Kansas State was enjoyable from day one. Getting back into the graduate education side of the endeavor made it even better.

When I was up for the promotion, the state congressman who had taken a lead role in sponsoring the Kansas Gulf War study, Dan Thimesch, provided a letter of recommendation on my behalf. So did Sid Warner from the Kansas Board of Regents.

What a difference!

The military-friendly, veteran-friendly nature of the K-State campus also allowed us to leverage research and graduate education opportunities with various branches of the Department of Defense. While almost all universities will happily take DOD money, most would prefer to never see anyone in uniform on their campus—as Congressman Solomon discovered in New York.

At K-State, we like having active-duty military personnel around. We appreciate what they're doing for the country . . . protecting America's freedoms. I suspect that it's been that way for quite some time here too, what with Fort Riley next door and lots of active duty and retired Army personnel living in Manhattan. Our next-door neighbor, John White, was a retired Army Command sergeant major. The woman living two doors up when we moved here, Alberta Anthony, was Bob Dole's physical therapist in the military when he was wounded in the Second World War. Alberta continued to get Christmas cards from him every year.

The magnitude of the difference was really driven home for me in 1999 though—October 15—by a thirty-year-old picture in the newspaper of a march down Poyntz Avenue. It was the Manhattan version of the Vietnam Moratorium that had drawn three thousand, plus or minus, in Whitewater as marchers, spectators, and basic hell-raisers back in 1969 . . . not one of my favorite days there.

The old photo told a different story in Manhattan.

The panoramic view down Poyntz showed a total of *four* marchers—PERIOD. There wasn't another soul visible anywhere; marching, gawking, or giving two shits whatsoever.

Yes, there's no question about it: relocating to Kansas wasn't a bad move . . . not a bad move at all.

SURVIVAL'S BOTTOM LINE . . . "WE *NOT* ME" . . . FREEDOM'S BOTTOM LINE

Enduring Truth: *True military-friendly, veteran-friendly shows; veiled hate does too.*

Chapter 22

PRIVATES, LIEUTENANTS, AND WANNABES

The good, the bad, and the ugly. What's wrong with this picture?

Mark Twain: *"If you tell the truth, you don't have
to remember anything."*[1]
[*Or make shit up*]

VIETNAM'S WAR OF HATE may well have gotten shelved permanently along the way had it not been for a few pesky friends and colleagues—Dolph Hatfield and his wife, Mary, prime among them—who kept pushing me to get it done.

Dolph worked at the National Institutes of Health, just outside Washington, D.C., and he's one of those few scientists in the world who worked on tRNA at one time or another. As a result, our scientific paths used to cross in out-of-the-way places periodically—Erlangen, Germany, Umeå, Sweden, Vancouver, British Columbia—and we stayed in touch after I became a research dropout.

Since my job took me to Washington every now and then, it was easy to catch margaritas with Dolph and Mary at La Casita or the Cosmos Club occasionally. At some point along the way, I had shared the early parts of the book with them way back when I was still at Ohio State. Dolph has insisted for years that the story was one that needed to be told, and he and Mary were persistent with their needling. That helped to keep me motivated.

In addition, Dolph was one of those who leaned toward the antiwar side of the issues back in the '60s . . . *but* he was not spouting treason, waving North Vietnamese flags, or burning buildings. As a result, I have always valued his "opposing team" perspective.

There was another viewpoint of importance back in Washington as well, that of a Vietnamese boat person—a lucky survivor, Dặng Văn Dông—who operated the Saigon Gourmet restaurant. I would visit with this young man from time to time during my trips back there, enjoying superb Vietnamese cuisine in the process—a bowl of *pho*, a spring roll with *nuoc mam* fish sauce.

Dặng told me of his escape from Vietnam as a youngster when his parents used jewelry they had hidden to bribe soldiers and guards. His mother and father stayed behind, but they made sure that their four children would depart at different times on different boats, knowing some would not survive.

Think about that. How bad it must have been for a mother and father to send their children off knowing some would die?

Dặng's parents were right too. Two—a son and daughter—were never heard from again, but Dặng and another son made it. And like so many Vietnamese I knew in 1969, Dặng was a terrific, caring person.

Yes, there were occasional reminders of those times in Vietnam . . . the cause and the people. The book couldn't be totally forgotten.

So even though I was enjoying my job at K-State—feeling motivated and enthused—and was always too busy to take a weekend to work on the book, I'd still find a minute or two sporadically to pen a few words here and there. Or, at least, I'd think about it.

There was never any big rush though, because I could never figure out how the book was going to end. Since the issues never seemed to go away and our attempts to resolve the problems never worked, I wasn't sure it was ever going to have a fitting conclusion. Maybe the lost welcome home couldn't be found.

How do you wrap up a story that never ends?

Nonetheless, the message VIETNAM'S WAR OF HATE was intended to deliver—that my experience wasn't all that unique—still seemed applicable multiple decades after the fact. It had been a slap in the face for me coming home at age twenty-five.

What must it have been like for proud 19- and 20-year-olds returning from their first extended stay away from home?

That issue did need to be raised, so I kept plodding along.

Occasionally, though, something would really fan the VIETNAM'S WAR OF HATE flames one way or another.

The 1995 revelations by Robert Strange McNamara in his book, *In Retrospect— The Tragedy and Lessons of Vietnam*,[2] should have poured lots of fuel on the fire, but they didn't. I had already decided he was a worthless piece of garbage, so his disclosure that he knew we should have gotten out of Vietnam in the early to mid '60s wasn't all that shocking. It sure as hell doesn't justify all the American lives lost after that, but it didn't serve as a motivator to get back to the book.

However, when the various articles were coming out nationally about discrimination against veterans on college campuses, Vietnam vets from around the country were tracking me down to provide stories about their own particular situation or location. One of those contacts stirred the embers quite a bit.

I got a call from a Vietnam veteran back east with a somewhat different perspective than I'd heard or thought about before. He worked for the board of education in Maine, and it was his contention that there are significant numbers of teachers at all levels—elementary, junior high, and high school, not just universities—that exhibit the same behaviors and biases we documented.

He felt that antimilitary, antiveteran prejudices are the norm, not the exception, for those in primary and secondary education who were on college campuses in the 1960s and '70s . . . for the males at least. Therefore, he thought we should consider expanding our studies.

He pointed out that another way to extend one's college deferral during the Vietnam War was to go into teaching, and teaching was obviously not the calling for many of them; it just helped them dodge the draft. He thought earning teaching credentials might have been utilized even more, since lots of guys didn't have the academic credentials to get into Ph.D. programs.

In thinking about it, that might have occurred by a couple different routes. First, I don't believe there was a time limit on earning a bachelor's degree prior to 1968. You just had to be a full-time student in good standing, that is, not on probation due to bad grades. So, switching to an education major late in one's undergraduate studies could have added a year or two to completion—graduation.

Alternately, enrolling in a postbaccalaureate master's in education program had the potential to extend one's draft deferment another couple years before 1968 when graduate deferments were ended. This wouldn't have been as advantageous as a four-to-five-year doctoral curriculum and dissertation project, but some might have qualified for a doctorate of education program after the master's degree.

And, clearly, these folks wouldn't have wanted unrepentant Vietnam vets around. Plus, they wouldn't have wanted anything factual about the Vietnam War to cloud their indoctrination of students in their charge.

That rather disturbing thought certainly got my attention! So even though he didn't have published data about S-2 deferments while getting teaching certifications, the concept was feasible. Plus, he saw the outcome.

It was bad enough thinking about the misinformation and propaganda being disseminated to college students. Now we had to worry about these spineless lowlifes poisoning the minds of our kids all the way down to elementary school?

Shit!

With only about 10 percent of the American population being military veterans at the time, we sure as hell didn't need a totally biased, one-sided point of view being delivered to our impressionable youth.

Who's going to present the other—*factual*—side of the story?

Not only did the study need to be done, I also needed to get back to the book and get it finished.

Damn!

Then, sometime later, a movie about the Second World War sparked the kindling even further. It provided the impetus to move a couple additional chapters from conceptual to actual.

When *Saving Private Ryan* came out in the theaters in 1998, lots of folks—various colleagues at K-State and my sister among them—asked my opinion of the movie. Everyone recommended it highly, and when I continued to make excuses for not having gone yet, most suggested that I should really see it on the big screen.

Somehow, I never managed while it was still showing in Manhattan. The whole thing was just too reminiscent of *Platoon*. I had heard those same arguments before.

Finally, however, when it came out on video, Marcy and I watched it at home. And unlike *Platoon*, it was good. Of course, anything with Tom Hanks in it tends

179

to be excellent. But, in my opinion, *Saving Private Ryan* was just good, so it was also disappointing.

Something was missing. I couldn't put my finger on it exactly, but it just didn't do it for me.

The battle scenes were intense and probably realistic, I guess.

That wasn't it.

Tom Hanks did his usual superb job portraying the lead character in the movie. That wasn't it.

I chewed on it . . . thought about it from various angles, but I couldn't figure it out. Still, something wasn't right. It just didn't click.

Then, at work a couple days later, I was asked by a colleague who knew I had rented it, what I thought. Without even thinking, I simply blurted out: "Well, if that was an authentic representation of those who fought in the Second World War, the guys I served with in Vietnam were better."

BINGO!

That was it.

The self-sacrifices, the comradeship—the do anything and everything to protect the guy next to you—the things I had seen time and time again in Vietnam weren't there in *Saving Private Ryan*. These were not the characteristics of just a few . . . of one or two soldiers in a squad or platoon—not in Vietnam. These attributes were damn near universal.

That didn't come through in the movie. Tom Hanks' character was about it . . . maybe a few others as well.

No question, that was the problem with *Saving Private Ryan*.

It was like reading a secondhand account of what combat is all about . . . something like the difference between the first half and second half of General Moore and Joe Galloway's book, *We Were Soldiers Once . . . and Young*,[3] only drastically more so. Moore and Galloway captured the intensity and reality of battle in the first half of the story—the part they experienced firsthand. They captured it in spades.

And even though Moore and Galloway understood combat *BIG TIME* based on their Herculean battle in the Ia Drang Valley and their book is terrific (the best I read about Vietnam), the authenticity wasn't the same in the second half. In the latter part, they were relaying what happened to their replacements . . . during the withdrawal out of the area.

Moore and Galloway weren't there.

Saving Private Ryan was like that, only on a much grander scale. It was like combat as imagined by people—movie directors, actors—who had heard all the stories and yarns, but who hadn't actually experienced it themselves. They wouldn't understand the absolute—no questions asked—trust of placing one's life in the hands of others around them.

Regardless, my off-the-cuff assessment was right on the money.

If *Saving Private Ryan* was an authentic representation of those who fought in the Second World War, the guys I served with in Vietnam were better . . . *much* better.

Of course, even when I first said it, I didn't believe it was true, that the guys I served with in Vietnam were better.

Did I think they were as good as those of the "greatest generation" who fought in the Second World War?

Yes, no doubt about it.

Better?

No, absolutely not!

But that's where the movie fell short. It didn't capture the reality of war . . . the reality of those who serve and sacrifice. It's not about individual soldiers or even just a few of them. It's about close units, a family . . . only closer than most. It's about intertwined members of a well-honed, dedicated team, each one willing to risk their life for the other . . . and each one doing so . . . day after day after day.

You most likely can't understand, much less depict, that nuance—the concern for your "family"—if you haven't experienced it firsthand. Only then will you know how universal "brothers-you'll-die-for" really is.[4-10, i]

Remarkably, General Moore could communicate that aspect about his men in a lecture format. I heard him in Joe Guilmartin's class prior to his book being published. The self-sacrificing reality of battle he managed to convey was absolutely amazing.

I wouldn't have thought it possible in an oral presentation just using slides, but even General Moore didn't manage to assimilate that subtlety into the secondhand part of his book. He wasn't there.

More importantly, it wasn't his family, his loved ones. He didn't know them like he knew his men.

That may help explain some of the phonies out there too, the wannabes who try to make themselves into heroes they aren't. They know they missed something; they just don't know what it is. As a result, their stories tend to be totally off-the-wall—self-centered overkill to the Nth degree.

Moreover, anyone who has been in combat can't brag about their own exploits— *there but for the grace of God* . . . If a buddy, a brother next to them died, they didn't do enough. There's a humility among true combat veterans that cowards and liars will never understand.

However, little did I realize the magnitude of the wannabe issue until I ran across the book *Stolen Valor: How the Vietnam Generation Was Robbed of Its Heroes and Its History*.[11]

Oh, I had at least one face-to-face encounter with an individual of that ilk at the Vietnam Memorial in New Mexico some years back—a scruffy individual in motorcycle leathers with all sorts of Vietnam-related patches and the like. He was a big dude and he sure looked the part of the hardened combat veteran he was trying to portray.

I was working at the kiosk, searching the database, and he asked for my help when I finished. He wanted to look up information on a friend who had died in Vietnam. They were both musicians there . . . traveling about the country entertaining the troops.

Musicians? (Are you kidding me?)

His friend had overdosed on heroin, so he wanted to look him up on The Wall's database. I helped, getting him started, but I don't know if his buddy showed up on The Wall . . . probably. At least this guy didn't actually pretend to be something he wasn't—except in appearance, of course.

However, when I was still in Columbus, I had heard about a Texas combat vet (Special Forces, I think) discovering that a significant number of homeless individuals claiming to be Vietnam veterans were, in fact, not, so I knew they were out there. But the magnitude documented in *Stolen Valor* is utterly staggering.

The Vietnam wannabes include people of note and (some might contend) stature: Senator Harkin of Iowa claimed to have been a combat air patrol pilot in Nam.[12] Actor Brian Dennehy maintained he had been wounded in action.[13] Both were in the military, but there is no evidence that either served in Vietnam as they asserted.

Zero!

Both slip significant notches in the stature category as a result.

A full chapter of *Stolen Valor* addresses story after story—in newspapers, magazines, and books, as well as on TV—about homeless "Vietnam veterans." In few instances did the "investigative" reporters even try to document that the individuals in question actually experienced combat in Vietnam as claimed . . . they just took people's word for it.

In most cases the authors of *Stolen Valor* could find no evidence that they did. Often there was no documentation of the person ever serving in the military, and if there was, the military records didn't substantiate the bogus Vietnam War stories the homeless guys were telling.

Apparently, it's less newsworthy if fatigue-clad derelicts are just failures, not traumatized, drugged-out Vietnam veterans.

Possibly the worst of the TV reporting exposed by *Stolen Valor* was a CBS piece entitled "The Wall Within," hosted by Dan Rather[14] . . . the medically-unfit-to-complete Marine boot camp, TV anchor, Dan Rather.[15] The Vietnam vets interviewed—and most of them checked out as Vietnam vets—supposedly suffered from PTSD caused by the ghastly atrocities they had committed in Nam.

In Dan Rather's words, these guys were "haunted by their deeds."

Of course, when their military records were examined, only one had actually been in combat. Five of the six couldn't have done the awful things they reported. Rear echelon support troops (cooks, clerk typists, and the like—the vast, vast majority of those who served in Vietnam) didn't have the opportunity. And—surprise, surprise—the professed 16-year-old Navy Seal trained assassin in Vietnam really wasn't.

Nonetheless, CBS stood by their "documentary."

Somehow, it's reminiscent of the NBC stance in 1968 regarding the Tet Offensive—who cares if Tet was a huge defeat for the Vietcong?

The American people believe otherwise, so forget about setting the record straight.

Damn dirt bags!

A couple decades later, CBS was going down the same road—so what if these guys aren't authentic? The American people know Vietnam vets are screwed up, so what difference does it make?

THANKS A LOT!

The stories about screwed up Vietnam vets are so uniformly accepted nobody seems to think it's important. However, I know lots of Vietnam veterans, and they're all doing quite well . . . some exceptionally well.

Considering the vast number of bogus Vietnam veterans exposed in *Stolen Valor*, it makes me wonder:

Are most of the losers highlighted by the media actually frauds?

That would sure help propagate the myth the militarily unfit Dan Rather-types of the world want people to believe.

Many of the things B.G. Burkett (the lead author of *Stolen Valor*) relayed about his own experiences in and after Vietnam were consistent with my own. And would you believe that he was another member of the 199th Light Infantry Brigade?

Perhaps it isn't so unexpected based on the relative numbers of those who served in various units, but it sure seems out of whack. The 199th was an independently operating brigade, not a division like so many served with in Vietnam. It's curious the number of authors . . . and would-be authors . . . from the 199th Redcatchers.

Burkett's work was another reason for me to get back to *VIETNAM'S WAR OF HATE*. More fact-based information is needed out there to help set the record straight.

In thinking about it though, *Stolen Valor* served as a relatively unemotional prompt for me all in all. It didn't get my blood boiling.

However, a much more personal reminder of why I needed to finish the book began permeating the national news around the September 10, 2000. It was a sports-related item few others would have associated with antiveteran bigots on America's college campuses.

That's the way it struck me though.

It was the firing of Bobby Knight at Indiana.

Considering I have no idea whether Coach Knight ever served in the military, my instantaneous reaction—a raw nerve going into voltage overload—might seem a bit odd. Well, Bobby wasn't the cause of that jolt . . . or the associated emotional flashback.

Nope! It was slug slime doing the firing.

The IU president had been the provost at Ohio State when I was up for advancement to full professor—the S.O.B. who tried to keep the promotion from going through. That worthless . . . miserable . . . rotten . . .

Yes, there's no question, the sports newsbytes sparked a few dormant synapses there for a while.

And a visit to K-State by another Whitewater, Wisconsin native about six months later may have triggered a few more troubling, pissed-me-off-type of recollections as well. The world-famous military historian Stephen Ambrose was coming to Manhattan to give a Landon Lecture on April 19, 2001—adding his name to the list of U.S. presidents and other notables to give Landon Lectures.

Being from my hometown, Whitewater, originally, I suppose Stephen Ambrose should have served as a source of inspiration for my book, but that isn't quite the way it worked. In fact, having heard lots of stories about the anti-Vietnam War rhetoric he and his wife spouted ad nauseam when he was employed at K-State many years earlier, it was more of an opposite effect.

I haven't even managed to read any of his books yet. Oh, maybe one of these days.

Of course, a holdover reaction from my youth—when Stephen Ambrose's father was our family doctor—might play in there as well. As a small child, the only adult I can recall absolutely *hating* to see show up at our house was Dr. Ambrose—pain or something bad was about to ensue. I'd really like to believe, though, that my reading prejudices are based on something more noteworthy . . . like an eminent war historian protesting against military intervention without actually worrying about the facts involved.

But, whatever the reason, I wasn't all that disappointed when I had to go to Washington and missed Ambrose's Landon Lecture. It's likely, nonetheless, that his visit did serve as a subtle bump, nudging me back toward my long-stagnant literary undertaking.

However, the big time "get back to the book attention-getter" exploded from out of nowhere the very next week. It hit with startling accusations against former Nebraska Senator Bob Kerrey . . . president of the New School in New York City at the time.

I first read about Kerrey's alleged war crimes in the *Manhattan Mercury*,[16] then got the full *New York Times* version.[17] A member of his unit in Vietnam reported that Lieutenant Kerrey had led a group of Navy SEALs in an operation in Thanh Phong that rounded up and killed women and children in 1969. At least one Thanh Phong villager confirmed the story that the reporter first relayed to Senator Kerrey in 1998 as a work in progress.

The *Times* and their collaborator, CBS's *Sixty Minutes II*, sat on the story for two-and-a-half years. Apparently, they didn't want the allegations to break prior to the national elections.

Now, why would that matter?

Bob wasn't running for anything . . . only from something, perhaps. Of course, it may have had something to do with his decision not to run against Al for a shot at the presidency, and he didn't run for the senate again either. The other shoe was bound to drop sometime.

Or would it?

Would the *Times* and CBS have delayed the story if Bob Kerrey had been an "R" instead of a "D?"

Looking at it that way, it's probably remarkable they reported it at all . . . EVER.

While I have no way of knowing whether the accusations are true or not, I did see most of a lengthy TV interview of Mr. Kerrey about the story . . . by Tim Russert, I think it was . . . and I wasn't impressed. Even though it was not what

I'd call a hardball interview (more like slow pitch softball), Bob's responses were neither straightforward nor convincing.

There was lots of double-talk—spin-doctoring—and excessive finger pointing to identify something else—the military, an amoral war—as the cause for *anything* that might have happened that night. Whatever it was couldn't have been his fault.

And what was my appraisal after hearing Bob's gyrating replies?

He did it. One doesn't need to spin the truth.

Damn!

Just what we need: Another high-profile son-of-a-bitch proving how awful U.S. troops were in Vietnam.

Although I had hoped my friend Admiral Zumwalt hadn't been hoodwinked into awarding Kerrey the Bronze Star for his actions in Thanh Phong, that's probably what happened. Bob doesn't even deny now that his men killed a number of women and children that night; it's the rounding up and executing part that's in contention.

However, women and children weren't noted in the paperwork for the Bronze Star for valor he "earned" for he and his men killing twenty-one VC that night. And Lieutenant Kerrey obviously knew it at the time.

How many of the twenty-one were women and children, Bob?

That certainly would have made it a lot less heroic and valorous.

It seems that young Bob had problems telling the truth, the whole truth, and nothing but the truth back then.

So, why should anyone believe old Bob today?

Bob must have missed the childhood "war etiquette" lessons in the movies with Audie and the Duke. Plus, he must have slept through the military justice part of his Navy training as well. We certainly had plenty of that instruction in the Army.

Wouldn't officers get that information routinely?

And the crap he spouts about "unwritten rules of Vietnam"[17] is little more than that . . . CRAP. You don't kill unarmed old men, women, and children—noncombatants, prisoners, or whatever—regardless.

That's bullshit, Bob, but "unwritten rules" seems to be the standard B.S. fallback for any of those who returned from Vietnam with no pride within.

And what about the Congressional Medal of Honor (CMH)?

You "felt like a pawn in Nixon's war," like you were "being used" when you took it?[17]

Give me a *fucking* break!

No one *forced you* to take it!

Having read a few citations for the CMH over the years—documenting astonishing, selfless feats of valor—the information I've seen about Bob Kerrey's appears marginal, at best. Hopefully, there was more to it than just doing his job as an officer and losing a leg. If not, lots more—*and lots better*—servicemen in Vietnam should have received that highest of all awards for heroism.

It was surprising to find out a couple weeks after the story broke that students at the New School were calling for Mr. Kerrey to resign.[18] Our data from Adrian's alma mater suggested a substantial problem for *un*repentant Vietnam veterans there.

However, as a repentant veteran, Bob should have still been welcome. Of course, these were graduate students calling for his resignation, not the old-line counter-culture faculty and administrators from the '60s and '70s who needed their unenlightened antiwar prejudices reinforced.

Maybe that explains it . . . young folks with intelligence and common sense. If it looks like crap, feels like crap, and smells like crap, it's probably crap—Advanced Scholarly Analysis 999.

The Kerrey excrement was definitely throwing my life out of balance there for a while . . . rekindling old agitations. *Not* good.

I was already dealing with some deteriorating health issues that started back in 1999 when I was nailed by a tick. I had been on and off antibiotics since that September, and the arthritic-type joint and back pain made moving (and even sleeping) extremely difficult . . . except when the antibiotics would knock things back. Old Arty was absolutely killing my knees, making it a suck-it-up struggle just to navigate a few stairs.

I was beginning to suspect that a wheelchair was in the offing . . . not that I could have wheeled it because my left elbow and hand probably hurt worse than my knees.

But pain still isn't an excuse.

Dr. Coonrod finally ran every test in the book in January 2001 to see if there was some odd critter to blame; the likely culprits checked for early on, then again later, all came up negative. And the winner was *Francisella tularensis* . . . the bug that causes rabbit fever, a.k.a., tularemia.

"Franci" is not a personal acquaintance I'd recommend. She can be an agonizing, unpredictable pain in more ways than one.

At least the diagnosis got me put back on antibiotics—that helped.

In late February, navigating much better, I got to travel with a small contingent from Manhattan and Junction City to visit the Army's National Training Center at Fort Irwin, California. We were there to watch a large armored detachment from Fort Riley test their skills against the resident aggressor force.

The two-star commander of Fort Riley, Major General St. Ange, was there as well, and I was surprised to learn that he had been with the 199th in Vietnam a year after I was there. Astonishingly, he had served as the platoon leader of Delta Company's 2nd Platoon—my old "No Sweat" unit—in 1970.

We earned our Combat Infantry Badges with the same platoon.

Talk about your small worlds.

The Fort Riley troops did exceptionally well in the exercises, and the massive tank battles were fun to watch. They were certainly *very* different from the squad, platoon, and company-size infantry operations I was used to in Vietnam.

Unfortunately, I came down with a really nasty cold somewhere along the line on that trip. The upper respiratory problems that developed were as bad or worse than I've ever experienced . . . probably because my intimate companion Franci was still lingering about, compounding the problem.

Franci even managed to get old Mort stirred up as well as Arty—fickle bitch!

186

With relentless aches and pains everywhere, massive upper respiratory problems, and a nearly chronic lack of sleep, the early part of 2001 was not going particularly well. It was not going well at all.

In addition, we were understaffed to beat hell at work at the time, which didn't help a lot either. That problem was finally rectified in April, but I was about out of gas by then.

Then, the Kerrey crap hit. Some, like him, should be "repentant" veterans.

There's no question: I was in need of a break. I had actually been losing vacation time *again* . . . not the smartest way to go.

You'd think I would have learned.

So, when an invitation came to attend a board meeting at the Vietnam Veterans Memorial on Sunday of Memorial Day weekend, I was tempted to go. I could use a few days off.

And, as additional motivation, my pal Adrian was going to be the featured speaker on Memorial Day. That provided additional appeal. I could use some of his "Goooooooooood Morning, Vietnam" enthusiasm.

Yes, I'd have to give it some serious thought.

ANTI-AMERICA AMERICANS . . . LADY LIBERTY'S ACHILLES' HEEL

— Screw-the-Public Profiteers —

Enduring Truth: *"WE not ME" patriots win battles;*
"ME/FU" profiteers lose wars.

Chapter 23

PRIDE ... USE IT OR LOSE IT

Finding that elusive "welcome home" hidden in the Land of Enchantment.

In spite of all the inducements bestowed by Franci, Arty, and Mort, the decision to head to New Mexico for the 2001 Memorial Day services in Angel Fire wasn't finalized until just a couple weeks before. There are always good reasons to stay chained to the desk, especially when you're having fun at your job . . . working like hell, but enjoying it nonetheless. But, with my buddy Adrian as the keynote speaker and in dire, dire need of some R&R, I finally booked the flights.

Marcy would look after the kids—our two dogs—at home.

This was the Vietnam Veterans Memorial's thirtieth anniversary and, remarkably, twenty years had passed since our first encounter with that inspirational swept-wing chapel on a hillside in the Moreno Valley.

Where did all the years go?

And how could this be only my third Memorial Day weekend there over that period of time?

Little did I realize when I finally got around to making my motel reservation that the motorcycles would be back as well . . . in force, just like the first time, only worse. Apparently Red River had set a goal of 20,000 or more bikers for their resuscitated, reinvigorated Memorial Day weekend rally.

As a result, I had lots of trouble finding a place to stay: There were no rooms available at the motels I called in Eagle Nest or Angel Fire —Red River, quaint or not, was not an option. I finally found one in Taos.

Recalling the sleepless nights back in '88, the Harleys could have put a real crimp in the R&R goal for the trip. They didn't, though, thanks to my boss and his wife who insisted that I cancel the motel room and stay at their place in Taos once they heard about my plans.

Thank you, Jim and Sharon, thank you.

It wasn't until I was packed and on my way to Kansas City to catch the flight that I thought about my old jungle hat and fatigue jacket. Those two items had gone along on my earlier Memorial Day treks to New Mexico in 1988 and 1993 . . . evidence, I guess, of my bona fides for my Vietnam comrades.

But they hadn't been packed this time and, somehow, that didn't seem to matter. I had nothing to prove to anyone and, besides, I knew there were far too many wearing the garb who didn't deserve to.

Why should I worry about a jungle hat and fatigue jacket just to look like some fraudulent wannabe misfit?

No sweat!

The flight down was uneventful, and New Mexico still looked great from the air as we came in for a landing. Albuquerque looked awfully good as well, except for freeway construction up the wazoo. However, just like 1988, the rental car was locked on a northward trajectory, hammer down.

Didi mau!

The R&R couldn't start until I reached the Enchanted Circle.

The Coffman's adobe retreat in Taos, while not all that easy to find, proved to be the perfect spot to rest and relax. It was quiet, well away from the roar of Harleys on every main drag around.

Except for being jolted into action at 0550 the first morning there when a hose on the washing machine burst, it was as peaceful as anywhere I've ever been. Of course, with cold water blasting up into 100-year-old unfinished adobe bricks in the utility room, it was a real eye opener dashing in there in my skivvies and being rained on by bone-chilling cold mud.

Otherwise, however, the evenings, nights, and early mornings were just what I needed to recuperate, even if the days were a bit chaotic racing around the Circle. There were friends to see on Saturday—Norma and John Hardesty in Ute Park and Betty Fleishner in Eagle Nest—and activities at the Memorial on Sunday . . . visiting at length with Dr. Westphall and attending the memorial board's meeting.

On Sunday evening I went to see two former K-State colleagues, John and Mary, who were at their place in Taos. Another friend of John's, Kim, was also visiting from back east. It turned out that Kim taught a course on Vietnam, along with other areas of history, at Dickinson College in Pennsylvania, so we had some spirited discussions that night.

Not surprisingly, the origin of antiveteran prejudices on today's college campuses was debated at length, along with the role of graduate deferments in creating the problem. Then, when Kim noted that history appears to end in 1945 for most high school students, that got us into the topic of extending student deferments to go into teaching—K-12—during Vietnam as well.

So, how did college-prone males legitimately avoid the draft back then?

Huge numbers of them continued on to graduate school immediately following their undergraduate studies (thereby explaining the three-fold jump in male enrollments until the graduate deferment ended in 1968). Those that didn't have the grades or inclination for graduate school went into teaching.

Yep! That's what I was told by a Maine board of education guy.

And where are these guys today?

Where, indeed! They're out there pervading the senior levels in America's educational system—in the primary and secondary schools and peppered throughout higher education.

And what do you suppose their attitudes might be with regard to military service and military veterans?

Gee, I wonder.

Of course, the worst part of it may not be the consequences for veterans. It's the fact that these draft dodgers, legitimate though some may be, were the people educating our youth . . . my grandson Zeke. They're serving as the kids' role models.

That's not reassuring.

The Sunday evening discussions also wandered off into the topic of my long-stalled literary undertaking, VIETNAM'S WAR OF HATE. My short synopsis—which turned out to be not all that short—hit on the fact that my first year back from Vietnam was orders of magnitude worse than being combat and some of the disquieting pitfalls encountered along the way. I also let them know where it stood as of May 27, 2001 . . . idling as it had been for years, not going anywhere.

I was astounded when John commented that he'd "never heard any of this before."

Really?

It sure seems like it would have come up during one of our many, random-topic discussions over the years at K-State. But, most of those were during the recent, stuck-in-idle phase though.

Regrettably, or perhaps not as it turned out, I also started running off at the mouth about the recent allegations concerning Bob Kerrey in Vietnam, and argued that the Navy should initiate a court-martial investigation. If the accusations were true that women and children were rounded up and killed, this would be no different than the situation with Lieutenant Calley at My Lai. As the officer in charge on the ground, Calley was court-martialed.

Why should Kerrey be any different?

I launched into my standard arguments that the vast majority of those who served in Vietnam did so honorably and eventually concluded that allowing this matter to go unchallenged was a slap in the face to the majority who served ethically . . . with honor, pride, and dignity. We didn't commit any war crimes and letting Kerrey off the hook—without investigating the matter—would only serve to confirm for the antiwar protesters that they were right all along. And that was bunk . . . another reason why I needed to complete the book.

As soon as I started down this path—bringing Bob Kerrey into the discussion—I regretted doing so. All it was likely to accomplish was getting me upset, which would make any potentially rational conclusions appear substantially less so. Once I shut up, I quickly apologized for getting emotional about it.

John, Mary, and Kim seemed to take it pretty well though, even if they may not have been convinced as to the appropriateness of the actions I was suggesting regarding "the honorable" (or is it formerly honorable . . . dishonorable) Mr. Kerrey. Anyhow, one thing was clear: The lively interchanges that occurred that evening were all supportive of me getting off my butt and finishing the book.

Well, I'd like to, but that's a little difficult since I still don't know how it ends.

I didn't realize as I said goodnight and backed out of their drive that evening—hearing the familiar crumbling sound of crushed limestone gnashing under the tires, just like at the farm in 1969—that I was right in the midst of the ending. The finish line was at hand.

The value of the R&R at the Coffman hacienda became apparent first thing the next morning, however, after another fantastic night's sleep.

Arising as the sun was coming up, I was really looking forward to an inspiring day at the memorial . . . listening to Lynn Anderson sing the Marine's Vietnam anthem, "I Never Promised You a Rose Garden," and hearing Adrian's inspirational "Gooooood Morning, Vietnam" address. And it looked to be one beautiful day out there.

It was the previous night's conversations, though, that were weaving through my mind and, bit-by-bit, things began to gel. Last night was not just about retelling the same old *VIETNAM'S WAR OF HATE* story; some critical pieces of the puzzle that never quite meshed were starting to come together. The pieces had probably been lying there—perhaps for some time—but I hadn't seen them or didn't know how they fit together.

Memorial Day morning, I did.

Thirty-three years after being drafted into the Army, I was finally experiencing the final chapter of the welcome home.

It all started with a simple, self-directed question: Why did I apologize for getting emotional last night?

I really wasn't. I expected to be—Kerrey-like topics have caused the pressure cooker to overheat and blow in the past. But heck, I'll bet my blood pressure didn't so much as twitch a point or two, much less spike. Oh, perhaps I was bit more emphatic in those parts of our conversation, but that was about it.

Boy, that's a significant change.

And there's no "morning after" nausea in reconsidering what the guy most likely did either. Another transformation.

Not that my opinion changed: Sure, he should stand in front of the court. No question about it. If found guilty, punishment appropriate to the crimes should be handed down. Absolutely. If innocent, so be it.

I'm not going to lose any sleep over it though. His alleged actions no longer seemed like a slap in the face for me . . . or for the guys I served with in Nam. We didn't do it. We can still be proud of our service, as we could all along.

The fact that Bob Kerrey isn't proud of his actions in Vietnam (something he admitted) is irrelevant. The fact that he doesn't deserve the citations for valor he received—something he also acknowledged—while despicable perhaps, is also irrelevant.

Moreover, it's irrelevant to the fallen comrades we'll be honoring at the memorial . . . on their special day. The vast, overwhelming majority served their country with honor and pride even if Bob didn't. And while it's unfortunate that so many of them were lost so early in their lives, it's not how long they lived; it's how

191

they lived. They deserve our admiration and respect, and we owe it to them to wear our pride in their selfless service openly for all to see—proudly.

The families need to know that there's no shame here. Sorrow, yes, but no shame . . . NONE . . . only pride.

Pride: Use it or lose it.

We won the battles. We fought well. We fought with honor. No one can take that from us. And those who served didn't choose to give it away . . . others chose that path.

The shame is theirs, not ours.

The Cambodian holocaust—the Killing Fields—it's their doing. They can take responsibility for the "boat people" . . . the multitude of women and children lost at sea . . . those wonderful people of South Vietnam—Chaum and his colleague from the North, Long. We fought and died to prevent it.

The "hell no, we won't go" crowd: They're the ones who refuse to see the harvests that ensued from the seeds they so righteously sowed.

The shame is theirs, not ours.

* * *

Wow! What a beautiful, sunny day out there.

I haven't felt this good for a long time. Even my aching knees, elbow, and hand don't seem to be hurting all that much.

I feel great!

New Mexico comes through again.

Showering, shaving, getting ready for the day's activities . . . everything was right with the world.

It was amazing, the absolute clarity of things that morning. Issues that had seemed baffling before—items I hadn't given much thought to—made perfect sense.

The victims: Vietnam provided the ideal excuse for all their failures in life.

"It isn't my fault. It was the war."

And, of course, it doesn't matter whether they were actually there or not. As documented in *Stolen Valor*, some claiming to be Vietnam veterans were never even in the military. But everyone knows how horrible it was in Vietnam, so people will easily believe any liar who blames his failed business, failed marriage, or failed anything else on what happened to him "in the war."

"I've been haunted by it for years!"

Yeah, you bet . . . asshole.

The wannabes: Vietnam probably *has* haunted these folks for years. Many of them were never there either, but they can't quite cope with the pride exhibited by the combat veterans who were.

The wannabes saw those war movies back in the '50s; they identified with the heroes. Apparently, they want to believe—or want others to believe—that they're just like Audie and the Duke up on the big screen back then.

192

Being a desk jockey on Okinawa, or even at Bien Hoa in Vietnam (living comfortably as a REMF), must not answer those nagging questions some of the wannabes keep asking themselves.

But, being a Green Beret, covert CIA agent, on special "ops" in Laos and North Vietnam, now that has some real appeal. And that scar on the forehead from falling down drunk coming out of a strip club in Bangkok, well, in thinking about it, might actually have come from a bayonet wound when their outpost was overrun north of the DMZ.

"Boy, could I tell you stories about what really happened when I was awarded my third Silver Star. General Westmoreland tried to get me to take the CMH for that one (he had sent me on the mission personally, but I can't go into that), but being on TV with the president would have blown my CIA cover."

And if they base their fantasies on what they've seen and heard about combat in Vietnam—*Apocalypse Now, The Deer Hunter*, Oliver's bullshit *Platoon*—there would have to be some horrific savagery involved. Everyone knows that's the way it was in Vietnam, so that would be a requirement in the story—the lie—to make it believable.

It sure is strange how far some of these guys go with their "make it up as they go" stories. But it's easy to see why they tend to clam up around someone who actually paid their dues across the big pond . . . in combat.

We know the truth.

And while I can't understand the lies, I probably can understand some of the questions and self-doubts they're dealing with. It goes along with that totally irrational feeling back in Vietnam . . . of being cheated if I hadn't been wounded. Questions were answered that wouldn't have been otherwise.

When people ask me about being commandeered into the infantry and ending up in Vietnam, I generally tell them, "Having lived through it, I wouldn't trade the experience." Of course, I usually follow that up with the smart-ass comment, "Had I not lived through it, I probably wouldn't say that."

But I really wouldn't trade the experience, and I know why. I don't have to be a wannabe. I've navigated the lowland in Psalm 23 they lie about—that "walk through the valley of the shadow of death." I've answered the questions of my youth, as well as those regarding evil in the valley . . . and a related, hellacious gully . . . Gully of the Shadows of Death.

The uncertainties nagging the wannabes probably can't be answered many other ways either: war is about it. All the frills of life are stripped away in combat.

Teetering on the brink of life and death—not knowing if the next breath (or the current one) will be your last—you'll find out what you're made of . . . for better or worse. If it's the former, that can be a powerful source of strength on down the road—something the wannabes can only yearn for, but never truly find.

The protesters: And if Vietnam is still haunting the wannabes (who want to believe they were brave when, in fact, they were never tested), it must be traumatizing the hell out of those guys who protested fervently while successfully dodging the draft. That should be rather tough to live with.

These aren't the Ali's out there who paid the price for their beliefs. They aren't the Bob Cedergren's . . . the guys who left the country based on heart-felt principles and were actually principled enough to give up their U.S. citizenship.

They aren't those who quietly and legitimately avoided the war either. I walked that path for a time.

Nope, these are the chicken shits who protested at the top of their lungs just to hide their fear—the ones with North Vietnamese flags who spit on returning veterans, literally and figuratively. They're the assholes that are still spitting on veterans today, too spineless to face up to the consequences of their actions . . . the ones Professor Berger argued, "must not walk away in silence,"[2] but did.

These lowlifes are well beyond wondering whether they would have been brave if given the chance. They confirmed to themselves decades ago what they are: gutless cowards to the core.

I'm sure glad I don't have to live with that.

It certainly helps explain, though, why they don't want any unrepentant veterans around . . . especially, any unrepentant combat veterans—Vietnam, Desert Storm, Afghanistan, or any other. And if the cause in Vietnam was worth fighting for, worth dying for (if it wasn't amoral and American soldiers weren't vicious monsters), that should pack a huge ration of additional guilt on top of the cowardice . . . if they actually confront the facts.

Having proud veterans in their midst would stain the already tarnished reflection they see in the mirror.

Having proud veterans around probably doesn't help those small numbers of Vietnam veterans who came back ashamed of their own actions either—the one guy we had in 2nd Platoon . . . Oliver Stone . . . John Kerry . . . Bob Kerrey, most likely. It's obvious why these guys would have protested against the war back then.

I knew with our guy from day one; it wasn't until recently that it made sense for Bob. There had to be someone else to blame for the less than honorable actions by the less than honorable few. The war, or those running it, had to be bad.

It couldn't have been Bob Kerrey who provided the moral sanctions for any amoral actions while he was in command. As he tried to pass the buck on TV: "the military provides these sanctions."

Not the military I knew, Bob, and we were there at the same time . . . in early 1969.

There was a remarkable clarity about things in the high desert air that morning . . . even about things I already knew: Clearly, there are things much worse than war. There are things much worse than dying in war.

Living with what these guys live with would be worse . . . much, much worse.

And the especially nice feature about all the a.m. revelations is that not once while dwelling on them was any of it upsetting. It was emotionally neutral. This was not one of those calms before the storm either; it was just calm and peaceful.

Everything was in balance. Everything made sense.

Well, almost everything. I probably never will understand the antiwar fanatics of the female persuasion back then . . . their passion for the cause and their ability to hate, instantly. That look in the eyes is something I'll never forget—like a crazed animal ready to kill.

The first time I saw the look in Whitewater I was shocked. Seeing it two decades later in Columbus still left me flabbergasted.

Why? Where's it coming from?

They weren't there. They didn't experience Vietnam *or* combat firsthand.

How can they automatically hate those who did?

Oh, well. It's their problem, not mine. They can figure out how to live with it . . . or not.

And I could recall the story of one woman with Vietnam experience who provided a stark, but illuminating, contrast. I think it was in Bob Greene's book . . . a female officer had eggs smeared on the ribbons of the Marine uniform she was wearing while waiting to catch a flight at a U.S. airport during the war. Her comment a couple decades later about the protesters indicated that her scars could hardly be seen, "but theirs will be with them forever."[3]

You know, maybe that's it.

Given enough time, our wounds—those of us who served honorably—have healed or will, but the scars created by unconscionable behavior probably never can. They'll just continue to fester and putrefy. Whether it's a radical, spit-in-your-face male or female protester—or Bob Kerrey, John Kerry, Oliver Stone—if there was no justification for their appalling, inexcusable actions back then or the horrific outcomes they caused, there still isn't.

The pride is ours, not theirs.

And just as with the "what war is all about" coed in 1970, the revelations made me feel—*almost*—like I should thank Bob. It was the stories about Thanh Phong in 1969 that got me thinking again about those times . . . about a Congressional Medal of Honor winner coming back from Vietnam and joining the protests.

Why would he do that . . . if he had really *earned* the CMH?

Yes, it was time to get back to the book. It had been left unfinished too long.

* * *

What a fantastic day!

In 2001 . . . having done reasonably well for a farm kid from Wisconsin who never figured out what he wanted to be when he grew up (and never grew up), I could look back over my life and find profound satisfaction in knowing that I've never done anything better than I did my job in Vietnam. Of course, I'll never know why I was so good at it—able to track and read sign. It went way beyond the shake 'n' bake training by the Army Rangers.

It was as if Geronimo or one of his contemporaries from the 1800s had moved in and taken control. But, whatever the reason, it helped keep my guys alive.

Yeah, I'm *damned* proud of the job I did over there.

I was lucky too . . . serving in the Vietnam War. In combat, you learn to appreciate—and I mean *really* appreciate—the value and the fragility of life. Life can be snuffed out in a whisper with absolutely no warning. When my time comes, I know there had better be no giant regrets still lingering.

Whether others believe it or not, I'm also convinced that the South Vietnamese were worth fighting for and dying for. Regardless of the outcome, I can take that to the grave, knowing I did what I could.

And then there are the guys I served with in Vietnam. They're the greatest generation, as far as I'm concerned.

Enyeart, Russell, Perry, and Petite; Cunningham, Hardison, and Rodriquez; Rogers, Martin, and Holmes, plus a whole bunch more. There were none better—*ever!*

I'd bet my life on it . . . *and did.*

The recollections and feelings I was experiencing Memorial Day morning in New Mexico were just like those dredged up that exhilarating dawn back in Oakland decades earlier: standing tall and walking proud. As an infantry soldier, I had fought beside some of the best ever . . . fearing no evil . . . ready to die for our country.

The pride was back, not forced or with any second-guessing or question marks associated. It was genuine. It was real. It was that old Second World War "mom and apple pie" sensation. We fought for mom and apple pie—honorably and proudly.

Wow! Check out that "see forever" turquoise sky! And the clean, untainted mountain air . . . the subtle aroma of sage, the pungent fragrance of pine . . . it just doesn't get any better.

Heading up Taos Canyon on my way to the memorial mid-morning, it was like floating on a calm sea . . . or the "cloud nine" I was on when I returned to the "real world" in August of 1969 . . . totally relaxing and peaceful.

There's a stretch of a few miles, after the tight turns in the lower part of the canyon and before you hit more switchbacks on the way up to Palo Flechado Pass, where the road has some long sweeping curves. The sun was shining; the temperature and clean dry air were perfect.

Without focusing on anything in particular, feeling absolutely content, I was tapping on the center of my chest with the fingers on my right hand, thinking: Everything is just fine in there. The ol' ticker is doing great, thank you . . . just like 1969.

Lost in thought, gazing at the road ahead, I caught a glimpse out of the corner of my eye of a sleek dark silhouette gliding over the pines. I wasn't sure what kind of bird it was at that point, but I was only halfway paying attention to it anyhow. The glistening black shape, gliding directly toward me, becoming ever larger in the upper left-hand corner of the windshield, suddenly—*astonishingly*—flipped over on its back for a moment then back upright again, startling me awake.

HELLO!

I'd never seen a bird do anything like that before, not even close. My oblivious expression burst into a grin from ear to ear as I focused on the aerial acrobat just for an instant before he flashed from view overhead, above the car.

Yes, Brother Raven, you're right. I should be smiling. It's a day to feel good and be happy about life while embracing reverence in the afterlife called for today.

Memorial Day: Commemorating, honoring, exalting the selflessness and pride in our comrades who fought and died for us.

Thank you for the aerobatic jolt . . . allowing the Light to enter.

It's time to greet my *"thou art with me"* brothers here in your sacred Land of Enchantment—those still present; those in the chapel, lost in the past. Yea, though we walked through the valley of the shadow of death together, *together* we feared no evil . . . or faced it *together*, regardless.

Yes, with you, my brothers, I'd walk it again.

And, yes, I'm sure we will . . . somewhere, sometime . . . together . . . again.

Welcome Home!!!

SURVIVAL'S BOTTOM LINE . . . "WE *NOT* ME" . . . FREEDOM'S BOTTOM LINE

Enduring Truth: *Valley of the shadow patriots:*
Guardians of Lady Liberty . . . ALWAYS!

Epilogue I

DEFENDING FREEDOM

Selfless "WE not ME"[1,i] *patriots must fight for freedom—AGAIN TODAY*

....

THE SPIRIT OF WE[2,ii]
. . . "WE *not* ME" . . .

A life best lived should always be about YOU,
It should never be about ME;
But, the times to really cherish and hold on to
Are those all too fleeting moments in life
That are truly about WE!

....

Selfless "WE *not* ME"[1] patriots are America's defenders of freedom in war, and "the Spirit of WE"[2] is my description of what I "cherish and hold on to" from Vietnam, experiencing combat selfless service firsthand. Maybe for lifelong civilians, "the Spirit of WE"[2] might sound more like a poem accompanying wedding vows than a verse about war, but the value is *NEVER* more consequential than in combat . . . ditto the cost. Your life is in the hands of those around you; their lives are in yours. Soldiers cannot be focused on "ME" in battle if most—*or some*—are going to survive.

As underscored in my 2021 article about Vietnam's Gully of the Shadows of Death[3]: "Remarkably, . . . in the midst of the very worst humankind has to offer—*WAR*—you see the very best humankind has to give. Repeatedly, there are young U.S. troops—18 and 19-year-olds—putting their own lives on the line to protect their brothers next to them . . . some of those brothers they may have known for only a few days.

Logic can't explain that selfless commitment—'WE' *versus* 'ME' in combat—to someone who hasn't been there; not in a way they'll feel to the core of their very being like those who've lived it. For anyone who has, those life and death fleeting moments reside deep within . . . *FOREVER*.

And for most, they're 100% about 'YOU' and 'WE'—0% 'ME.'"[3,iii]

Yes, "the Spirit of WE"[2] exists in war—*your next breath bet on it, dependent on it*—like nowhere else.

198

....

Martin Luther King, Jr: *"No one really knows why they are alive until they know what they'd die for."*[4]

....

Dr. King's statement is prophetic for soldiers in war as I learned in Vietnam and noted in my "Time Warp"[1] article based on VIETNAM'S WAR OF HATE. "In Delta, everyone knew 'what they'd die for'—their 'WE *not* ME' brothers. After a firefight, those remaining knew 'why they are alive'—thanks to their 'WE *not* ME' brothers.

Combat is horrific, but those extraordinary MLK moments illuminated the very best within: love of brothers, love of country, love of life. The former led to a willingness to sacrifice the latter.

Thus, I left Vietnam knowing we are all ONE."[1]

These truths seem obvious to me now, but it took 50 years to align all "the Spirit of WE"[2] reflections flickering in the distant past. For decades, there was just that cryptic, intangible "mom and apple pie" feeling of pride I was treasuring from the second-most horrific time in my life.

As VIETNAM'S WAR OF HATE detailed, the worst was coming home from Vietnam, the first eight to ten months . . . hands down.

Strangely, though, the past few years, I've actually felt sorry for those who've never experienced that powerful pride and comradeship—"we are all ONE"—while serving in combat. However, it wasn't until 2019 that words to describe it, "the Spirit of WE,"[2] came to me . . . where "WE" means more than "ME" a thousand times over. It was a TV discussion about veterans' suicides that delivered the eureka moment to me.[iv]

What could be causing military veterans to be killing themselves in such high numbers today?

They're out of the warzone. They're home . . . safe!

I'd known about the terrible, twenty-plus per day suicide rate for veterans for a few years, but watching *Fox and Friends* on March 30, 2019—listening to three individuals tackling the problem—is when "the Spirit of WE"[2] revelation emerged as the title for a vague poem bouncing around in my head. It was somewhere in the midst of their "battle buddies" discussion.

Those with battle buddies—others touched by "the Spirit of WE"[2] in war, I believe—are better able to drag themselves out of the quicksand that's pulling them under . . . drowning them. A place where death shines brighter than life, drawing them to it.

* * *

But what is it that keeps combat veterans from readapting easily to civilian life, going back to who they were prior to serving in the military?

That should be a "piece of cake" as the saying goes . . . as I felt it would be coming home from Vietnam. Nonetheless, it wasn't; it isn't.

I learned that fifty-plus years ago, expecting—*no, KNOWING*—it would be a piece of cake for me after only nineteen months on active duty.

How could it be otherwise?

I'd spent 94 percent of my life as a civilian; 6 percent as an Army *draftee*.

I wasn't some gung-ho volunteer. Hell, I dodged the draft with a student deferment for years.

Piece o' cake!

Regardless, I've said for years, my first year back from Vietnam was orders of magnitude worse than being in combat in Vietnam.

That's nuts . . . even back in the Vietnam, spit-on-soldiers era. The rationale for that assessment came out in my 2021 "Last Rites for 'WE' in America"[2] article:

> However, it took me fifty years—1969 to 2019—to find words to describe it. For decades, I just told people, "Having lived through it (Vietnam), I wouldn't trade the experience; had I not lived through it, I probably wouldn't say that." Probably not.

The reason I wouldn't trade the experience is because of the bond formed with my brothers in combat. Looking back, there was something to cherish about it. It was about a life best lived, oddly serene . . . bordering on spiritual . . . eternal . . . but extremely difficult to put into words. When every person focuses on YOU, not ME, it makes WE a powerful force that MIGHT be beatable, but it's 100 percent UNBREAKABLE. Brothers would DIE for one another . . . and did.[2]

Today, I'm convinced it's "the Spirit of WE"[2] that those of us from that war— ANY WAR—share with one another; a recurring "Yea, thou I walk through the valley of the shadow of death"[5] reality for combat troops. Or perhaps a gully, not a valley, for some.

Of course, that assumes you're able to look back as a proud member of team "WE." And from my relatively short stint in Vietnam, that would be 98 percent of my comrades-in-arms.

As *VIETNAM'S WAR OF HATE* articulated, they were *AWESOME!*

Delta Company's 2nd Platoon—Enyeart, Russell, Perry, and Petite; Cunningham, Hardison, and Rodriquez; Rogers, Martin, and Holmes; plus, innumerable others— were the personification of "WE *not* ME"[1] soldiers in Vietnam. They defined "the Spirit of WE"[2] brotherhood for me in 1969 even though I didn't know how to describe it or what to call it at the time. We just lived it together, placing our lives in each other's hands.

As civilians, we may have shared few commonalities, but in combat, we were brothers. "Black, white, pink, purple—TOTALLY irrelevant.

I placed my life in their hands; they placed their lives in mine. That's just the way it is in battle: it's your family."[1] Unfortunately, it was not 100 percent.

About one in fifty—2 percent—during my stint in Nam focused on only themselves . . . "ME/FU." Mercifully, though, they were few and far between; the outliers who, when tested under fire, failed the test.

Going back to the "real world," they were undoubtedly the atypical Vietnam vets that protested against the war. And, *obviously*, they would; "THE WAR" had to be the culprit. No way could the dysfunctional poser they looked at in the mirror everyday be the problem.

Having no pride within, they would have aligned with the antiwar creeps spitting on honorable troops coming home. The "ME/FU" guys could convey "firsthand" accounts of warmongers in Vietnam; those being the majority who put their lives on the line to save their brothers and South Vietnamese allies while the "ME/FU" guys contributed their worth—*NADA, ZIP, ZERO!*

Yep, they belonged together, returning "ME/FU" slime congealing with chicken-shit hide-at-home slime.

However, the biggest problem with the 2-percenters wasn't that they were "ME/FU" cowards in Vietnam and lying slugs back home. Nope. It's that some of them most assuredly got one or more of their selfless brethren killed. Not protecting their brothers' backs—looking out for only themselves—could have that outcome; *a terminal "ME/FU" ending.*

··

Martin Luther King, Jr: *"A man who won't die for something is not fit to live."*[6]

··

Dr. King's second maxim is particularly applicable to "ME/FU" guys.

Perhaps that's a bit harsh for the two-cents-worth, but not really. They earned no respect in Vietnam, so they deserve no respect at home. Not when worthy "WE *not* ME"[1] brothers may have died because of them.

VIETNAM'S WAR OF HATE provided some probable examples, but too few are identified publicly as *"not fit to live"* per Martin Luther King, Jr. principles. Of course, these folks had no principles . . . ditto their spitting comrades.

Appallingly, fifty years after coming home from Vietnam, I'm seeing far too many similarities to the unhinged hatefulness I encountered back then.

The five vomit-inducing flavors of anti-America anarchists of the 1960s and '70s detailed in *VIETNAM'S WAR OF HATE* have been proliferating again, totally out of control. As I underscored in "Anti-America Americans Synergizing Again,"[7] just like a half century ago, there are the vile, despicable: "socialist-loving 'intellectuals;' screw-the-public profiteers; mass media manipulators; antimilitary/antiauthority zealots; and sanctimonious amoral moralists."[7, v]

The rebirth of anti-America Americans is scary as hell!

Also scary is the knowledge that domestic anti-America Americans are identical to the 2-percenters in Vietnam; they adhere to the same self-serving, "ME/FU" philosophy. In the 1960s and '70s, it's unlikely they amounted to a huge percentage of the U.S. population; they just had the biggest mouths. Thus, they overwhelmed everyone else—the old "silent majority"—in every news cycle.

Problematically, today, the number of "ME/FU" extremists appears to have increased exponentially, becoming a significant percentage nationally. And if their ranks seemed to have grown inordinately by the spring of 2019, that pales by comparison to where things were by the summer of 2020 . . . in the aftermath of COVID-19 and George Floyd.

When "all lives matter" is racist and "defund the police" is not insane, the country is teetering on the edge. Say goodbye to liberty and freedom.

Anti-America Americans were Lady Liberty's Achilles' heel when VIETNAM'S WAR OF HATE was written; they were tearing the country apart. Twelve chapters illuminated their appalling destruction[vi]; others corroborated it. In recent years, they've been back at it, becoming America's Achilles' heel once again.

Do you think America's enemies aren't watching . . . salivating?

Do you think they won't use these anti-America "ME/FU" Americans to their advantage . . . making us pay . . . AGAIN?

Well, guess what?

They already are, and it could get worse . . . LOTS worse.

North Vietnam, in cahoots with her Chinese and Soviet allies, used the 1960s and '70s anti-America Americans—our Achilles' heel—to conquer South Vietnam. The Vietcong Minister of Justice, Truong Nhu Tang, detailed that point explicitly in his book after the war.[8]

That's a fact; VIETNAM'S WAR OF HATE validated it. For additional proof, read Tang's book or check out "'Stupid Is as Stupid Does' in Vietnam and Afghanistan."[9, vii]

Tang was the VIETCONG justice minister. *He knew.*

So, how are China and Russia using anti-America Americans today?

That should ring a bell for Pavlov's mass-media dogs out there. But, it won't since they're the mouthpiece for the communists-at-heart, anti-America Americans, manipulating public opinion on their behalf.

The urgent question now is: Which U.S. Achilles will be ruptured next as a result?

They're taking "ME/FU" to all-time extremes and the outcomes for today's "land of the free" won't be good. "Free" could be a thing of the past at the rate we were going.

The George Floyd outrage was warranted. The path we went down as a result was shear lunacy with relevant lessons from 1969 and 1970: "I left Vietnam knowing we're all ONE. I came home to discover we're NOT."[4] But, deep down, I still knew ONE was true; we are all equal, as God[10] and Country[11] intended. "The Spirit of WE"[2] proved that to me in Vietnam.

Fifty years later, the life-saving value of "WE *not* ME"[1] is crystal clear, as is the life-annihilating devastation of "ME/FU" as well. And neither is limited to wars in foreign lands. They're just as meaningful at home and especially so in today's world.

"The Spirit of WE"[2] must be a reality in America too.

THE SPIRIT OF WE[2]
... "WE *not* ME" ...

A life best lived should always be about YOU,
It should never be about ME;
But, the times to really cherish and hold on to
Are those all too fleeting moments in life
That are truly about WE!

And as noted in the prologue: All [the anarchists] must be confronted and exposed for what they are: anti-America "ME/FU" self-servants bent on destroying liberty and freedom as we know it. They failed fifty years ago; they could still succeed this time. Stopping them will require American patriots—believers in the U.S. Constitution and in "We the People"—to be "WE *not* ME" selfless servants and fight back.

Being a patriot—on the backside of over-the-hill, but a patriot nonetheless—I felt compelled to raise the alarm.

Learn from history for Christ's sake!

"WE" can't keep going through this crap.

WAKE UP, AMERICA!!!

Epilogue II

DESTROYING FREEDOM

Half-Century "Time Warp:"[1, i] *"Anti-America Americans Synergizing Again"*[2, ii]

....

**THE SELF-SERVICE OF ME
... "ME/FU" ...**

*A life worthlessly lived is always about ME,
It will NEVER be about YOU;
As the times self-servants cherish and hold on to
Are their all too frequent moments in life
That are exclusively about ME . . . FU!*

....

It took me three decades to find that elusive welcome home, and two decades later, the United States catapulted backward in time. America in 2019 to 2020 became America in 1969 to 1970 . . . AGAIN.

"Antifa is the Weather Underground of 50-years ago, just without the bombs—YET! Same guerilla tactics; same goal: destroy America."[1]

My conclusion: "What I've seen in 2019 and 2020 is a mirror image of what I lived in 1969 and 1970. A fifty-year time warp."[1]

Appallingly, the same five groups of anti-America Americans responsible for the anarchy a half century ago are the ones undermining democracy and liberty in America once more. Understanding the overt and covert interactions among them will be essential if they are to be defeated.

And they MUST be defeated.

Maybe VIETNAM'S WAR OF HATE insights can help facilitate their undoing.

"Anti-America Americans Synergizing Again,"[2] published in early 2021, detailed the threats:

> Having been dumped into the middle of the mayhem when I returned from Vietnam in 1969, I came face-to-face with the anti-America revolutionaries far too frequently. Along the way, I was able identify five distinct, but interacting components: (1) socialist-loving "intellectuals"; (2) screw-the-public profiteers; (3) mass-

204

media manipulators; (4) antimilitary/antiauthority zealots; and (5) sanctimonious amoral moralists.[2]

The chapter-ending enduring truths in VIETNAM'S WAR OF HATE entitled, "Anti-America Americans . . . Lady Liberty's Achilles' Heel" focused on these five anarchist classes. They wrapped up twelve of the twenty-three chapters.[iii] Obviously, I felt both the threats and the truths would persist, but I didn't anticipate that the threats would be dominating again in my lifetime. At least, I hoped they wouldn't . . . *but they are.*

These domestic threats to U.S. freedom must be confronted. And as detailed in the article above:

From an old combat vet perspective, #1 and #2 would categorize as strategic threats, #3 and #4 as tactical threats, and #5 as worthless threats. The last one can't be ignored though, since those blowholes own a bully pulpit.[2]

STRATEGIC THREAT #1—SOCIALIST-LOVING "INTELLECTUALS"[iv]

As articulated in the *American Thinker* article:

Since serving in combat in 1969, I've spent a half century inside the ivory tower. That has convinced me the intelligentsia [*socialist-loving "intellectuals"*] are the #1 threat to American freedom. University Marxists/Leninists/Stalinists gave birth to today's "woke" cancel culture while simultaneously administering last rites to higher education quality in America.

Beyond that, they educate the other four anarchist elements—profiteers, manipulators, zealots, and moralists—to serve themselves, not others; especially, *not* America. And, of course, they continually propagate more of their own . . . with the in-breeding generating precisely what genetics predicts.[2]

To expand on that, the #1 ranking was because colleges:

a) Self-perpetuate the next generation(s) of *socialist-loving "intellectuals"* within academe which is truly bad; worse yet, they brainwash new teachers going into the K-12 system as well;
b) Teach socialistic political science to the next generation of *screw-the-public profiteers* in federal, state, and local government . . . both elected officials and bureaucrats;
c) Instruct the next generation of *mass-media manipulators* in journalism (if you can call it that) and mass "communistation" (mass communication back when honesty still existed within their ranks);
d) Lead and advocate for the causes propagated by the rabid *antimilitary/ antiauthority zealots* on campus and off; and
e) Provide liberal performing arts "education" to *sanctimonious amoral moralists* of the future in Hollywood and elsewhere.

As a result, significant effort must be focused on fixing the flaws within America's educational system. It's the bedrock—*strategic*—underpinning for most of the problems patriotic Americans now face.

One big problem with the politically driven grievance culture in higher education today is that they've turned self-serving "ME/FU" individuals into "WE/FU" victims' groups and Marxist "WE/FU" collectives. Either allows them to band together and bitch without having to perform individually. BUT, diversity of thought is NOT allowed; every victim in the group is required to sing from the same grievance song-sheet. If they don't, they'll lose their membership rights and any benefits those rights produced.

"Fixing America's education system will be a long war of attrition at best, but knowing the cause is essential to achieving the desired outcome. And success will come down to basic supply and demand economics—education consumers *not* spending their money at grossly anti-America universities. All have anti-America faculty, but some fewer than others.

It's the almighty tuition dollars, folks. You control those payments, so *control them!*"[3v]

Finally, as noted in Chapter 21:

The social engineering carried out by the university thought police is still in the mold of Hitler and Stalin . . . it's just less obvious in the campus ivy-clad stalag/gulag.

That enduring truth must not be overlooked going forward. It has already killed quality higher education and it's in the process of killing America.

....

STRATEGIC THREAT #2—SCREW-THE-PUBLIC PROFITEERS[vi]

Ronald Reagan: *"Politics is supposed to be the second-oldest profession.
I have come to realize that it bears a very close resemblance to the first."*[4]

....

"Anti-America Americans"[2] leveraged Reagan's quote: "One could argue that politicians and bureaucrats—government pimps and prostitutes using Reagan's analogy—are the #1 threat. However, they receive their political science degrees from Marxist faculty prior to heading to D.C. to 'socialize' the country. Thus, *screw-the-public profiteers* finish below their mentors as threat #2 . . . #2 being apt in multiple ways.

The pimps and prostitutes profit at taxpayer's expense, fleecing the country they're supposed to serve. Logic might say the pimps are more culpable, but [similar to prostitutes with pimps] bureaucrats service the acts politicians negotiate.

Yes, Mr. President, that's 'a very close resemblance' to the oldest profession.

There were countless deep-state, 'insurance policy' examples in 2019. Civil servants [*sic*] might not accrue immediate financial gains, but covert abuses yield IOUs.

And 2020's COVID-19 offered examples daily of elected swamp dwellers being swamp slime. Some bog amphibians can regenerate limbs; D.C.-types need backbones and morals."[2]

Elected profiteers—pimps—will always be the screw-the-public winners with regard to big-time strategic consequences, but deep-state bureaucrats/profiteers/racketeers—prostitutes—are the ones that implement the strategies and ensure that screw-the-public outcomes occur. Each plays a crucial, detrimental role that must be not only considered, but confronted whenever and wherever possible.

Patriots can vote elected profiteers out of office and put pressure on the new ones to fix the bureaucrat problem . . . not that the swamp will ever be drained as effectively as it needs to be.

However, if that's not done repeatedly and long-term, it's highly likely Washington's elected *screw-the-public profiteers* will be at the helm of the USS Titanic when America hits the iceberg. D.C.'s *screw-the-public profiteer* prostitutes (bureaucrats) will then commandeer all the lifeboats for themselves.

....

TACTICAL THREAT #1—MASS MEDIA MANIPULATORS[vii]

....

"Whenever leftist anarchy rears its ugly head, the nearly universal response seems to be: close your eyes; don't look! The mob violence yesterday at the U.S. Capitol, on the other hand, will be a tool for establishment repression of conservatives."[2]

That was my lead with the "Anti-America Americans"[2] piece on January 7, 2021 and the mass media proved it to be true almost instantly . . . manipulating away. They set the national dialogue and all threats from that point on for four years were on the right ONLY.

Nonetheless, my article focused on highlighting the media biases fifty years ago and today. They're much more alike than most would recognize.

Few people knew how bad the reporting was in the '60s and '70s, since the hacks still feigned being truthful. Their stilted propaganda was subtle, but effective—regurgitate bile repeatedly until others swallow it.

That's still true today; reporters just don't fake honesty anymore.

"The mainstream was bad in the Vietnam era, but it's worse now. It resembles the Mekong Delta fifty years ago when human excrement from villages went straight into the rivers and streams. 'Keep your mouth shut' was advised when crossing or bathing in them. That's difficult bathing in 2021's polluted mainstream."[2]

Because of that ocean of bile regurgitated repeatedly in the 1960s and 1970s about those serving in Vietnam—making all of us out as blood-thirsty war criminals—it's my hope that *VIETNAM'S WAR OF HATE* corrected some of those misperceptions. I'm more convinced today than ever before that the 98 percent honorable, 2 percent dishonorable I experienced was closer to the norm throughout the war. War criminals would have been within the 2 percent camp. *Mass-media manipulators* projected it the other way around . . . SLUGS!

Now, a correction must be made to one of the op-ed articles I published. In "Big Tech—SS—Gestapo,"[5, viii] I made the case for Big Tech being a stand-alone strategic threat. However, given more time to ruminate on it, that's wrong. Big Tech is today's premier *mass-media manipulator*. That moves it from a secondary strategic threat to a top tactical threat within the *mass-media manipulators* category.

TACTICAL THREAT #2—ANTIMILITARY/ANTIAUTHORITY ZEALOTS[ix]

Again, from the *American Thinker* article[2]:

In-the-streets anarchists were the most visible anti-America Americans back in the '60s and '70s as they often are today. But, they're just destructive thugs empowered by the classless classes above.

As noted previously, "Antifa is the Weather Underground of fifty years ago, just without the bombs—YET!"[1] Body counts and building rubble will go up when they access explosives.

Burgess Owens remarked recently, "Whether it be Antifa, a terrorist group, whether it be BLM, a terrorist group, I tell you one thing they have in common with the KKK: They're cowards and bullies."[6] Cowards become bullies in mobs, just like fifty years ago with the Weathermen and Students for a Democratic Society. "Cowardly anti-Americans" defines them all.[2]

As also highlighted in, "Tested Under Fire: Relevant on the Battlefield and in the Streets:"[7, x]

Listening to city leaders pontificate about defunding the police while anarchy is erupting in their streets has been but one of numerous moronic storylines playing out on the news over the past few months. It's another area where there are far too many appalling similarities to the late 1960s, early 1970s. That's when mayhem in the streets was the "in" thing for many of today's leaders on the left . . . another sordid "time warp."[1, 7]

All of it was brought about by *antimilitary/antiauthority zealots* who don't care a lick about America. They want others to shed their blood and give up their lives. Cowardly, lawless anarchists do what they do best . . . run their mouths as part of a mob where their gutlessness won't show. Most are drawn from one or more of the other four anti-America American categories, but their roles as *antimilitary/antiauthority zealots* must be called out. They *are* the boots-on-the-ground tactical implementers.

WORTHLESS THREAT #1—SANCTIMONIOUS AMORAL MORALISTS[xi]

And lastly from the "Anti-America Americans"[2] article:

Hollywood narcissists and allied wind-bags are anarchists-light at best. They'll stoke the flames, taking few risks themselves.

They pontificated from sheltered soapboxes a half century ago as they're doing again in the new Millennium. One amoral old retread moved from advocating the killing of U.S. soldiers to attacking climate change,[8] but that affirmative action was brief. Thankfully, she hasn't contributed patriot names to any walls of late, but her zealot comrades have.[2]

Today, 99 percent of Hollywood's beautiful people would fill the bill as *sanctimonious amoral moralists*, proving it every time they open their mouths. Whether it's the old antiwar hag Jane "ME/FU" Fonda, Alyssa "ME/FU" Milano, Debra "ME/FU" Messing, Robert "ME/FU" De Niro, Alec "ME/FU" Baldwin, or whomever, they're all barf bags.

* * *

The five classes of anti-America "ME/FU" Americans were worthless scum in the 1960s and 1970s. They're even more worthless today—advocating socialism openly. And just like the "ME/FU" 2 percent in Vietnam, they look out for one thing and one thing only: themselves. You don't count; America doesn't count.

....

THE SELF-SERVICE OF ME
— "ME/FU" —

A life worthlessly lived is always about ME,
It will NEVER be about YOU;
As the times self-servants cherish and hold on to
Are their all too frequent moments in life
That are exclusively about ME . . . FU!

....

Returning from combat in 1969, I had no clue I'd be doing battle for decades with these five synergizing groups of anarchists. My "Welcome Home" from Vietnam wasn't thanks to them. . . .

American patriots need to understand: These anarchists want to end U.S. democracy. The conspirators failed a half century ago; they might succeed this time.

Pre-400 BC, Sophocles recognized, "There is no greater evil than anarchy."[2, 9]

So, it's time to *"wake up, America!* U.S. liberty and freedom may soon be gone."[10, xii]

FIGHT BACK . . . *before it's too late.*

Epilogue III

INHERITING FREEDOM

America's "We the People" beneficiaries: Heirs no more if "ME/FU" wins

....

THE SPIRIT OF WE THE PEOPLE
... "WE *the* PEOPLE *not* ME"[1, i] ...

A life best lived should always be about YOU,
It should never be about ME;
But, the times to really cherish and hold on to
Are those all too fleeting moments in life
That are truly about WE;
"WE the PEOPLE not ME!"

....

"We the People of the United States, in Order to form a more perfect Union, establish Justice, insure domestic Tranquility, provide for the common defence,[ii] promote the general Welfare, and secure the Blessings of Liberty to ourselves and our Posterity, do ordain and establish this Constitution for the United States of America."[2]

That's the preamble to the Constitution as written in 1787.

For the individual goals listed to be met, those seeking independence were required to step up to make them happen. The framers of the Constitution couldn't do it, and neither could any follow-on president or congress. It was going to take "We the People of the United States" back then, just as it still takes "We the People of the United States" now.

Regrettably, We the People have been failing at every preamble objective far too often.

1. The Union has been less perfect recently than at any time during my eight decades here on earth.
2. Justice has been an outright farce.
3. Domestic Tranquility is frequently nonexistent.
4. Common defense was focused on woke rubbish rather than defending the nation in recent years.
5. General Welfare has been in the toilet.

6. The Blessings of Liberty existed for only two groups . . . the privileged elite and illegal aliens.

And, finally, our Posterity was taking it in the posterior; none of the rights in the U.S. Constitution would be left to our descendants if things didn't change. Hopefully, the November 2024 election has America on the right path.

....

D.L. Lewis: *"Liberty was fought with bullets, Blood was shed for independence, Sacrifices were made for freedom"*[3]

....

Liberty and freedom come at a cost, and few Americans seem willing to step up and pay those costs anymore. As I noted in a 2021 opinion piece: Today it's all, "ME! ME! ME!" often followed by a two-word term-of-endearment [*sic*]. And, NO, it's not "LOVE YOU!"[4, iii] Close thought; the second word is the same and the first still has four letters, "XXXX YOU!" You guessed it. That does not bode well for We the People as America approaches her 250th birthday in 2026.

Essentially every article I've written from 2020-2024 has been related to my combat service in Vietnam and the more gruesome war I encountered coming home. They are instructive as to what We the People must do today.

The colorblind brotherhood in battle was a central component of the first article written about a half-century "time warp" I witnessed firsthand.[5] In combat, my brothers were just that: BROTHERS; black, white, pink, purple—TOTALLY irrelevant. That led to perhaps the most important take-home lesson from my time in Southeast Asia: Thus, I left Vietnam knowing we are all ONE.

My opinion about that has never changed, even though my welcome home from Vietnam bombarded me with just the opposite. I came home to discover we're NOT because that's what the anarchists back then were out to prove. They've been trying even harder today and far too many Americans caved to their lies.

How do I know they are lies?

It's pretty easy, actually. I experienced the truth on the battlefield where life and death were the defining metrics. Brothers in combat focused on keeping their brothers alive, routinely risking their own lives in doing so.

And, again, black, white, pink, purple—TOTALLY irrelevant.

As one of my other titles highlighted, "The Gully of the Shadows of Death Disproved Critical Race Theory [CRT] Over 50-Years Ago."[6, iv] My brothers and I encountered that gully on Groundhog Day in 1969 and too many did not survive the shadows. Nonetheless, it proved conclusively, we are all ONE.

Nothing tops the altruism of "WE *not* ME" selfless service in combat.[4] The collateral on the line is your life, and in 1969 nearly 100 percent of my brothers in Vietnam placed it there knowingly . . . willingly.

It's probably unrealistic to ask We the People today to commit to that level. Domestic wars are different than foreign wars. However, the same principles are needed if liberty and freedom are to survive, something equivalent to "WE *not* ME" in combat . . . "WE *the* PEOPLE *not* ME," perhaps. It encompasses the neighbors helping neighbors approach of my parents' generation, a reality I saw play out repeatedly on the small dairy farm where I was raised.

Today, mothers and fathers standing up against tyrannical school boards and teachers' unions cramming CRT and related hogwash down their children's throats is a great start. We the People must rally around them. The actual racists pushing the CRT/equity agenda must be illuminated for what they are . . . Marxist bigots and race-baiters.

Authoritarians come to power when significant portions of the population become dependent on them, and the CRT/equity agenda created the requisite, needy victims' groups. "ME! ME! ME! XXXX YOU!" moaners are brought together in Marxist collectives where they can blame others for something—anything—and then demand reparations (equity) to make up for it.[1] Thankfully, these issues are being confronted within the federal government in 2025.

But, there's one additional truism to consider as well . . . an old one.

....

John Adams: *"Our Constitution was made only for a moral and religious people. It is wholly inadequate to the government of any other."*[7]

....

In other words, "it is wholly inadequate to the government of" immoral and godless people. Maybe John Adams' statement more than two centuries ago explains more precisely who is causing the problems in America today . . . immoral and godless Marxist bigots and race-baiters.

There was certainly no shortage of immoral and godless people in America in 2022 when my article was written, which raised the question: "Have Americans become a people who no longer deserve their Constitution?"[8, v]

As a reminder, John Adams was "America's first vice president and second president, who served on the First Continental Congress and helped draft the Declaration of Independence."[8] Thus, he should know who the Constitution was made for and who it wasn't.

Considering the Constitution preamble per Adams, then, "We the People of the United States" means "We the [moral and religious] People of the United States . . . do ordain and establish this Constitution." It does not mean, "We the [immoral and godless] People."

That difference really could explain many of the ongoing problems in America today.

Anti-America anarchists are abusing the Constitution and constitutional rights as America approaches her 250th birthday in 2026. Increasing numbers of citizens have endorsed socialism as the national model, an oppressive ideology that destroys liberty and freedom.

So, perhaps John Adams pegged it over two centuries ago. Maybe the issues today come down to morality and religion or, more accurately, a lack thereof. Both have been in states of precipitous decline.

It was moral and religious people who wanted "to form a more perfect Union, establish Justice, insure domestic Tranquility," etc. That seems logical for ethical beings attempting to escape religious persecution elsewhere in the world.

Would immoral, godless types want those things?

Probably not. A less perfect union would likely be their goal. Certainly, less justice would and, preferably, no justice. That appeared to be the trajectory the United States was on in 2022.

Tranquility?

No!

Those lacking scruples and spirituality would surely have less tranquility—that is, turmoil—in mind. Immoral people profit by exploiting mayhem, not being constrained by ethical norms good people respect. And godless heathens don't worry about the next life; they just smash and grab everything they want in this life. *Mine!* That seems a lot like where the United States has been recently or was getting darn close to being.

Defunding the police insanity decapitated justice while trashing tranquility as well. The closet communists running big cities trampled two constitutional objectives at once with that and kicked the bejesus out of "general Welfare" and "the Blessings of Liberty" to boot.

As noted in 2022: Turn on the TV; see what's going on across America. Look at what's happening on airplanes. . .in elevators. . .on Main Street, USA. It's ugly and getting uglier day by day.

For an old academic like me, 'our Posterity' (i.e., children) mentioned in the preamble seem especially out of touch with the goals our forefathers set. Far too few young people today have a clue about the value of the Constitution, democracy, and capitalism. That does not bode well for the future.

In 2019, Alyssa Ahlgren, a college student working on her MBA, articulated the problem in an article entitled, "My Generation Is Blind to the Prosperity Around Us."[9] She highlighted that "the United States of America has lifted more people out of abject poverty, spread more freedom and democracy, and has created more innovation in technology and medicine than any other nation in human history." Knowing this, she can't understand why many of those her age are attracted to socialism.

Ms. Ahlgren also noted, "We don't have a lack of prosperity problem. We have an entitlement problem, an ungratefulness problem, and it's spreading like a plague." That was before China's viral plague hit and infected the United States with Maoist prosperity-killing internment dictates. Locked away, "a lack of prosperity problem" became a reality.

The essay concluded by noting that Ahlgren's "generation is becoming the largest voting bloc in the country." They can either "continue to propel us forward with the gifts [of] capitalism and democracy" or they "can fall into the trap of entitlement and relapse into restrictive socialist destitution."

Too many have been leaning in the latter direction.

Where we stand today, it's clear that moral and religious people of all ages must unite. Multiple generations must come together to reaffirm the importance of America's Constitution.

Vote to rebuild every parameter called for in the Constitution:

A more perfect union—*Yes!*
Justice—*Yes!*
Domestic tranquility—*Yes!*
Common defense—*Yes!*
General welfare—*Yes!*
Blessings of liberty—*Yes!*

You don't know how to vote for those?

Find those politicians who endorse *all* Constitution components and vote for them. Better yet, find non-politicians who love America and are willing to shoulder the burden of getting the United States back on track—that is, they are willing to run for public office. Vote for them.

"Our Constitution was made only for a moral and religious people." It's time for every moral and religious person in America to help ensure the Constitution survives. Anyone standing on the sideline is, by default, voting "*no*" on every principle therein.[8]

* * *

So, stay off the sidelines before the United States of America's grand experiment in democracy is killed by the anti-America "ME/FU" Americans. That's all the "socialist-loving 'intellectuals,' screw-the-public profiteers (politicians and bureaucrats), mass media manipulators, antimilitary/antiauthority zealots, sanctimonious amoral moralists,"[10, vi] and every other Marxist/Maoist element out there.

Destroying freedom is what they do.

Patriotic Americans—moral and religious Americans—must stand together against the "ME/FU" mob. We're all in this together and—just as in combat—*we are all ONE!* As a result, "WE *not* ME" applies, but saving America makes it about "WE *the* PEOPLE *not* ME."

....
THE SPIRIT OF WE THE PEOPLE
... "WE *the* PEOPLE *not* ME"[1] ...
A life best lived should always be about YOU,
It should never be about ME;
But, the times to really cherish and hold on to
Are those all too fleeting moments in life
That are truly about WE;
"WE the PEOPLE not ME!"
....

214

Anti-America Marxists and Maoists have had America teetering on the brink of her own Gully of the Shadows of Death . . . the death of America. China and Russia are rooting for their communist comrades in the United States, stealthily, but ready to help nudge America over the edge.

Will our children's children be inheriting freedom?

"We the People" get to choose. We can "secure the Blessings of Liberty to ourselves and our Posterity"[2] . . . or NOT!

Freedom's survival—America's survival—is up to "We the People."

CHOOSE WISELY!!!

Appendix A

AUTHOR'S BIOGRAPHY

R.W. Trewyn, PhD
Vice President for Research Emeritus
Kansas State University

Raised on a 102-acre dairy farm in Wisconsin, Ron Trewyn was trained and employed as an accountant prior to starting college at Wisconsin State University–Whitewater (WSU-W) in January 1964. Becoming intrigued with marine biology, he transferred to the University of Hawaii in 1965, but after two years concluded it wasn't his calling. Taking a semester off to decide what research path to pursue, he ended up having more time when his draft notice arrived two days before Christmas in 1967.

Following basic and advanced infantry training, he attended the Army NCO candidate course graduating as a staff sergeant, E-6. He served with the 199th Light Infantry Brigade in Vietnam until his tour was cut short by shrapnel 2 inches from his heart. He nearly chose to go back, though, when welcomed home to incessant, rabid hatred.

Enduring the hostility, he completed his bachelor's degree, magna cum laude, at WSU-W (now the University of Wisconsin–Whitewater) in 1970. A month later he enrolled in graduate school at Oregon State University and earned a Ph.D. in 1974, majoring in microbial physiology with minors in biochemistry and genetics.

Following four years of postdoctoral cancer research at the University of Colorado Health Sciences Center, he was a professor of medical biochemistry at Ohio State for sixteen years (1978–94). He guided research on cancer development, diagnostics, and therapeutics as a member of the OSU Comprehensive Cancer Center, while directing the center's tumor procurement service, teaching biochemistry to medical students, and mentoring graduate students. Getting involved in military veteran advocacy activities (a–c), he and his colleagues exposed widespread discrimination against Vietnam-era veterans on college campuses in violation of federal law (d–n).

He assumed a research administration position at Kansas State University in 1994 and served in multiple leadership roles over the next two-and-a-half decades. Those included: president of the KSU Research Foundation; vice provost for research and dean of the graduate school; and vice president for research. He had a principal role in winning a national site selection that brought the $1.25 billion National Bio and Agro-defense Facility to the KSU campus. While serving on two

216

Agent Orange federal study committees (o–p), he helped disclose major analytical flaws in a twenty-five-year, $145 million Air Force veterans' health analysis (q–s).

He retired in 2022 as vice president for research emeritus at Kansas State.

Seeing parallels today to the anti-America anarchy of the 1960s and 1970s, he has written multiple op-ed articles based on lessons from VIETNAM'S WAR OF HATE (Appendix D).

Military Veteran Advocacy

(a) R.W. Trewyn: Judicial appointee to the Franklin County Veterans Service Commission, Columbus, OH, providing >$1 million in annual emergency relief to veterans, 1992 to 1994.

(b) R.W. Trewyn: Elected as the 1st Commander of the Colonel David H. Zook AMVETS Post 1974 established on the Ohio State University campus; March 5, 1992.

(c) James A. Stever, R.W. Trewyn and Abe Miller: 501(c)(3) Cofounders and Trustees, *Center for the Study of Veterans in Society,* Hamilton, OH, 1992 to 2010.

(d) R.W. Trewyn: "Protests aided resolve of the North Vietnamese." *The Columbus Dispatch,* Feb. 16, 1991.

(e) James A. Stever and R.W. Trewyn: "The campus war." *The Ohio AMVET,* 7: 14–15, 1992.

(f) R.W. Trewyn: "Veterans' rights: Correcting old wrongs." *Main Street Business Journal,* Columbus, Ohio, July 1992.

(g) R.W. Trewyn: "Does Political Correctness Relate to Anti-Veteran Bias on the College Campus?" *Political Correctness in Ohio.* Ohio Association of Scholars, Columbus, OH, November 20, 1992.

(h) R.W. Trewyn and James A. Stever: "Veterans' Rights: What Went Wrong?" Reserve Officers Association. *68th Annual State Convention.* Cincinnati, Ohio, April 23, 1993.

(i) R.W. Trewyn and James A. Stever: "Title 38, United States Code, Section 4212: Implementation & Enforcement by the U.S. Department of Labor." Written testimony to the U.S. House of Representatives' Veterans Affairs Committee, October 14, 1993.

(j) R.W. Trewyn: "Unequal Employment Opportunity for Military Veterans." Keynote address at the *Council of Scholars Colloquium* sponsored by the Vietnam Veterans Institute. Army Navy Club, Washington, D.C. November 12, 1993.

(k) R.W. Trewyn: "Discrimination against veterans by the federal agency charged with protecting veterans' rights." *Journal of the Vietnam Veterans Institute* 3: 22–36, 1994.

(l) R.W. Trewyn: Inducted into the Ohio Veterans Hall of Fame for his efforts to prevent employment discrimination against veterans on college campuses. November 1, 1994.

(m) R.W. Trewyn, James A. Stever and William E. Weber: "Employment Disparities and the Vietnam Veteran." *The History and Legacy of Those Who Served in Vietnam;* Keynote by General William C. Westmoreland. Hoffberger Center for Professional Ethics, University of Baltimore, Baltimore, Maryland. November 8 to 9, 1994.

(n) R.W. Trewyn and James A. Stever: "Academe: Not so hallowed halls for veterans." *Journal of the Vietnam Veterans Institute* 4: 63–75, 1995.

Agent Orange Health Effects Activities

(o) R.W. Trewyn: Appointed by the U.S. Secretary of Health and Human Services (HHS) to the HHS Advisory Committee on *Long-Term Health Effects of Phenoxy Herbicides*. Recommended by Admiral Elmo R. Zumwalt, Jr. Served from 1995 to 1999 and 2001 to 2006.

(p) R.W. Trewyn: National Institute for Environmental Health Sciences' Ad Hoc Panel on *Vietnam-U.S. Studies of Agent Orange/Dioxin*, 2000 to 2002.

(q) R.W. Trewyn: "U.S. Army Infantry Operations in Vietnam." Invited testimony to the National Academy of Sciences' Institute of Medicine Committee, *Health Effects in Vietnam Veterans of Exposure to Herbicides*, Irvine, CA. February 8, 1993.

(r) R.W. Trewyn: "Inadequacies of Federal Agent Orange Studies." Invited testimony to the U.S. House of Representatives' National Security, Veterans Affairs, and International Affairs Subcommittee, *Air Force Ranch Hand* Study on the Health Effects of Agent Orange*, Washington, D.C. March 15, 2000.

(s) R.W. Trewyn: "Air Force Agent Orange Health Study Flaws." *Nightline* interview by Ted Koppel in New York about the twenty-five-year, $145 million Vietnam Ranch Hand* health effects analysis, November 17, 2005.

---

* Ranch Hand was the name for the herbicide spraying missions in Vietnam.

Appendix B

GLOSSARY OF ABBREVIATIONS AND TERMS

A general meaning is provided for abbreviations, acronyms, slang, and jargon, as well as Vietnamese words, phrases, and terms used in *VIETNAM'S WAR OF HATE*. Some may not be precise, but represent the author's understanding or use of the terms.

Agent Blue	A cacodylic acid (arsenic-based) herbicide
Agent Orange	Herbicide mixture of 2,4-D and 2,4,5-T + dioxin
Airmobile	Transportation of infantry troops by helicopter
AK or AK-47	Russian Kalashnikov assault rifle
AMVETS	A military veterans' service organization
Arty	Slang for artillery in Vietnam; slang for author's arthritis pains
ARVN	Army of the Republic of Vietnam (South Vietnam)
Beaucoup	French for "big" or "a lot"; used in Vietnamese street jargon
Big Pond	The Pacific Ocean
C-4	A plastic explosive used in Vietnam
Cache	A hiding place for enemy supplies and materials
Cherry	A new guy in the field in Vietnam
Chieu Hoi	Vietnamese for surrender or give up; amnesty program
CIB	Combat Infantry Badge; earned only by being in combat
CMH	Congressional Medal of Honor
CO	Commanding officer
CS	A non-lethal tear gas
CSVS	Center for the Study of Veterans in Society
CV	Curriculum vitae
Dau Tranh	Vietnamese for warfare on all fronts; military, political, etc
DAV	Disabled American Veterans; veterans' service organization
D.C.	Washington, D.C.
Det Cord	An explosive cord used in Vietnam
DIC	Draft Information Club; a faculty-sponsored group at WSU-W

219

Didi Mau	Vietnamese for move out of the area rapidly
Diên Câu Dâù	Vietnamese for crazy
DMZ	Demilitarized zone
DOD	Department of Defense
DRV	Democratic Republic of Vietnam (North Vietnam)
Dustoff	Army medical evacuation by helicopter
E-1	Private; lowest Army enlisted rank
E-2	Private 2nd class; next to the lowest Army enlisted rank
E-3	Private 1st class; PFC in the Army
E-4	Corporal or specialist 4th class (Spec-4) in the Army
E-5	Sergeant or specialist 5th class (Spec-5); lowest NCO rank
E-6	Staff sergeant (SSG) or specialist 6th class (Spec-6)
E-7	Sergeant first class or specialist 7th class (Spec-7)
E-8	First sergeant or master sergeant
ESP	Extra-sensory perception
GI	Second World War slang for soldier; stands for government issue
GPA	Grade point average
GRE	Graduate record exam
Grunt	Infantry soldier
Huey	Bell UH-1 Army helicopter
IV	Intravenous
Jolly Green Giant	Sikorsky HH-53 Air Force rescue helicopter
KIA	Killed in action
KSU	Kansas State University, also K-State
LIB	Light Infantry Brigade
LRRP	Long-range reconnaissance patrol
LZ	Landing zone
Medevac	Medical evacuation
MIA	Missing in action
MF	Motherfucker
Mort	Slang for the piece of mortar shrapnel in the author's lung
MOPH	Military Order of the Purple Heart
MOS	Military occupational specialty, that is, job assignment
NCO	Noncommissioned officer; ranks of E-5 to E-9
Number 1	Vietnamese street slang for "the best"
Number 10	Vietnamese street slang for "the worst"
Nùóc Mâm	Vietnamese fish sauce; very aromatic (smells awful)
NVA	North Vietnamese Army

OCS	Officer Candidate School
OFCCP	Office of Federal Contract Compliance Programs
OSBP	Ohio State Biochemistry Program
OSU	*The* Ohio State University
PFC	Rank of private first class, E-3
Phở	Vietnamese soup
POW	Prisoner of war
PT	Physical training
Punji Pit	A pit with sharpened bamboo stakes dipped in feces
R&R	Rest and recuperation
REMF	Rear echelon motherfucker; non-infantry personnel
RNA	Ribonucleic acid
RPG	Rocket-propelled grenade
RTO	Radiotelephone operator
RVN	Republic of Vietnam
Same-same	Vietnamese street slang for "same as" or "likewise"
SDS	Students for a Democratic Society
Sin Loi	Vietnamese for "sorry about that" or "tough shit" by GIs (Sin Loi MF)
TDC	Teachers for a Democratic Society
Ti Ti	Vietnamese term for "tiny" or "small"; pronounced "tee tee"
UDI	Union of Democratic Intellectuals
VVA	Vietnam Veterans of America; veterans' service organization
VC	Vietcong
Victor Charlie	VC, that is, Vietcong
VFW	Veterans of Foreign Wars; veterans' service organization
WIA	Wounded in action
Willy Peter	Slang for white phosphorous explosive
WSU-W	Wisconsin State University–Whitewater (now UW-W: University of Wisconsin–Whitewater)

Appendix C

ENDURING TRUTHS

Chapter-Ending Lessons Learned Still Relevant Today

COMBAT ... THE "EASY" PART

Chapter 1: Pride ... Now You See It; Now You Don't

Adios, Mother! Hello, mom and apple pie.

Enduring Truth: *Pride serving honorably in war is timeless . . . valued by others or not.*

Chapter 2: Patriotism to Hell and Back

Grasping the fundamentals . . . right or wrong.

Enduring Truth: *Patriotism learned early inspires standards and expectations for life.*

Chapter 3: Vietnam

The agony and the ecstasy . . . death and "dry" socks.

Enduring Truth: *Pay attention! Lessons about death might really be lessons about life.*

Chapter 4: Okinawa

Recovering from the wounds; reflecting on the battles.

Enduring Truth: *Valley of the shadow memories can beckon more fear than the walk.*

Chapter 5: Reincarnation

The first weeks at home. A dead man gets a reprieve.

Enduring Truth: *Soldier to civilian should be easy—"no sweat!" Bet on it, you'll lose.*

COMING HOME . . . HOSTILE AND DEADLY

Chapter 6: Back to School

Walk-in-the-park student life . . . where the grizzly carnage really begins.
Enduring Truth: *Wounds suffered in war heal. Wounds inflicted at home persevere.*

Chapter 7: Hiding Out

Ducking incoming rounds. Where's the Goddamn DMZ?
Enduring Truth: *Antiwar rants ravage the hearts and souls of patriots who've served.*

Chapter 8: Surrounded by Traitors

Time to reenlist; time to go back to the Delta.
Enduring Truth: *Life or death? Unrelenting hate can turn the latter into the chosen path.*

ANTI-AMERICA AMERICANS . . .
LADY LIBERTY'S ACHILLES' HEEL
(A) *STRATEGIC THREATS*

1) *SOCIALIST-LOVING "INTELLECTUALS"*

Chapter 13: Ambushed by Friendly Fire

Pinned down; hunkered in the academic bunker.
Enduring Truth: *Antimilitary bigots lurk among the sham "intellectual elite" [sic/ sick].*

Chapter 19: Repent and Ye *Might* Be Employed

Or go hide in the closet. That works just as well . . . probably better.
Enduring Truth: *Unrepentant vets gave us freedom; the "elite" gave their worth: SHIT!*

Chapter 20: Not So Hallowed Halls

The feds' assessment: "harassment, intimidation and coercion."
Enduring Truth: *Elitist third-rate intellects vilify first-class patriots as second-class citizens.*

(C) *WORTHLESS THREATS*

5) *SANCTIMONIOUS AMORAL MORALISTS*

Chapter 10: Screw the Bastards

Enough is enough; the rotten bastards don't have the right.
Enduring Truth: *Only the war fighters truly know "what war is all about" . . . ASK!*

Chapter 12: SOS

Platoon: Served by Lee Iacocca with shit-on-a-shingle.
Enduring Truth: *Lies unchallenged become truth; truth dishonored begets more lies.*

SURVIVAL'S BOTTOM LINE . . . "WE *NOT* ME"
. . . FREEDOM'S BOTTOM LINE

Chapter 14: Retreat

Hiding in the West and rediscovering pride on sacred ground.
Enduring Truth: *Memorials to selfless servants are best built with citizens' hearts.*

Chapter 21: Goodbye Columbus

Good riddance is more like it.
Enduring Truth: *True military-friendly, veteran-friendly shows; veiled hate does too.*

Chapter 23: Pride . . . Use It or Lose It

Finding that elusive "welcome home" hidden in the Land of Enchantment.
Enduring Truth: *Valley of the shadow patriots: Guardians of Lady Liberty . . . ALWAYS!*

Appendix D

OP-ED ARTICLES INSPIRED BY *VIETNAM'S WAR OF HATE*

All have been based in part on VIETNAM'S WAR OF HATE and they have fallen into three general categories: (A) Combat in Vietnam and America; (B) Americanism/Patriotism; and (C) Destroying Liberty and Freedom. They are listed in the author's suggested order of importance.

A. Combat in Vietnam & America

1. Trewyn, R.W., "Time Warp: 1969/70 Anarchy . . . Recycle 2019/20," *Canada Free Press*, Dec. 3, 2020; https://canadafreepress.com/article/time-warp-1969-70-anarchy-recycle-2019-20

2. Trewyn, R.W., "Anti-America Americans Synergizing Again," *American Thinker*, Jan. 7, 2021; https://www.americanthinker.com/articles/2021/01/antiamerica_americans_are_synergizing_again.html

3. Trewyn, R.W. "Off to Vietnam as an NCO." *ARMY Magazine*, 73 (04): 57-58, Apr. 2023

4. Trewyn, R.W., "Correcting the Record About Vietnam Veterans' Service," *ARMY Magazine*, 72 (11): 23-25, Nov. 2022

5. Trewyn, R.W. "Vietnam's Medevac 'Saints' Provided a Crucial Lifeline." *ARMY Magazine*, 73 (08): 49-51, Aug. 2023

6. Trewyn, R.W., "'Stupid is as Stupid Does' in Vietnam and Afghanistan," *American Thinker*, Aug. 18, 2021; https://www.americanthinker.com/blog/2021/08/stupid_is_as_stupid_does_in_vietnam_and_afghanistan.html

7. Trewyn, R.W., "Vietnam's Role in Government Putrefaction Today," *American Thinker*, Jul. 31, 2021; https://www.americanthinker.com/articles/2021/07/vietnams_role_in_government_putrefaction_today.html

8. Trewyn, R.W., "In Vietnam, 'Enemy' Scouts Fought Alongside US Soldiers," *ARMY Magazine*, 73 (12): 56-58, Dec. 2023

9. Trewyn, R.W. "The Incompetence is Stunning," *Canada Free Press*, Apr. 18, 2023; https://canadafreepress.com/article/the-incompetence-is-stunning

10. Trewyn, R.W., "The Gully of the Shadows of Death Disproved Critical Race Theory Over 50-Years Ago," *Canada Free Press*, Jun. 29, 2021; https://canadafreepress.com/article/the-gully-of-the-shadows-of-death-disproved-critical-race-theory-over-50-years-ago

11. Trewyn, R.W., "Tested Under Fire: Relevant on the Battlefield and in the Streets," *Canada Free Press*, Feb. 2, 2021; https://canadafreepress.com/article/tested-under-fire-relevant-on-the-battlefield-and-in-the-streets

B. Americanism/Patriotism

1. Trewyn, R.W., "Army Combat Leadership Lessons for Life," *ARMY Magazine*, 74 (02): 11-12, Feb. 2024;
2. Trewyn, R.W. "Think You Can!" *American Thinker*, Jun. 27, 2023; https://www.americanthinker.com/blog/2023/06/think_you_can.html
3. Trewyn, R.W., "'WE' . . . the Only Pronoun that Truly Matters!" *Canada Free Press*, July 13, 2022; https://canadafreepress.com/article/we-the-only-pronoun-that-truly-matters
4. Trewyn, R.W., "Have Americans Become a People Who No Longer Deserve Their Constitution?" *American Thinker*, Jan. 12, 2022; https://www.americanthinker.com/blog/2022/01/have_americans_become_a_people_who_no_longer_deserve_their_constitution.html
5. Trewyn, R.W., "WE the PEOPLE not ME," *Canada Free Press*, Dec. 14, 2021; https://canadafreepress.com/article/we-the-people-not-me
6. Trewyn, R.W., "Last Rites for 'WE' in America—Last Rites for America?" *Canada Free Press*, Aug. 31, 2021; https://canadafreepress.com/article/last-rites-for-we-in-america-last-rites-for-america
7. Trewyn, R.W., "Hijacked the Flag?" *Canada Free Press*, Dec. 15, 2020; https://canadafreepress.com/article/hijacked-the-flag

C. Destroying Liberty & Freedom

1. Trewyn, R.W. "Is It DEI, IED or DIE? Yes, It Is!" *American Thinker*, Feb. 22, 2023; https://www.americanthinker.com/articles/2023/02/is_it_dei_ied_or_die_yes_it_is.html
2. Trewyn, R.W., "What's Causing Today's Epidemic Pathology?" *Canada Free Press*, December 7, 2022; https://canadafreepress.com/article/whats-causing-todays-epidemic-pathology
3. Trewyn, R.W. "Ayn Rand has some prescient thoughts about Democrats' avoidance of reality," *American Thinker*, Jul. 18, 2023; https://www.americanthinker.com/blog/2023/07/ayn_rand_has_some_prescient_thoughts_about_democrats_avoidance_of_reality.html
4. Trewyn, R.W., "Crying 'Racist!' is the Waterboarding of the Left," *American Thinker*, May 27, 2021; https://www.americanthinker.com/blog/2021/05/crying_racism_is_the_waterboarding_of_the_left.html
5. Trewyn, R.W., "What? The University of North Carolina is Banning DEI?" *American Thinker*, Feb. 28, 2028; https://www.americanthinker.com/blog/2023/02/what_the_university_of_north_carolina_is_banning_dei.html

6. Trewyn, R.W., "The Birth of Cancel Culture and the Death of Education," *American Thinker*, December 22, 2020; https://www.americanthinker.com/articles/2020/12/the_birth_of_cancel_culture_and_the_death_of_education_.html

7. Trewyn, R.W., "Vultures or Eagles? What's the Character of the Creatures in Residence?" *Canada Free Press*, Jun. 28, 2022; https://canadafreepress.com/article/vultures-or-eagles-whats-the-character-of-the-creatures-in-residence

8. Trewyn, R.W., "Biden Our Time . . . Ruining Our Time (BOT ROT)," *Canada Free Press*, Mar. 28, 2023; https://canadafreepress.com/article/biden-our-time-ruining-our-time-bot-rot

9. Trewyn, R.W., "Dave, Walter or Joe?" *Canada Free Press*, Aug. 11, 2022; https://canadafreepress.com/article/dave-walter-or-joe

10. Trewyn, R.W., "Cancel Culture M&Ms: Marxists & Maoists," *Canada Free Press*, Jun. 15, 2021; https://canadafreepress.com/article/cancel-culture-mms

11. Trewyn, R.W., "Big Tech—SS—Gestapo," *Canada Free Press*, Mar. 30, 2021; https://canadafreepress.com/article/big-tech-ss-gestapo

12. Trewyn, R.W., "Urinating with Skunks," *Canada Free Press*, January 5, 2021; https://canadafreepress.com/article/urinating-with-skunks

13. Trewyn, R.W., "Dysfunctional Airbags Potentially Deadly," *Canada Free Press*, January 12, 2021; https://canadafreepress.com/article/dysfunctional-airbags-potentially-deadly

ENDNOTES

Dedication

i. "WE *not* ME" is my shorthand description for combat selfless service and it was published initially in: Trewyn, R.W. "Time Warp: 1969/70 Anarchy . . . Recycle 2019/20," *Canada Free Press*, December 3, 2020.[1] That was also my first op-ed publication based on *VIETNAM'S WAR OF HATE*.

ii. "Number 1" was street jargon in Vietnam for "the best" as noted in Appendix B, Glossary of Abbreviations and Terms.

iii. "Number 10" was street jargon in Vietnam for "the worst" as noted in Appendix B, Glossary of Abbreviations and Terms.

Prologue

i. "The Spirit of WE" is a poem I composed about combat selfless service, and it was published in: Trewyn, R.W. "Last Rites for 'WE' in America—Last Rites for America?" *Canada Free Press*, August 31, 2021.[1] The poem included the following proviso in the article: "I believe 'the Spirit of WE' is an original work but can't rule out that I heard the poem sometime and it stuck with me. If that's the case, I would happily cite the poet."

ii. A complete Glossary of Abbreviations and Terms can be found in Appendix B.

iii. As touched on in the dedication endnote, "WE *not* ME" is my description of the combat selfless service I experienced firsthand in Vietnam. It was described in: Trewyn, R.W. "Time Warp: 1969/70 Anarchy . . . Recycle 2019/20," *Canada Free Press*, December 3, 2020. As noted therein, "In combat, unity equates to survival. It's all about 'WE *not* ME.' Living to see tomorrow takes race, ethnicity, and everything else out of the equation. If there were civil rights problems in the military in 1969, they were utterly undetectable within my Delta Company family. My brothers were just that: BROTHERS; black, white, pink, purple—TOTALLY irrelevant."[2]

iv. The infantry NCO Candidate Course at Fort Benning, GA was in place from 1967 to 1972 to address the significant shortage of NCOs in combat units in Vietnam. "Shake 'n' bake" was likely coined by old-line NCOs to pimp the graduates, but it became a proud trademark for many of us who made it through the course successfully.

v. Gully of the Shadows of Death encountered on Groundhog Day in 1969 was first used in print in: Trewyn, R.W. "The Gully of the Shadows of Death Disproved Critical Race Theory Over 50-Years Ago." *Canada Free Press*, June 29, 2021. As noted therein: "For anyone who experiences combat, it will likely be a difference-maker, positive and negative, for the rest of their lives. Remarkably, though, in the midst of the very worst humankind has to offer—WAR—you see the very best humankind has to give. Repeatedly, there are young U.S. troops—18 and 19-year-olds—putting their lives on the line to protect their brothers next to them . . . some of those brothers they may have known only a few days. . . .

Logic can't explain that selfless commitment—'WE' versus 'ME' in combat—to someone who hasn't been there; not in a way they'll feel to the core of their very being like those who've lived it. For anyone who has, those life and death fleeting moments will reside deep within . . . FOREVER! And for most, they're 100% about 'YOU' and 'WE'—0% 'ME.'"[3]

vi. See the "Enduring Truths" at the end of chapters 9–13, 15–20, and 22. A summary for all twenty-three chapters can be found in Appendix C.

vii. The five categories of anti-America Americans were described in: Trewyn, R.W. "Anti-America Americans Synergizing Again," *American Thinker*, Jan. 7, 2021. As noted therein, "From an old combat vet perspective, #1 and #2 would categorize as strategic threats, #3 and #4 as tactical threats, and #5 as worthless threats. The last one can't be ignored though, since those blowholes own a bully pulpit.

American patriots need to understand: these anarchists want to end U.S. democracy. The conspirators failed a half century ago; they might succeed this time."[4]

Chapter 2

i. Trewyn, R.W. "WE the PEOPLE not ME," *Canada Free Press*, Dec. 14, 2021. "Liberty and freedom come at a cost, and few Americans seem willing to step up and pay those costs anymore."[2]

ii. Trewyn, R.W. "Hijacked the Flag?" *Canada Free Press*, Dec. 15, 2020. "When you've walked the valley of the shadow of death with comrades-in-arms in uniform—any uniform, anytime, anywhere; every color, every culture, every religion—the American flag and national anthem have a higher, 'thou art with me' meaning."[6]

Chapter 3

i. A 2023 opinion article was written based on this Henry Ford quotation and my experiences in Vietnam as documented in *VIETNAM'S WAR OF HATE*: Trewyn, R.W. "Think You Can!" *American Thinker*, Jun. 27, 2023.[2]

ii. *VIETNAM'S WAR OF HATE* excerpts in the second freelance article of mine acquired by *ARMY Magazine*: Trewyn, R.W. "Off to Vietnam as an NCO." *ARMY Magazine*, 73 (04): 57–58, April 2023.[3]

iii. As noted in the prologue, the infantry NCO candidate course was in place from 1967 to 1972 to address the significant shortage of NCOs in combat units in Vietnam. "Shake 'n' bake" was likely coined by old-line NCOs who earned their stripes the old way, through years and years of hard work, rank by rank.

iv. Trewyn, R.W. "The Gully of the Shadows of Death Disproved Critical Race Theory Over 50-Years Ago," *Canada Free Press*, Jun. 29, 2021.[4] "Our last of multiple assaults on the enemy position began at 1813, entry #135, and we finally made it well inside the tree line to a massive ravine . . . the Gully of the Shadows of Death.
BOOM! Then, '[SH]IT' hit the fan – BIG TIME!!!
With the first machinegun burst from a shadowy hole in the side of the gully, our KIA/WIA numbers jumped again. . . . [Soon], Delta's commander joined his troops lost that day."[4]

v. *VIETNAM'S WAR OF HATE* excerpts in the fourth freelance article acquired by *ARMY Magazine*: Trewyn, R.W. "In Vietnam, 'Enemy' Scouts Fought Alongside US Soldiers," *ARMY Magazine*, 73 (12): 56–58, Dec. 2023.[5]

vi. *VIETNAM'S WAR OF HATE* excerpts in the third freelance article acquired by *ARMY Magazine*: Trewyn, R.W. "Vietnam's Medevac 'Saints' Provided a Crucial Lifeline," *Army Magazine*, 73 (08): 49–51, Aug. 2023.[6]

Chapter 4

i. This MLK quotation was used in my first published article from *VIETNAM'S WAR OF HATE*: Trewyn, R.W. "Time Warp: 1969/70 Anarchy . . . Recycle 2019/20," *Canada Free Press*, Dec. 3, 2020. "In Delta, everyone knew 'what they'd die for'—their 'WE *not* ME' brothers. After a firefight, those remaining knew 'why they are alive'—thanks to their 'WE *not* ME' brothers.
Combat is horrific, but those extraordinary MLK moments illuminated the very best within: love of brothers, love of country, love of life. The former led to a willingness to sacrifice the latter.
Thus, I left Vietnam knowing we are all ONE. I came home to discover we're NOT."[2]

Chapter 6

i. This Dr. Martin Luther King, Jr. quotation provided the impetus for another opinion article based on *VIETNAM'S WAR OF HATE*: Trewyn, R.W. "'WE' . . . the Only Pronoun that Truly Matters!" *Canada Free Press*, July 13, 2022. As noted therein, "Selfless service in war is real, as is the colorblind brotherhood in war. It proved to me that 'we must live together as brothers or perish together as fools.'"[1,2]

Chapter 7

i. This colorblind point was expanded upon in my first publication based on *VIETNAM'S WAR OF HATE*: Trewyn, R.W. "Time Warp: 1969/70 Anarchy . . .

Recycle 2019/20," *Canada Free Press*, December 3, 2020. "In combat, unity equates to survival. It's all about 'WE *not* ME.' Living to see tomorrow takes race, ethnicity, and everything else out of the equation. If there were civil rights problems in the military in 1969, they were utterly undetectable within my Delta Company family. My brothers were just that: BROTHERS; black, white, pink, purple—TOTALLY irrelevant.

I placed my life in their hands; they placed their lives in mine. That's just the way it is in battle: it's your family."[2]

Chapter 9

i. I was able to tell the Old Main story 50-years later: Trewyn, R.W. "Time Warp: 1969/70 Anarchy . . . Recycle 2019/20," *Canada Free Press*, December 3, 2020. "In 1970, Weathermen and accomplices infiltrated 'nonviolent' [*sic*] protests and torched the land-mark structure on campus, Old Main, destroying 107,000 square feet of teaching space.

I started my education—literally, kindergarten—in the building I watched burn."[2]

ii. *VIETNAM'S WAR OF HATE* excerpts in my first free-lance article acquired by *Army Magazine*: Trewyn, R.W. "Correcting the Record About Vietnam Veterans' Service," *Army Magazine*, 72 (11): 23–25, Nov. 2022.[4] The stop-action image of the tower pinnacle falling is still as clear as it was that cold night in February 1970.

Chapter 10

i. Trewyn, R.W. "What's Causing Today's Epidemic Pathology?" *Canada Free Press*, December 7, 2022. "BOOM! Her soft, glimmering eyes exploded into dagger-emitting magma and the initially attractive young lass transformed into a malicious witch."[2]

ii. Trewyn, R.W. "Cancel Culture M&Ms: Marxists and Maoists," *Canada Free Press*, June 15, 2021: "On-campus today, the most senior 'artistic, social, or political' M&Ms got their training during the Vietnam antiwar riots of the 1960s/70s or soon thereafter. They didn't serve the country, so hating their country came easy. Marx and Mao were their heroes. And, of course, the antiwar, antimilitary, anti-America faculty of the Vietnam era trained the next generation of faculty members who joined their ranks. That indoctrinated group trained the next generation and so on."[5]

Chapter 11

i. This Ayn Rand quotation, and some of her others, became the subject of another opinion article inspired by *VIETNAM'S WAR OF HATE* that was submitted with the nonpartisan title, "America . . . Stop Avoiding Reality!" The online editors opted to change it to: Trewyn, R.W. "Ayn Rand has some prescient thoughts about Democrats' avoidance of reality," *American Thinker*, July 18, 2026.[2]

Chapter 18

i. I highlighted this issue from Minister Tang's book in an article published in 2021, many years after writing chapter 18: Trewyn, R.W. "'Stupid Is as Stupid' Does in Vietnam and Afghanistan," *American Thinker*, Aug. 18, 2021.[15]

ii. This topic in Guenter Lewy's book was also highlighted in my 2021 article: Trewyn, R.W. "'Stupid Is as Stupid' Does in Vietnam and Afghanistan," *American Thinker*, Aug. 18, 2021.[15]

iii. This topic from Minister Tang's book was also highlighted in the article many years after writing chapter 18: Trewyn, R.W. "'Stupid Is as Stupid' Does in Vietnam and Afghanistan," *American Thinker*, Aug. 18, 2021.[15]

iv. Professor Berger's article was cited in this essay many years after I wrote Chapter 18 as well: Trewyn, R.W. "Vietnam's Role in Government Putrefaction Today," *American Thinker*, July 31, 2021.[25]

Chapter 19

i. "Daggers of hate in American eyes" is the pathology discussed in this article and Sue was one of two who inspired the article: Trewyn, R.W. "What's Causing Today's Epidemic Pathology?" *Canada Free Press*, Dec. 7, 2022.[6]

ii. Trewyn, R.W. "Urinating with Skunks," *Canada Free Press*, Jan. 5, 2021.[13] This article focused on the local, state, and federal insanity in 2019 and 2020; stupidity like defunding the police. It came out the day before the Capitol Hill "issues" in Washington, D.C. where pissing contests with skunks became highly relevant.

Chapter 21

i. The committee didn't find out until the project was nearly finished that the Air Force was not required to implement any of our recommendations.

ii. My service on the committee was from 1995 to 1999 and 2002 to 2006 when the final report was completed. At the meeting in 1999, we found out that one-third of the study control group had been stationed in Vietnam. That meant they were exposed to Agent Orange since all the military bases there were sprayed with herbicides routinely. Thus, the statistical analyses were meaningless, and I objected vociferously. That may have been why I wasn't reappointed until 2002, but I was invited to testify before congress about it:
Trewyn, R.W. "Inadequacies of Federal Agent Orange Studies." Requested testimony to the U.S. House of Representatives' National Security, Veterans Affairs, and International Affairs Subcommittee, *Air Force Ranch Hand Study on the Health Effects of Agent Orange*, Washington, D.C., March 15, 2000.[8]
Unbelievably, we found out in 2005 that the statistical flaws were not being corrected in the final report being prepared by the Air Force; they were sticking

with the original study protocol. I protested again and that led to a national television interview by Ted Koppel:

Trewyn, R.W. "Air Force Agent Orange health study flaws with the 25-year, $145 million Vietnam Ranch Hand analysis," *Nightline*, Nov. 17, 2005.[9]

After the broadcast, two retired Air Force colonels sent a letter to the K-State president demanding that I be fired for making slanderous comments about the study they designed.

Chapter 22

i. A focus of my writing most recently has been to convey the message of selfless service in the military; how universal "WE *not* ME" really is. The following are examples:

Trewyn, R.W. "Time Warp: 1969/70 Anarchy . . . Recycle 2019/20," *Canada Free Press*, Dec. 3, 2020;[4]

Trewyn, R.W. "Tested Under Fire: Relevant on the Battlefield and in the Streets," *Canada Free Press*, Feb. 2, 2021;[5]

Trewyn, R.W. "The Gully of the Shadows of Death Disproved Critical Race Theory Over 50-Years Ago," *Canada Free Press*, June 29, 2021;[6]

Trewyn, R.W. "'Stupid Is as Stupid Does' in Vietnam and Afghanistan," *American Thinker*, Aug. 18, 2021;[7]

Trewyn, R.W. "Last Rites for 'WE' in America—Last Rites for America?" *Canada Free Press*, Aug. 31, 2021;[8]

Trewyn, R.W. "WE the PEOPLE not ME," *Canada Free Press*, December 14, 2021;[9]

Trewyn, R.W. "'WE' . . . the Only Pronoun that Truly Matters!" *Canada Free Press*, July 13, 2022.[10]

Epilogue I

i. "WE *not* ME" is relevant again today because of what was pointed out in the following article: Trewyn, R.W. "Time Warp: 1969/70 Anarchy . . . Recycle 2019/20," *Canada Free Press*, Dec. 3, 2020. "What I've seen in 2019/20 is a mirror image of what I lived in 1969/70."[1]

ii. That mirror image makes the poem particularly relevant as well: Trewyn, R.W. "Last Rites for 'WE' in America—Last Rites for America?" *Canada Free Press*, Aug. 31, 2021. "When every person focuses on YOU, not ME, it makes WE a powerful force that MIGHT be beatable, but it's 100% UNBREAKABLE."[2]

iii. Trewyn, R.W. "The Gully of the Shadows of Death Disproved Critical Race Theory Over 50-Years Ago," *Canada Free Press*, June 29, 2021. "But HOW, exactly, did the Gully of the Shadows of Death disprove CRT?
It's quite simple actually: 'WE *not* ME.' On Groundhog Day in 1969, I learned that the often-described brotherhood in battle is real. 'WE' means EVERY combat brother."[3]

iv. I was going to speak about the relevance of combat leadership—"Follow Me" and "battlefield vision"—to academic leadership a mere six days later at Lisa Freeman's investiture as the Northern Illinois University president. As a result, I was thinking about Vietnam and selfless service more than I had for years in preparing for that talk; I was anticipating a hostile audience (it wasn't). Nonetheless, that may have been what finally allowed me to connect all the loose ends.

v. Trewyn, R.W. "Anti-America Americans Synergizing Again," *American Thinker*, Jan. 7, 2021. "Fully comprehending the interplay took 30 years, but that got me to the rank order above. From an old combat vet perspective, #1 and #2 would categorize as strategic threats, #3 and #4 as tactical threats, and #5 as worthless threats. The last one can't be ignored though, since those blowholes own a bully pulpit."[7]

vi. See the "Enduring Truths" at the end of Chapters 9–13, 15–20, and 22. A summary for all twenty-three chapters can be found in Appendix C.

vii. Trewyn, R.W. "Stupid Is as Stupid Does in Vietnam and Afghanistan," *American Thinker*, Aug. 18, 2021. "How Afghanistan will compare to Vietnam in the long run is to be determined, but 'stupid is as stupid does' is what comes when politicos don't learn from history. Unfortunately, it's the norm in Washington, D.C. where the I.Q. of a cabbage—*skunk cabbage*—is as good as it ever gets."[9]

Epilogue II

i. The first article written from VIETNAM'S WAR OF HATE: Trewyn, R.W. "Time Warp: 1969/70 Anarchy . . . Recycle 2019/20," *Canada Free Press*, Dec. 3, 2020. "ALL LIVES MATTER!"[1]

ii. It's the anti-America Americans who are destroying freedom: Trewyn, R.W. "Anti-America Americans Synergizing Again," *American Thinker*, Jan. 7, 2021. "American patriots need to understand: these anarchists want to end U.S. democracy. The conspirators failed a half century ago; they might succeed this time."[2]

iii. See the "Enduring Truths" at the end of chapters 9–13, 15–20, and 22. A summary for all twenty-three chapters can be found in Appendix C.

iv. Enduring truths for Chapters 13, 19 and 20; see Appendix C for a complete list.

v. From: Trewyn, R.W. "The Birth of Cancel Culture and the Death of Education," *American Thinker*, December 22, 2020: ""Vietnam draft dodgers and allied haters of those who serve assumed control of U.S. universities decades ago. They and their trainees vilify America and American patriots, making national pride an alien concept on most college campuses."[3]

vi. Enduring truth for Chapters 15 and 17; see Appendix C for a complete list.

vii. Enduring truths for Chapters 18 and 22; see Appendix C for a complete list.

viii. Trewyn, R.W. "Big Tech—SS—Gestapo," *Canada Free Press*, March 30, 2021.[5] The Nazis' "Schutzstaffel" (SS) becomes "Speech Slaughtering" with Big Tech.

ix. Enduring truths for Chapters 9, 11, and 16; see Appendix C for a complete list.
x. Trewyn, R.W. "Tested Under Fire: Relevant on the Battlefield and in the Streets," *Canada Free Press*, Feb. 2, 2021. "The images from today's cities with rioting and looting ongoing—a.k.a., mostly peaceful protests—have illuminated clear analogies regarding what infantry troops face on the battlefield and police officers face in the streets."[7]
xi. Enduring truths for Chapters 10 and 12; see Appendix C for a complete list.
xii. This became the subject of another opinion article inspired by *VIETNAM'S WAR OF HATE* that was submitted with the nonpartisan title, "Today's Woke Waterboarding Threat to U.S. Freedom." The online editors opted to change it to: Trewyn, R.W. "Crying 'Racism!' is the Waterboarding of the Left," *American Thinker*, May 27, 2021. "When those screaming 'you are racist' are the de facto racists and the power brokers in America let them get away with it—*and benefit from it*—it's time for American patriots to take a stand and fight."[10]

Epilogue III

i. Trewyn, R.W. "WE the PEOPLE not ME," *Canada Free Press*, Dec. 14, 2021.[1] The article is reproduced verbatim after the verse except for the last two paragraphs.
ii. The British spelling of defense.
iii. From: Trewyn, R.W. "Last Rites for 'WE' in America—Last Rites for America?" *Canada Free Press*, August 31, 2021. "'We the People' was how it all began and 'WE' had a good run . . . almost 250 years. Tragically, 'WE' died somewhere along the way, RECENTLY"[4]
iv. Trewyn, R.W. "The Gully of the Shadows of Death Disproved Critical Race Theory Over 50-Years Ago," *Canada Free Press*, June 29, 2021. "Critical race theorists—i.e., critical racists—DON'T BELIEVE in the U.S. Declaration of Independence, July 4, 1776: 'We hold these truths to be self-evident, that all men are created equal . . .' They don't WANT YOU TO BELIEVE in it either."[6]
v. Trewyn, R.W. "Have Americans Become a People Who No Longer Deserve Their Constitution?" *American Thinker*, Jan. 12, 2022.[8] The essay is reproduced here with minor modifications at the beginning to merge it with the other article.
vi. Trewyn, R.W. "Anti-America Americans Synergizing Again," *American Thinker*, Jan. 7, 2021. "American patriots need to understand: these anarchists want to end U.S. democracy. The conspirators failed a half century ago; they might succeed this time."[10]

BIBLIOGRAPHY

General References

Abbott, Bill. "Names on the Wall," *Vietnam Magazine*, June 1993.

Army and Navy Publishing Company, Inc. *127th Infantry*, Baton Rouge, Louisiana, 1941.

Atkinson, Rick. *The Long Gray Line*, Pocket Books, New York, 1989.

Banerian, James. *Losers Are Pirates: A Close Look at the PBS Series "Vietnam: A Television History,"* Sphinx Publishing, Phoenix, Arizona, 1985.

Berger, Peter L. "Indochina and the American conscience," *Commentary*, February 1980.

Bergerud, Eric M. *Red Thunder, Tropic Lightning*, Penguin Books, New York, 1993.

Blakeley, Major General H.W., USA, Ret. *The 32D Infantry Division in Second World War*, Bureau of Purchases, State Capital, Madison, Wisconsin, 1955.

Bowman, John S. *The Vietnam War: Day by Day*, Brompton Books Corporation, Hong Kong, 1989.

Braestrup, Peter. *Big Story*, Yale University Press, New Haven, 1978.

Brody, Jeffrey. "Vietnamese Ignored in Films," *The Columbus Dispatch*, February 25, 1990.

Burkett, B.G. and Glenna Whitley. *Stolen Valor: How the Vietnam Generation was Robbed of its Heroes and its History*, Verity Press Dallas, 1998.

Burleigh, Nina. "After Years of Silence, the Healing Begins," *Chicago Tribune*, May 28, 1989.

Chavez, Linda. "Vietnam a Mistake? Fewer finding fault," *USA Today*, April 19, 1995.

Coate, Richard. "The Forgotten War," *The Columbus Dispatch*, April 22, 1990.

Collier, Peter, and David Horowitz. *Destructive Generation: Second Thoughts about the Sixties*, Summit Books, New York, 1989.

Collier, Peter. "At Home: The Left's Anti-War Follies, (Tet: Twenty-Five Years Later)," *The American Legion*, February, 1993.

Davidson, Lt. Gen. Phillip B., USA (Ret.). *Vietnam at War: The History 1946-1975*, Presidio Press, Novato, California, 1988.

------. *Secrets of the Vietnam War*, Presidio Press, Novato, California, 1990.

Downs, Jr., Frederick. *Aftermath: A True Story*, Berkley Books, New York, 1985.

Duc, Nguyen Qui. *Where the Ashes Are*, Addison-Wesley Publishing, Reading, Massachusetts, 1994.

Eckhardt, Mary. "Regents Deny Recognition of Faculty Teamsters Local," *Royal Purple*, May 4, 1970.

Edelman, Bernard. *Dear America: Letters Home from Vietnam*. Pocket Books, New York, 1985.

Eilert, Rick. "Hollywood's War Against Vietnam Veterans," *American Legion Magazine*, July, 1990.

Elegant, Robert. "How to Lose a War," *Encounter*, August 1981.

Engelmann, Larry. *Tears Before the Rain: An Oral History of the Fall of South Vietnam*, Oxford University Press, New York, 1990.

Esper, George. "Vietnam Plus 15: Divisive War Lives on in Minds of Many Vets," *The Columbus Dispatch*, April 29, 1990.

Franklin, H. Bruce. "The Antiwar Movement We Are Supposed to Forget," *The Chronicle of Higher Education*, October 20, 2000.

Gabrenya, Frank. "'Born on Fourth' Opens More Eyes," *The Columbus Dispatch*, February 4, 1990.

Goebel, Ulf. *Sgt. Ed Arthur's Nam*, Dakar Publishing, Westerville, Ohio, 1974.

Gottlieb, Sherry Gershon. *Hell No We Won't Go! Resisting the Draft During the Vietnam War*, Viking Penguin, New York, 1991.

Greene, Bob. *Homecoming*, G.P. Putnam's Sons, New York, 1989.

Guilmartin, John. *America in Vietnam: The Fifteen Year War*, Military Press, New York, 1991.

Hammond, William M. *Public Affairs: The Military And The Media, 1962-1968*, U.S. Government Printing Office, Washington, D.C., 1988.

Hasse, John. "Protest Challenges Academic Freedom, Burrows Participates in Discussion," *Royal Purple*, May 4, 1970.

Hearden, Patrick J. *The Tragedy of Vietnam*, Harper Collins Publishers, New York, 1991.

Horton, Stan. "Hollywood's War on Vietnam Vets," *VFW Magazine*, November 1989.

Innerst, Carol. "Lawmaker Unveils Plight of Vietnam Veterans," *Washington Times*, July 31, 1996.

Jacoby, Jeff. "When Jane Fonda Spoke Out," *Boston Globe*, June 17, 1999.

Janesville Gazette. "Ex-UW-W Chief Recalls War Days," February 23, 1989.

Karnow, Stanley. *Vietnam: A History*, Penguin Books, New York, 1984.

Kimball, Roger. *Tenured Radicals*, Harper Perennial, New York, 1990.

Kiryio, Maria. "Coming home: Nurses Find the Road Back From Vietnam Long, Hard," *Chicago Tribune*, May 28, 1989.

Landsberg, Mitchell. "1968: The Year of Living Dangerously," *The Columbus Dispatch*, February 7, 1993.

Lanning, Michael Lee. *The Only War We Had: A Platoon Leader's Journal of Vietnam*, Ivy Books, New York, 1987.

------ and Dan Cragg. *Inside the VC and the NVA: The Real Story of North Vietnam's Armed Forces*, Ivy Books, New York, 1992.

Lewy, Guenter. *America in Vietnam*, Oxford University Press, New York, 1978.

Lifton, Robert Jay. *Home from the War*, Beacon Press, Boston, 1992.

Mayo, Lida. *Bloody Buna*, Doubleday and Company, Garden City, New York, 1974.

MacNeil, Robert. *The Right Place at the Right Time*, Penguin Books, New York, 1990.

MacPherson, Myra. *Long Time Passing: Vietnam and the Haunted Generation*, Doubleday and Company, Garden City, 1984.

Massie, Jim. "Saigon: Joy, Regret and a Temple Dog," *The Columbus Dispatch*, April 29, 1990.

McBride, Barb. "Professor Believes Dissent Great Social Value," *Royal Purple*, November 6, 1969.

McDaniel, Dorothy. *After the Hero's Welcome: A POW Wife's Story of the Battle Against a New Enemy*, Bonus Books, Chicago, 1991.

McDaniel, Eugene "Red." "In Hanoi: Inside, Looking Out, (Tet: Twenty-Five Years Later)," *The American Legion*, February 1993.

Mittelman, Captain Joseph B. *Eight Stars to Victory*, The Ninth Infantry Division Association, Washington, D.C., 1948.

Moore, Lt. Gen. Harold (Ret.) and Joseph L. Galloway. *We Were Soldiers Once . . . and Young*, Random House, New York, 1992.

Nolan, Keith William. *The Battle for Saigon: Tet 1968*, Pocket Books, New York, 1996.

Oconomowoc Enterprise. "25 Years Ago Company G Left for World War II," October 21, 1965.

O'Neill, John E. and Jerome R. Corsie. *Unfit for Command: Swift Boat Veterans Speak Out Against John Kerry.* Regnery Publishing, Inc., Washington, D.C., 2004.

Page, Tim, and John Pimlott. *Nam: The Vietnam Experience 1965-75*, Hamlyn Publishing, London, 1990.

Reinberg, Linda. *In the Field: The Language of the Vietnam War*, Facts on File, New York, 1991.

Roberts, Leslie. "Vietnam's Psychological Toll," *Science*, 241: 159–61, 1988.

Royal Purple. "Students Plan National Anti-War Demonstration," October 6, 1969.

------. "Fire destroys Old Main," February 9, 1970.

------. "'Whitewater 4' Speak of Past Events; Also Talk of Future Academic Freedom," March 12, 1970.

Ruesch, Tom. "Teamsters Begin Picketing Hope to Gain Recognition," *Royal Purple*, May 14, 1970.

Rusher, William. "Missing the Point About Vietnam," *Washington Times*, April 21, 1995.

Santoli, Al. *Everything We Had: An Oral History of the Vietnam War by Thirty-three American Soldiers Who Fought It*, Balentine Books, New York, 1981.

Scharnberg, Ken. "Vietnam: Twenty-Five Years After Tet," *The American Legion*, February, 1993.

------. "Someone Is Screaming: It's You, (Tet: Twenty-Five Years Later)," *The American Legion*, February 1993.

Sorley, Lewis. *A Better War: The Unexamined Victories and Final Tragedy of America's Last Years in Vietnam*, Harcourt Brace and Company, Orlando, 1999.

Spector, Ronald. "In the Field: The Stalemate Continues (Tet: Twenty-Five Years Later)," *The American Legion*, February 1993.

Stevens, Michael E. *Voices from Vietnam*, State Historical Society of Wisconsin, Madison, 1996.

Stone, Andrea. "Chicago '68: Revisiting the Storm," *USA Today*, August 21, 1996.

Strempf, Tony. "Distorted 'Lessons' From the Vietnam War," *Academic Questions*, Transaction Periodicals Consortium, New Brunswick, Winter, 1992–93.

Summers, Colonel Harry G., Jr. *On Strategy: A Critical Analysis of the Vietnam War*, Dell Publishing, New York, 1984.

------. *Vietnam War Almanac*, Facts on File Publications, New York, 1985.

------. "In Washington: Defeat Snatched From Victory (Tet: Twenty-Five Years Later)," *The American Legion*, February 1993.

Tang, Truong Nhu, David Chanoff and Doan Van Toai. *A Vietcong Memoir: An Inside Account of the Vietnam War and its Aftermath*, Vintage Books, New York, 1985.

Thompson, Leroy. *The US Army in Vietnam*, David & Charles Publishers, Devon, England, 1990.

Vien, General Cao Van. *The Final Collapse*, Center of Military History, U.S. Army, Washington, D.C., 1985.

Webb, James. "Can He Come Home Again?" *Wisconsin State Journal Parade*, April 2, 1989.

------. "The Media's War on Vietnam Vets," *Wall Street Journal*, July 15, 1998.

Weikel, Dan. "U.S. Finds Job Bias Against Veterans at Cal State Long Beach," *Los Angeles Times*, August 15, 2000.

West, Diana. "Does 'Born on the Fourth of July' Lie?" *Washington Times*, February 23, 1990.

Westphall, Victor. "The DAV Vietnam Veterans National Memorial: A Brief History," *DAV Vietnam Veterans National Memorial*, November 1990.

Whitewater Register. "Moratorium Day Parade Appears Orderly," October 16, 1969.

Wyatt, Clarence R. *Paper Soldiers: The American Press and the Vietnam War*, W.W. Norton & Company, New York, 1993.

Cited References

Dedication

1. Trewyn, R.W. "Time Warp: 1969/70 Anarchy . . . Recycle 2019/20," *Canada Free Press*, Dec. 3, 2020; https://canadafreepress.com/article/time-warp-1969-70-anarchy-recycle-2019-20

Prologue

1. Trewyn, R.W. "Last Rites for 'WE' in America -- Last Rites for America?" *Canada Free Press,* Aug. 31, 2021; https://canadafreepress.com/article/last-rites-for-we-in-america-last-rites-for-america
2. ------. "Time Warp: 1969/70 Anarchy . . . Recycle 2019/20," *Canada Free Press*, Dec. 3, 2020; https://canadafreepress.com/article/time-warp-1969-70-anarchy-recycle-2019-20
3. ------. "The Gully of the Shadows of Death Disproved Critical Race Theory Over 50-Years Ago," *Canada Free Press*, June 29, 2021; https://canadafreepress.com/article/the-gully-of-the-shadows-of-death-disproved-critical-race-theory-over-50-years-ago
4. ------. "Anti-America Americans Synergizing Again," *American Thinker*, Jan. 7, 2021; https://www.americanthinker.com/articles/2021/01/antiamerica_americans_are_synergizing_again.html

Chapter 1

1. https://www.scrapbook.com/quotes/doc/41379.html

Chapter 2

1. https://motivationgrid.com/21-inspiring-quotes-by-albert-einstein/
2. Trewyn, R.W. "WE the PEOPLE not ME," *Canada Free Press*, December 14, 2021; https://canadafreepress.com/article/we-the-people-not-me
3. Blakeley, Major General H.W., USA, Ret. *The 32D Infantry Division in Second World War*, p. 127, Bureau of Purchases, State Capital, Madison, Wisconsin, 1955.
4. Mayo, Lida. *Bloody Buna*, p. 170, Doubleday and Company, Garden City, New York, 1974.
5. Blakeley, Major General H.W., USA, Ret. *The 32D Infantry Division in Second World War*, p. 95, Bureau of Purchases, State Capital, Madison, Wisconsin, 1955.
6. Trewyn, R.W. "Hijacked the Flag? *Canada Free Press*, December 15, 2020; https://canadafreepress.com/print_friendly/hijacked-the-flag

Chapter 3

1. https://www.goodreads.com/author/quotes/203714.Henry_Ford
2. Trewyn, R.W. "Think You Can!" *American Thinker*, Jun. 27, 2023; https://www.americanthinker.com/blog/2023/06/think_you_can.html
3. Trewyn, R.W. "Off to Vietnam as an NCO." *ARMY Magazine*, 73 (04): 57–58, April 2023.
4. Trewyn, R.W. "The Gully of the Shadows of Death Disproved Critical Race Theory Over 50-Years Ago," *Canada Free Press*, June 29, 2021; https://

canadafreepress.com/article/the-gully-of-the-shadows-of-death-disproved-critical-race-theory-over-50-years-ago
5. Trewyn, R.W. "In Vietnam, 'Enemy' Scouts Fought Alongside US Soldiers," *ARMY Magazine*, 73 (12): 56–58, Dec. 2023.
6. Trewyn, R.W. "Vietnam's Medevac 'Saints' Provided a Crucial Lifeline." *ARMY Magazine*, 73 (08): 49–51, August 2023.

Chapter 4

1. https://www.birminghamtimes.com/2018/01/some-of-dr-martin-luther-king-jr-s-profound-quotes/
2. Trewyn, R.W. "Time Warp: 1969/70 Anarchy . . . Recycle 2019/20," *Canada Free Press*, Dec. 3, 2020; https://canadafreepress.com/article/time-warp-1969-70-anarchy-recycle-2019-20
3. https://www.kingjamesbibleonline.org/Psalms-23-4/

Chapter 5

1. https://www.brainyquote.com/quotes/gad_saad_998516

Chapter 6

1. https://www.brainyquote.com/quotes/martin_luther_king_jr_101309
2. Trewyn, R.W. "'WE' . . . the Only Pronoun that Truly Matters!" *Canada Free Press*, July 13, 2022; https://canadafreepress.com/article/we-the-only-pronoun-that-truly-matters
3. *Royal Purple*. "Students Launch Anti-War Campaign," Oct. 2, 1969.

Chapter 7

1. https://www.brainyquote.com/quotes/edwin_louis_cole_170162
2. Trewyn, R.W. "Time Warp: 1969/70 Anarchy . . . Recycle 2019/20," *Canada Free Press*, Dec. 3, 2020; https://canadafreepress.com/article/time-warp-1969-70-anarchy-recycle-2019-20

Chapter 8

1. Greene, Bob. *Homecoming: When the Soldiers Came Home from Vietnam*, p. 236. G.P. Putnam's Sons, New York, NY, 1989.
2. *Royal Purple*. "Reaction to Vietnam Speech," Nov. 6, 1969.
3. McBride, Barb. "Professor Believes Dissent Great Social Value," *Royal Purple,* Nov. 6, 1969.
4. *Royal Purple*. "Dr. Adams Examines Educational Functions," Oct. 9, 1969.

5. ------. "DeAntonio's Controversial War Film Displays 'Immorality Of Involvement,'" Dec. 8, 1969.
6. Beattie, Leal, and Cygan, John. "Anti-ROTC students march, presents demands to Carter," *Royal Purple*, Dec. 15, 1969.

Chapter 9

1. https://www.brainyquote.com/quotes/friedrich_nietzsche_124387
2. Trewyn, R.W. "Time Warp: 1969/70 Anarchy . . . Recycle 2019/20," *Canada Free Press*, Dec. 3, 2020; https://canadafreepress.com/article/time-warp-1969-70-anarchy-recycle-2019-20
3. *Whitewater Register*. "Last Big Fire All but Destroyed North Wing," Feb. 12, 1970.
4. Trewyn, R.W. "Correcting the Record About Vietnam Veterans' Service," *ARMY Magazine*, 72 (11): 23–25, Nov. 2022.
5. *Royal Purple*. "State Rules Arson in Blaze," Feb. 9, 1970.

Chapter 10

1. https://www.goodreads.com/quotes/721301-fear-is-a-reaction-courage-is-a-decision
2. Trewyn, R.W. "What's Causing Today's Epidemic Pathology?" *Canada Free Press*, Dec. 7, 2022; https://canadafreepress.com/article/whats-causing-todays-epidemic-pathology
3. *Royal Purple*. "Monday's edition was Roger's worst," May 7, 1970.
4. ------. "In Memoriam: Allison Krause, Sandy Scheuer, Jeffrey Miller, William Schroeder; Died Monday, May 4, 1970, Kent State University," May 7, 1970.
5. Trewyn, R.W. "Cancel Culture M&Ms: Marxists and Maoists," *Canada Free Press*, June 15, 2021; https://canadafreepress.com/article/cancel-culture-mms
6. *Royal Purple*. "Anti-war Moratoriums Forecasted for Spring," February 23, 1970.
7. ------. "Robert Burrows, Chairman of the Department of English," February 26, 1970.
8. ------. "Carter Suspends English Teachers," March 5, 1970.
9. ------. "Doyle Orders University to Admit Suspended Faculty," March 9, 1970.
10. ------. "English Faculty Affiliates With Teamsters Local 579," April 9, 1970.

Chapter 11

1. https://www.goodreads.com/quotes/7204254-you-can-avoid-reality-but-you-cannot-avoid-the-consequences
2. Trewyn, R.W. "Ayn Rand Has Some Prescient Thoughts About Democrats' Avoidance of Reality," *American Thinker*, July 18, 2023; https://www.americanthinker.com/blog/2023/07/ayn_rand_has_some_prescient_thoughts_about_democrats_avoidance_of_reality.html

Chapter 12

1. https://www.brainyquote.com/quotes/helen_keller_383771

Chapter 13

1. https://www.pinterest.com/pin/103442122670140174/

Chapter 14

1. https://susanershler.com/inspirational-quote-pain-is-temporary-pride-is-forever/

Chapter 15

1. https://www.brainyquote.com/quotes/will_rogers_411692

Chapter 16

1. https://www.brainyquote.com/quotes/miguel_de_cervantes_157071

Chapter 17

1. https://www.brainyquote.com/quotes/george_s_patton_130444
2. Lewy, Guenter. *America in Vietnam*, p. 4, Oxford University Press, Oxford, 1978.
3. ------. p. 160.
4. Thompson, Leroy. *The US Army in Vietnam*, p. 77, David & Charles Publishers, Devon, England, 1990.
5. Lanning, Michael Lee. *The Only War We Had: A Platoon Leader's Journal of Vietnam*, p. 19, Ivy Books, New York, 1987.
6. ------. p. 181.
7. https://www.historyplace.com/unitedstates/vietnam/index-1965.html
8. https://www.thefridaytimes.com/2020/05/22/march-in-support-of-vietnam-war-1970/
9. Summers, Jr., Harry G. *On Strategy*, p. 137, Dell Publishing, New York, 1984.
10. ------. p. 138.
11. Davidson, Phillip B. *Secrets of the Vietnam War*, p. 110, Presidio Press, Novato, California, 1990.
12. Hammond, William M. *Public Affairs: The Military and the Media, 1962-1968*, p. 364, Center of Military History, United States Army, Washington, D.C., 1988.
13. Braestrup, Peter. *Big Story*, p. 356, Yale University Press, New Haven, 1978.
14. Epstein, Edward J. *Between Fact and Fiction*, p. 225, Vintage, New York, 1975.
15. Braestrup, Peter. *Big Story*, p. 134, Yale University Press, New Haven, 1978.

16. Hammond, William M. *Public Affairs: The Military and the Media, 1962-1968*, p. 370, Center of Military History, United States Army, Washington, D.C., 1988.

Chapter 18

1. https://www.brainyquote.com/quotes/aldous_huxley_161359
2. Karnow, Stanley. *Vietnam: A History*, p. 500, Penguin Books, New York, 1984.
3. ------. p. 442-443.
4. ------. p. 530.
5. ------. p. 488.
6. ------. p. 610.
7. ------. p. 653.
8. Lewy, Guenter. *America in Vietnam*, p. 40, Oxford University Press, Oxford, 1978.
9. Reinberg, Linda. *In the Field: The Language of the Vietnam War*, p. 106, Facts on File, New York, 1991.
10. Lewy, Guenter. *America in Vietnam*, p. 198, Oxford University Press, Oxford, 1978.
11. Davidson, Phillip B. *Secrets of the Vietnam War*, p. 156, Presidio Press, Novato, California, 1990.
12. Lewy, Guenter. *America in Vietnam*, p. 202, Oxford University Press, Oxford, 1978.
13. ------. p. 202.
14. Tang, Truong Nhu, David Chanoff and Doan Van Toai. *A Vietcong Memoir: An Inside Account of the Vietnam War and its Aftermath*, p. 220, Vintage Books, New York, 1985.
15. Trewyn, R.W. "'Stupid Is as Stupid Does' in Vietnam and Afghanistan," *America Thinker*, Aug. 18, 2021; https://www.americanthinker.com/blog/2021/08/stupid_is_as_stupid_does_in_vietnam_and_afghanistan.html
16. Lewy, Guenter. *America in Vietnam*, p. 208, Oxford University Press, Oxford, 1978.
17. Tang, Truong Nhu, Chanoff, David, and Doan Van Toai. *A Vietcong Memoir: An Inside Account of the Vietnam War and its Aftermath*, p. 229, Vintage Books, New York, 1985.
18. Banerian, James. *Losers Are Pirates*, p. 339, Sphinx Publishing, Phoenix, 1985.
19. Greene, Bob. *Homecoming: When the Soldiers Returned from Vietnam*, p. 10, G.P. Putnam's Sons, New York, 1989.
20. ------. p. 59.
21. ------. p. 61.
22. Karnow, Stanley. *Vietnam: A History*, p. 466, Penguin Books, New York, 1984.
23. Tang, Truong Nhu, David Chanoff and Doan Van Toai. *A Vietcong Memoir: An Inside Account of the Vietnam War and its Aftermath*, p. 282, Vintage Books, New York, 1985.

24. Berger, Peter L. *Commentary*, "Indochina and the American Conscience," pp. 29–39, February 1980.
25. Trewyn, R.W. "Vietnam's Role in Government Putrefaction Today," *American Thinker*, July 31, 2021; https://www.americanthinker.com/articles/2021/07/vietnams_role_in_government_putrefaction_today.html
26. Associated Press. "Hong Kong Kicks Out Boat People," *The Columbus Dispatch*, December 12, 1989.

Chapter 19

1. https://www.brainyquote.com/quotes/eleanor_roosevelt_161321
2. Snell, Roger and Tim Doulin. "Professor Says OSU Is Ignoring Vets Job Law." *The Columbus Dispatch*, Jan. 23, 1991.
3. Gottlieb, Martin. "History of Vietnam Protesters Being Altered," *The Columbus Dispatch*, Jan. 31, 1991.
4. Trewyn, R.W. "Protests Aided Resolve of North Vietnamese," *The Columbus Dispatch*, Feb. 16, 1991.
5. Doulin, Tim and Roger Snell. "Veterans Group to Review OSU's Hiring Policy." *The Columbus Dispatch*, Jan. 29, 1991.
6. Trewyn, R.W. "What's Causing Today's Epidemic Pathology?" *Canada Free Press*, Dec. 7, 2022; https://canadafreepress.com/print_friendly/whats-causing-todays-epidemic-pathology
7. Snell, Roger. "OSU Hired 1 Vietnam Vet in '90," *Akron Beacon Journal*, May 18, 1991.
8. Vickers, Gaylon. "'Unrepentant Veteran' Phrase Opened Doors," *Northwest Columbus News*, May 29, 1991.
9. ------. "OSU Slights Vietnam Veterans," *Worthington Suburbia News*, June 5, 1991.
10. Doulin, Tim. "OSU Ignoring Law on Vets' Rights, Task Force Charges," *The Columbus Dispatch*, Sept. 19, 1991.
11. ------. "Probe of OSU Focuses on Veterans' Issue," *The Columbus Dispatch*, Sept. 20, 1991.
12. ------. "Gee Rips Report on Veterans," *The Columbus Dispatch*, Oct. 11, 1991.
13. Trewyn, R.W. "Urinating with Skunks," *Canada Free Press*, Jan. 5, 2021; https://canadafreepress.com/article/urinating-with-skunks
14. Froning, Jodi. "Gee Supports Office of Veteran's Affairs Despite Objections to Committee's Results," *The Lantern*, Oct. 14, 1991
15. Doulin, Tim. "OSU to Set Up Office of Veterans Affairs," *The Columbus Dispatch*, Nov. 2, 1991.

Chapter 20

1. https://www.brainyquote.com/quotes/henry_kissinger_103671
2. Holland, Earle. "A Peacetime War," *Ohio State Quest*, Winter, 1992.

3. Doulin, Tim. "Long-Awaited Post Is Established at Ohio State," *The Columbus Dispatch*, March 6, 1992.

4. Blais, Steve. "King Verdict Prompts Rally; OSU Students Set Flag Afire," *The Lantern*, May 4, 1992.

5. Silver, Stacey. "Flag Donated at Peace Rally," *The Lantern*, May 5, 1992.

6. Corvo, Kevin. "Student Honored for Flag's Return," *The Lantern*, May 21, 1992.

7. Bowen, William G., Sarah E. Turner and Marcia L. Witte. "The B.A.-Ph.D. Nexus," *Journal of Higher Education*, 63: 65–86, 1992.

8. Trewyn, R.W. "Protests Aided Resolve of the North Vietnamese." *The Columbus Dispatch*, Feb. 16, 1991.

9. Stever, James A. and R.W. Trewyn. "The Campus War." *The Ohio AMVET*, 7: 14–15, 1992.

10. Trewyn, R.W. "Veterans' Rights: Correcting Old Wrongs." *Main Street Business Journal*, Columbus, Ohio, July 1992.

11. ------ and James A. Stever: "Academe: Not so hallowed halls for veterans." *Journal of the Vietnam Veterans Institute* 4: 63–75, 1995.

12. ------. "Does Political Correctness Relate to Anti-Veteran Bias on the College Campus?" *Political Correctness in Ohio*. Ohio Association of Scholars, Columbus, OH, November 20, 1992.

13. ------ and James A. Stever: "Veterans' Rights: What Went Wrong?" Reserve Officers Association. *68th Annual State Convention*. Cincinnati, Ohio, April 23, 1993.

14. ------, James A. Stever and William E. Weber. "Employment Disparities and the Vietnam Veteran." *The History and Legacy of Those Who Served in Vietnam,* Hoffberger Center for Professional Ethics, University of Baltimore, Baltimore, Maryland. November 8–9, 1994.

15. ------ and James A. Stever. "Title 38, United States Code, Section 4212: Implementation & Enforcement by the U.S. Department of Labor." Written testimony to the U.S. House of Representatives' Veterans Affairs Committee, October 14, 1993.

16. Gee, E. Gordon. "From the President's Desk," *On Campus*, June 11, 1992.

17. Conciliation Agreement between the U.S. Department of Labor, Office of Federal Contract Compliance Programs and The Ohio State University, Sept. 16, 1992.

18. Snell, Roger. "GAO Probes OSU's Alleged Failure to Hire Vietnam Vets," *Akron Beacon Journal*, Dec. 5, 1992.

19. Trewyn, R.W. "U.S. Army Infantry Operations in Vietnam." Invited testimony to the National Academy of Sciences' Institute of Medicine Committee, *Health Effects in Vietnam Veterans of Exposure to Herbicides*, Irvine, CA. Feb. 8, 1993.

20. Ohio Colleges and Universities Veterans Affairs General Questionnaire submitted by Vice President Linda Tom, The Ohio State University, 26 July 1993, to Representative Mark A. Malone, Chairman, Ohio House and Senate Select Committee #51.

21. United States General Accounting Office. "Federal Contractor Hiring – Effect of Veteran Hiring Legislation Is Unknown," GAO/GGD-94-6, Oct. 1993.

22. *The Chronicle of Higher Education.* "House May Bar Grants to Campuses That Ban Military," June 1, 1994.

23. Trewyn, R.W. "Discrimination Against Veterans by the Federal Agency Charged With Protecting Veterans' Rights." *Journal of the Vietnam Veterans Institute* 3: 22–36, 1994.

24. ------. "Unequal Employment Opportunity for Military Veterans." Keynote address at the *Council of Scholars Colloquium* sponsored by the Vietnam Veterans Institute. Army Navy Club, Washington, D.C. Nov. 12, 1993.

25. Lanning, Michael Lee. *The Only War We Had: A Platoon Leader's Journal of Vietnam*, Ivy Books, New York, 1987.

26. Trewyn, R.W. "Welcome Home!" Invited presentation of original prose at, *An Evening of Blues, Poetry, and Prose.* Adrian Cronauer (*Good Morning, Vietnam!* screenplay author), Master of Ceremonies. Arts Club of Washington, Washington, D.C., November 12, 1993.

Chapter 21

1. https://www.brainyquote.com/quotes/mahatma_gandhi_135180

2. Mathews, Jay. "No Glory, No Parades, No Jobs?" *Washington Post*, April 29, 1995.

3. Morin, Richard. "Missing in Action: Vietnam Vets in the White House." *Washington Post*, April 9, 1995.

4. Trewyn, R.W. and James A. Stever. "Academe: Not So Hallowed Halls for Veterans," *Journal of the Vietnam Veterans Institute*, 4: 63–75, 1995.

5. ------. "Discrimination Against Veterans by the Federal Agency Charged With Protecting Veterans' Rights," *Journal of the Vietnam Veterans Institute*, 3: 22–36, 1994.

6. Angrist, Joshua D. "Lifetime Earnings and the Vietnam Era Draft Lottery: Evidence From Social Security Administration Records," *The American Economic Review*, 80: 313–336, 1990.

7. MacPherson, Myra. *Long Time Passing: Vietnam and the Haunted Generation*, Doubleday and Company, Garden City, New York, 1984.

8. Trewyn, R.W. "Inadequacies of Federal Agent Orange Studies." Requested testimony to the U.S. House of Representatives' National Security, Veterans Affairs, and International Affairs Subcommittee, *Air Force Ranch Hand Study on the Health Effects of Agent Orange*, Washington, D.C., March 15, 2000.

9. ------. "Air Force Agent Orange Health Study Flaws With the 25-Year, $145 Million Vietnam Ranch Hand Health Effects Analysis," *Nightline*, Ted Koppel interview, Nov. 17, 2005.

Chapter 22

1. https://www.brainyquote.com/quotes/mark_twain_133066

2. McNamara, Robert S. with Brian Van De Mark. *In Retrospect – The Tragedy and Lessons of Vietnam*, Random House, New York, 1995.

3. Moore, Lt. Gen. Harold (Ret.) and Joseph L. Galloway. *We Were Soldiers Once . . . and Young*, Random House, New York, 1992.
4. Trewyn, R.W. "Time Warp: 1969/70 Anarchy . . . Recycle 2019/20," *Canada Free Press*, December 3, 2020; https://canadafreepress.com/article/time-warp-1969-70-anarchy-recycle-2019-20
5. ------. "Tested Under Fire: Relevant on the Battlefield and in the Streets," *Canada Free Press*, Feb. 2, 2021; https://canadafreepress.com/article/tested-under-fire-relevant-on-the-battlefield-and-in-the-streets
6. ------. "The Gully of the Shadows of Death Disproved Critical Race Theory Over 50-Years Ago," *Canada Free Press*, June 29, 2021; https://canadafreepress.com/article/the-gully-of-the-shadows-of-death-disproved-critical-race-theory-over-50-years-ago
7. ------. "'Stupid Is as Stupid Does' in Vietnam and Afghanistan," *American Thinker*, August 18, 2021; https://www.americanthinker.com/blog/2021/08/stupid_is_as_stupid_does_in_vietnam_and_afghanistan.html
8. ------. "Last Rites for 'WE' in America—Last Rites for America?" *Canada Free Press*, Aug. 31, 2021; https://canadafreepress.com/article/last-rites-for-we-in-america-last-rites-for-america
9. ------. "WE the PEOPLE not ME," *Canada Free Press*, Dec. 14, 2021; https://canadafreepress.com/article/we-the-people-not-me
10. ------. "'WE' . . . the Only Pronoun that Truly Matters!" *Canada Free Press*, July 13, 2022; https://canadafreepress.com/article/we-the-only-pronoun-that-truly-matters
11. Burkett, B.G. and Glenna Whitley. *Stolen Valor: How the Vietnam Generation was Robbed of its Heroes and its History*, Verity Press, Dallas, 1998.
12. ------. p. 182.
13. ------. p. 164.
14. ------. p. 87–108.
15. ------. p. 107.
16. *Manhattan Mercury*. "Survivor Tells of Raid by Kerrey Commandos," April 29, 2001.
17. Vistica, Gregory L. "One Awful Night in Thanh Phong," *The New York Times*, April 25, 2001.
18. *Lawrence Journal World*. "Students Urge Kerrey to Resign," May 12, 2001.

Chapter 23

1. https://wholenesshealing.com/wholeness-healing-today/the-wound-is-the-place-where-the-light-enters-you-rumi/
2. Berger, Peter L. *Commentary*, "Indochina and the American Conscience," pp. 29–39, Feb. 1980.
3. Greene, Bob. *Homecoming*, p. 210–213, G.P. Putnam's Sons, New York, 1989.

Epilogue I: Defending Freedom

1. Trewyn, R.W. "Time Warp: 1969/70 Anarchy . . . Recycle 2019/20," *Canada Free Press*, Dec. 3, 2020; https://canadafreepress.com/article/time-warp-1969-70-anarchy-recycle-2019-20

2. ------. "Last Rites for 'WE' in America—Last Rites for America?" *Canada Free Press*, Aug. 31, 2021; https://canadafreepress.com/article/last-rites-for-we-in-america-last-rites-for-america

3. ------. "The Gully of the Shadows of Death Disproved Critical Race Theory Over 50-Years Ago," *Canada Free Press*, June 29, 2021; https://canadafreepress.com/article/the-gully-of-the-shadows-of-death-disproved-critical-race-theory-over-50-years-ago

4. https://www.birminghamtimes.com/2018/01/some-of-dr-martin-luther-king-jr-s-profound-quotes/

5. https://www.kingjamesbibleonline.org/Psalms-23-4/

6. https://www.inspiration-daily.com/said/man-die-something-not-fit-80/

7. Trewyn, R.W. "Anti-America Americans Synergizing Again," *American Thinker*, Jan. 7, 2021; https://www.americanthinker.com/articles/2021/01/antiamerica_americans_are_synergizing_again.html

8. Tang, Truong Nhu, David Chanoff and Doan Van Toai. *A Vietcong Memoir: An Inside Account of the Vietnam War and its Aftermath*, pp. 220–229, Vintage Books, New York, 1985.

9. Trewyn, R.W. "'Stupid Is as Stupid Does' in Vietnam and Afghanistan," *American Thinker*, Aug. 18, 2021; https://www.americanthinker.com/blog/2021/08/stupid_is_as_stupid_does_in_vietnam_and_afghanistan.html

10. https://www.biblegateway.com/passage/?search=Genesis+1%3A27&version=ESV

11. https://www.archives.gov/founding-docs/declaration

Epilogue II: Destroying Freedom

1. Trewyn, R.W. "Time Warp: 1969/70 Anarchy . . . Recycle 2019/20," *Canada Free Press*, Dec. 3, 2020; https://canadafreepress.com/article/time-warp-1969-70-anarchy-recycle-2019-20

2. ------. "Anti-America Americans Synergizing Again," *American Thinker*, Jan. 7, 2021; https://www.americanthinker.com/articles/2021/01/antiamerica_americans_are_synergizing_again.html

3. ------. "The Birth of Cancel Culture and the Death of Education," *American Thinker,* Dec. 22, 2020; https://www.americanthinker.com/articles/2020/12/the_birth_of_cancel_culture_and_the_death_of_education_.html

4. https://hartian.com/ronald-reagan-politics-is-supposed-to-be-the-second-oldest-profession/

5. Trewyn, R.W. "Big Tech – SS – Gestapo," *Canada Free Press*, March 30, 2021; https://canadafreepress.com/article/big-tech-ss-gestapo

6. Schultz, Marisa. "Utah Rep.-elect Burgess Owens, Former NFL player, Compares Antifa, Black Lives Matter to Ku Klux Klan," *Fox News*, Dec. 12, 2020; https://www.foxnews.com/politics/utah-rep-elect-burgess-owens-compares-antifa-to-kkk

7. Trewyn, R.W. "Tested Under Fire: Relevant on the Battlefield and in the Streets," *Canada Free Press*, Feb. 2, 2021; https://canadafreepress.com/article/tested-under-fire-relevant-on-the-battlefield-and-in-the-streets

8. https://www.foxnews.com/entertainment/jane-fonda-dismisses-critics-of-her-climate-protests-those-people-dont-matter

9. https://www.quotetab.com/quote/by-sophocles/there-is-no-greater-evil-than-anarchy

10. Trewyn, R.W. "Crying 'Racist!' Is the Waterboarding of the Left," *American Thinker*, May 27, 2021; https://www.americanthinker.com/blog/2021/05/crying_racism_is_the_waterboarding_of_the_left.html

Epilogue III: Inheriting Freedom

1. Trewyn, R.W. "WE the PEOPLE not ME," *Canada Free Press*, Dec. 14, 2021; https://canadafreepress.com/article/we-the-people-not-me

2. https://constitutioncenter.org/interactive-constitution/preamble

3. https://www.goodreads.com/quotes/tag/we-the-people

4. Trewyn, R.W. "Last Rites for "WE" in America—Last Rights for America?" *Canada Free Press*, Aug. 31, 2021; https://canadafreepress.com/article/last-rites-for-we-in-america-last-rites-for-america

5. ------. "Time Warp: 1969/70 Anarchy . . . Recycle 2019/20," *Canada Free Press*, Dec. 3, 2020; https://canadafreepress.com/article/time-warp-1969-70-anarchy-recycle-2019-20

6. ------. "The Gully of the Shadows of Death Disproved Critical Race Theory Over 50-Years Ago," *Canada Free Press*, Feb. 2, 2021; https://canadafreepress.com/article/the-gully-of-the-shadows-of-death-disproved-critical-race-theory-over-50-years-ago

7. https://www.brainyquote.com/authors/john-adams-quotes

8. Trewyn, R.W., "Have Americans Become a People Who No Longer Deserve Their Constitution?" *American Thinker*, Jan. 12, 2022; https://www.americanthinker.com/blog/2022/01/have_americans_become_a_people_who_no_longer_deserve_their_constitution.html

9. Ahlgren, Alyssa. "College Student: My Generation Is Blind to the Prosperity Around Us," *Foundation for Economic Education*, April 24, 2019; https://fee.org/articles/college-student-my-generation-is-blind-to-the-prosperity-around-us/

10. Trewyn, R.W., "Anti-America Americans Synergizing Again," *American Thinker*, Jan. 7, 2021; https://www.americanthinker.com/articles/2021/01/antiamerica_americans_are_synergizing_again.html

INDEX